Empire State

How the Roman Military Built an Empire

Simon Elliott

LIBRARY OF CONGRESS
SURPLUS
DUPLICATE

OXBOW | books

Oxford & Philadelphia

Published in the United Kingdom in 2017 by
OXBOW BOOKS
The Old Music Hall, 106–108 Cowley Road, Oxford OX4 1JE

and in the United States by
OXBOW BOOKS
1950 Lawrence Road, Havertown, PA 19083, USA

© Oxbow Books and the individual contributors 2017

Paperback Edition: ISBN 978-1-78570-658-5
Digital Edition: ISBN 978-1-78570-659-2 (epub)

A CIP record for this book is available from the British Library

Library of Congress Control Number: 2017940793

All rights reserved. No part of this book may be reproduced or transmitted in any form or by any means, electronic or mechanical including photocopying, recording or by any information storage and retrieval system, without permission from the publisher in writing.

Printed in Malta by Gutenberg Press Ltd
Typeset in India by Lapiz Digital Services, Chennai

For a complete list of Oxbow titles, please contact:

UNITED KINGDOM
Oxbow Books
Telephone (01865) 241249, Fax (01865) 794449
Email: oxbow@oxbowbooks.com
www.oxbowbooks.com

UNITED STATES OF AMERICA
Oxbow Books
Telephone (800) 791-9354, Fax (610) 853-9146
Email: queries@casemateacademic.com
www.casemateacademic.com/oxbow

Oxbow Books is part of the Casemate Group

Front cover: Porta Nigra Roman fortified city gate in Trier, built from large sandstone blocks without mortar in the late 2nd century. Photo: Simon Elliott.
Back cover: Roman amphitheatre at the legionary fortress of Caerleon; Town walls of the Caerwent (Roman *Venta Silurum*); Burgh Castle. Photos: Simon Elliott.

Contents

List of Tables

To my loving wife Sara for your endless
patience and support.

Introduction

The Roman state was the principal political force within the empire, intricately involved in all economic activities geared to supporting its infrastructure and own continuance. Yet, as a patrician institution, it also had other responsibilities, with political, economic and social roles which were often related. In an age before the advent of a civil service, nationalised industries and a free market able to fund major capital expenditure projects, to fulfil these responsibilities it turned to the only tool at its disposal, namely the military, the largest institution within the empire.

These armed forces of Rome, particularly those of the later Republic and Principate, are rightly regarded as some of the finest military formations ever to engage in warfare. In their time, the legions, auxilia and regional navies of Rome were pre-eminent, masters of most fields and seas of battle in which they engaged. Less well known however is their use by the State as tools for such non-military activities in political, economic and social contexts. In this capacity, they were central instruments for the emperor and his provincial governors and procurators to ensure the smooth running of the Empire, making sure each province paid its keep into the imperial *fiscus* (treasury). As Goldsworthy (2003, 145) says:

> Roman Emperors governed with the aid of only a very small civilian bureaucracy, and frequently called upon the army to perform many non-military tasks, simply because there was no one else available.

The use of the military in this regard also served another function, namely to keep the various components of the armed forces of Rome busy when not engaged in military activity. Simply put, it was not wise to allow such elite troops to lie idle for too long lest they begin to agitate.

In this book, the use of the military for such non-conflict related duties is considered in detail for the first time. To enable the narrative to run freely, the book is specifically broken down into a number of chapters each telling a key part of this story. In the first instance in Chapter 1, the scene is set for the following chapters by providing background on the Roman Principate, by giving detail on the Roman transport network so vital to the military in all of its roles, and finally discussing the nature of the Roman economy. Chapter 2 then takes the story forward with a detailed consideration of all aspects of the Roman military with a particular focus on the legionaries, auxilia and regional navies and including a discussion on current thinking with regard to Roman military identity, with Chapter 3 then examining the command and control of the empire from the emperor downwards to explore the means by which the military would have been employed by the state for non-military tasks. Here, the first detailed scrutiny of the military in such major roles is examined, namely administering and policing the empire, providing a firefighting resource and facilitating the games in the arena.

Sequential chapters will then review in detail the use of the military in very specific non-conflict roles. The first, and best known, is in their capacity as engineers. Today there is a very clear distinction between the activities of military and civil engineers, this in a British context dating back to at least 1760 when John Smeaton advertised himself as an engineer for hire. In the Roman world, however, there was no such clear distinction, and so if the state required a great engineering task to be undertaken then it was the military who were deployed in this capacity. The military was a resource well capable of such tasks, with even the lowliest legionary, auxilia or naval *milites* (a catch-all term for soldier) being a trained engineer, and with the major military formations featuring specialist engineers of all kinds (note that this work specifically doesn't cover siege engineering in the field). A separate chapter will then look at the role of these military engineers of all levels and kinds in some of the great construction projects of the empire.

Next, the role of the Roman military in the running of industry across the Roman Empire is examined, particularly the *metalla*[1] mining and quarrying industries. The subject of my own MA research at the Institute of Archaeology, UCL, and more recently my PhD research at the University of Kent, this is an area of particular importance to this work given the new findings and interpretations I will present.

A final specific focus of this work will be an examination of the role played by the military in agriculture throughout the empire. Despite the headline-grabbing nature of the military's role facilitating industry, it was agriculture that was by far the most important component of the Roman economy, and therefore the military's role in this regard is particularly important. This chapter will be followed by a conclusion which includes a review of the preceding chapters to present a holistic appraisal of the use of the Roman military in a non-fighting capacity as a key tool of the state, an analysis of how this role changed as the empire progressed from its Principate to Dominate phase (with a particular focus on the reform of the imperial administration by Diocletian in his reformation), and finally a reflection on how this research has enabled us to see the Roman military in a way distinct from the view that they were

1. Hirt (2010, 50), in his detailed examination of imperial mine and quarry administration, says that most contemporary literary sources (for example the 1st- and 2nd-century jurist Ulpian) understood the term *metallum* to mean a location where stone, metals and other resources were extracted, with *metalla* thus being a term appropriate for both mines and quarries. That convention is therefore used here.

'other' when compared to the rest of the society they served. The book also has four appendices to act as guides for the relevant chapters in the book, beginning with a review of the geology of the south-east of Britain which is very pertinent to Chapter 4's study of the Roman military as engineers and Chapter 6's analysis of Roman *metalla* in Britain (given the examples I use). Next featured is a distribution table for Upper Medway Valley ragstone across the south-east of Britain, again to inform Chapters 4 and 6, followed by a distribution table showing the locations and totals of *Classis Britannica* stamped tiles, to inform the relevant section on the Roman tile and brick industries in Chapter 4. Finally, given the importance in the book of examples from Britain, I include a timeline of the key developments in the province throughout its occupation by Rome. The book ends with a list of references and bibliography to allow the reader to pursue their own research on the subjects covered here.

Note that this work features both a re-examination of existing appreciations of the Roman military carrying out various civilian activities, though uniquely bringing together the various strands and themes in this regard into a single volume for the first time, together with some new cutting edge research found here in print, also for the first time. This latter is specifically with regard to my PhD research into the Roman military running state industries in the province of Britain, and particularly the industrial scale iron manufacturing industry in the Weald and ragstone quarrying industry of the Upper Medway Valley (which built a large amount of Roman London). Until their demise in the mid-3rd century these industries, and their supporting industrial and transport infrastructure, effectively represented the industrial heartland of Roman Britain (on a scale never to be replicated through the rest of the occupation). They are specifically addressed as two case studies in Chapter 6.

In terms of chronology, given the vast breadth of the subject matter, the focus of this book is mainly on the military forces of the Principate (namely from the coming to power of Augustus in 27 BC to the end of the 'Crisis of the 3rd Century' with the accession of Diocletian in AD 284). That is not to say that the Roman military were not similarly employed in non-conflict tasks in the Republic or later during the Dominate phase, but focusing on the empire at its Principate height allows a tighter focus on specific examples. It was during the Principate that the empire expanded to its greatest extent, under the great soldier Emperor Trajan, with his conquests in Dacia north of the Balkans and along the eastern frontier. After his reign, however, the continuous outward expansion experienced by the empire ceased, to be replaced from Hadrian onwards with a policy of consolidation (D'Amato, 2016, 6). It is from this time we begin to see the formalisation of the borders of the empire, with for example the construction of Hadrian's Wall (dubbed *limes Britannicus*) in Britain and the *limes Germanicus* along the Rivers Rhine and (partially) Danube. This transition, broadly, from offence to defence is reflected in the use of the military for non-conflict purposes and is a journey evident in the chapters that follow. Also of note, given the focus of the research presented here on the Principate, while the book does consider in detail the early military reforms of Septimius Severus in the late 2nd and early

3rd centuries AD, it doesn't those of Diocletian or Constantine from the late 3rd into the 4th centuries AD (excepting referencing them in the conclusion in Chapter 8).

Evidence of all kinds underpins the research which has allowed me to write this book to the level of detail I intended when I first set out on the project. The starting point was my PhD and earlier MA research (including an earlier MA in War Studies from KCL), particularly that focusing on Roman industry (iron manufacturing, ragstone quarrying and millstone production) in Kent during the occupation, and the role the military played therein. Types of evidence used in the research include the archaeological record, which has provided much of the hard data on which my theories are based, the historical record (including wherever possible primary sources, contemporary epigraphy and itineraries, though noting in the case of the first their often questionable impartiality), scientific observation, analogy and (where appropriate) anecdote. Where the data has been ambiguous or contradictory I have used common sense to make a judgment on what I believe to be the truth, particularly where primary references on key issues such as the mechanisms of imperial government are few and far between and only describe events in a particular snapshot of time.

Regarding classical and modern names, I have attempted to ensure that the research is as accessible as possible. For example, I have used the current name when a place or city is mentioned, referencing the Roman name at its first point of use. Meanwhile, where a classical name for a given post or role is well understood, for example *legate*, I use that, referencing the modern name in brackets at the point of first use. When emperors are detailed in the main body of the text, which is a frequent occurrence as one might imagine, I have listed the dates of their reign when each individual is first mentioned. Meanwhile, where permanent fortifications are detailed (as opposed to marching camps), I have used the hierarchy currently used by those studying the Roman military, this based on their size. Specifically, these are fortress (a permanent base for one or more legions, of some 20ha or more), vexillation fortress (a large fort of between 8 and 12ha, holding a mixed force of legionary cohorts and auxiliaries), fort (a garrison outpost occupied by an auxiliary unit or units, some 1 to 6ha in size) and fortlet (a small garrison outpost large enough to hold only part of an auxiliary unit).

In this book, the province of Britannia is frequently used as an example, and therefore a note of explanation regarding its political organisation is required. Until the reforms of Britain by Septimius Severus/Caracalla in AD 211/212 (initiated in AD 197), the term 'province' in relation to this north-western most outpost of Empire references the original single province of Britannia. After their reforms the term references either *Britannia Superior* or *Britannia Inferior* depending on the context, sometimes in fact both. After the Diocletianic reformation, with its establishment of the *diocese* of Britannia with its four (and perhaps later five) provinces, given the complexity the full name of each is detailed for clarity. The four definite later provinces within the *diocese*, as detailed on the Verona List of AD 303–314, are *Maxima Caesariensis*,

Flavia Caesariensis, *Britannia Prima* and *Britannia Secunda*. These are then listed again a century later in the *Notitia Dignitatum* which adds the fifth province, namely *Valentia*.

Again relevant specifically to the province of Britannia but equally important elsewhere, with regard to the academic terminology I use in this book I have specifically steered away from the concept of Romanisation popular in Roman archaeology since Millett (1990a, 1) definitively promoted the idea to a contemporary audience. This is because from the onset of the Roman occupation in Britain many processes and social changes unfolded, and in that regard I want to avoid being side-tracked in the debate about its perceived inability to capture the processes and outcomes of cultural change, and the tendency to associate the term with modern concepts of Imperialism (Gardner, 2013, 2). I have, however, retained the word *Romanitas*, given its usefulness as a descriptor for manifestations of (especially elite) Roman culture that are visible in the Roman landscape (in the form for example of villas, coin use and modes of burial).

Given the importance of the built environment to this work a framework is also required to define different types of settlement. For towns, I have used the convention of three different kinds, each with a different legal status. The first were the *coloniae*, chartered towns featuring Roman citizens who were often discharged veteran troops. Good examples in Britain include Colchester, Gloucester and Lincoln, all featuring strong evidence of the use of the Roman military in their construction and maintenance. Secondly there are the *municipia*, also chartered towns but with a mercantile origin, in Britain being represented by St Albans among others. Finally, one has *civitas* capitals, the Roman equivalent in Britain of a county town featuring the local government of a given region. These were most often located on the site of their equivalent pre-Roman centres, for example Canterbury, previously the principal settlement of the Cantiaci (Mattingly, 2006, 260). Next, moving down in scale, one has small towns (first definitively distinguished from their larger counterparts by Malcolm Todd, 1970, 114), which are defined as a variety of diverse settlements which existed throughout the Empire and which usually had an association with a specific activity, for example administration, industry or religion (with many also being located at key transport nodes). Continuing down the scale, one then has villa-estate settlements, mostly rural in nature but in the context of this work sometimes also associated with industry (where a link with the Roman military may be evident, see Chapter 6). These are then followed by non-villa settlements, those where there is a lack of evident displays of *Romanitas* as defined above, and finally – and again important to this work – industrial sites (which could be of any size, see discussion in The Roman Economy in Chapter 1 below).

Also important in this book, especially when discussing the administrators of the Roman Empire and the officers of the Roman military, is the social structure of Roman society, especially at the upper end. In terms of the ranking of the 'leisure classes', at the top was the senatorial class, endowed with 'moral excellence', wealth and high birth. These were followed by the equestrian class, with slightly less wealth but a reputable lineage, and finally the curial class (again with the bar set slightly lower). The latter were largely mid-level landowners and merchants, they making up a large percentage of the town councillors across the empire.

Lastly, I would like to thank those who have made this work on the Roman military in all of their non-conflict roles possible. Firstly, Professor Andrew Lambert of the War Studies Department at KCL, Dr Andrew Gardner at UCL's Institute of Archaeology, and Dr Steve Willis at the University of Kent for their ongoing guidance and encouragement. Standing on the shoulders of giants indeed! Next, my publisher, Clare Litt of Oxbow Books, for believing in this work. Also Dr Paul Wilkinson of the Kent Archaeological Field School, Dr Gustav Milne at UCL, Jeremy Hodgkinson of the Wealden Iron Working Group, Sam Moorhead at the British Museum, Dr Ian Betts at Museum of London Archaeology, Meriel Jeater at the Museum of London, Professor Sir Barry Cunliffe of the School of Archaeology at Oxford University, Professor Martin Millett at the Faculty of Classics, Cambridge University, Ray Chitty of the Medway River Users Association, Jim Bowden for his guidance regarding engineering and construction techniques and finally my patient proof readers Adrian Nash and my lovely wife Sara. All have contributed greatly and freely to my wider research, enabling this work to reach fruition. Finally, of course I would like to thank my family, including my always supportive and tolerant wife Sara once again, children Alex (himself a student of military history) and Lizzie, brother Tim and his family, and my mum and dad. All have been a terrific source of encouragement. Thank you all.

Simon Elliott
December 2016

Chapter 1

Background

In this chapter, a number of themes relevant to all aspects of the use of the Roman military in non-conflict roles are examined in detail to provide background for all subsequent chapters, the aim being to create foundations for a deeper understanding of the concepts and ideas which follow. The specific themes are a broad though concise description of the Roman Empire during the Principate, a description of the Roman transport network (a vital thread running through the entire book), and finally an outline of the Roman economic system to provide context for the civilian roles of the military.

The Principate Empire

As detailed in the Introduction, the Principate is the name given to the Roman Empire from the accession of Augustus in 27 BC (died AD 14) to the ending of the 'Crisis of the 3rd Century' with the accession of Diocletian in AD 284 (died AD 311, though having abdicated as emperor in AD 305). The name is derived from the term *princeps* (meaning chief or master), the principal citizen of the empire in the form of a single emperor, thus carrying on the deceit that the emperor was simply Rome's leading citizen. In this way, particularly with regard to the early emperors, the empire could be explained away to contemporary audiences as a simple continuance of the earlier Republic. This masquerade was formally abandoned with the onset of the Dominate (based on the word *Dominus*, meaning master or lord) from which point the sanctity of the emperor was officially promoted as something extraordinary, separating him from the rest of the Roman citizenry, this reflecting eastern despotic customs.

The official title adopted by Augustus (originally Octavian), when he emerged victorious from the vicious round of Roman civil wars following the assassination of Julius Caesar in 44 BC, was *princeps senatus/princeps civitatis* (first among senators/ first among citizens), intended to disguise the fact that he was in reality the emperor. It is from this time that we talk about the Roman Empire, not Republic. His timing couldn't have been better, with the political leadership and people of Rome willing to accept a degree of dictatorial control after the preceding political turbulence that had seen vast swathes of the Roman aristocracy backing the wrong horse in the various bids for power and suffering the often fatal consequences (this peace dubbed the *Pax Romana*). He chose his title carefully, particularly the *princeps senatus* component which traditionally referenced the eldest member of the Senate who was allowed to speak first in a debate. This fiction that the emperor continued with the governing traditions of the Republic existed for much of the Principate, even when Augustus' dynastic ambitions emerged early on. Successive emperors wrapped themselves in the archaic traditions of the Republic to maintain a pretence that in reality few citizens fell for, manifest in the continued adoption by the State of the phrase *Senatus Populusque Romanus* (the Senate and People of Rome, SPQR) to describe their system of rule (which referenced the pre-imperial oligarchic self-rule of the Republic). In reality though, the Senate now only issued its *senatus consulta* (decrees) at the pleasure of the emperor. The position of the emperor within this Principate system of government was later formalised by Emperor Vespasian (AD 69–79), with the position of the *princeps* becoming an entity in its own right, though still within a system which maintained the pretence of being a republic. The major change now, in addition to the adoption of the term *imperator* (emperor) for the first time, was that the ruler had the right to nominate his successor (even though this had in fact been the practice since the time of Augustus) rather than having to dress this up as an imperial nomination based on *auctoritas* (merit).

Within the Principate there were distinct dynasties which provide a chronological framework for the wider study of the Roman military in their non-conflict activities. These are as follows (Kean, 2005, 18):

- The Julio-Claudian dynasty from the accession of Augustus in 27 BC (though taking in the preceding civil wars) to the death of Nero in AD 68 (having become emperor in AD 54). This included the beginnings of empire, the destruction of three legions at the hands of the Germans in the Battle of Teotoberg Forest in AD 9, and the initial conquest campaigns in Britain.
- The Year of the Four Emperors in AD 69.
- The Flavian dynasty from the accession of Vespasian to the death of Domitian in AD 96 (having become emperor in AD 81). This included the conclusion of the Jewish Great Revolt of AD 66–70.
- The Nervo-Trajanic dynasty from the accession on Nerva in AD 96 (died AD 98) to the death of Hadrian in AD 138 (having become emperor in AD 117). This included Trajan's (emperor AD 98–117) conquest of Dacia in two campaigns from AD 101–102 and AD 105–106, famously recorded for posterity on Trajan's Column in Rome. Under Hadrian, it also marked the point at which the empire ceased to be one always on the offensive and looking to expand its territory, becoming one of consolidation and ultimately defence.
- The Antonine dynasty from the accession of Antoninus Pius in AD 138 (died AD 161) through to the death of Commodus in AD 192 (having become emperor in AD 180). The 23-year reign of Pius was one of comparative peace, with the empire at its most stable and mature. However, it is from the time of Marcus Aurelius

(Emperor AD 161–180) that we begin to see genuine pressure beginning to build across the frontiers of Rome to the north and east.

- The Year of the Five Emperors in AD 193 and the subsequent civil wars, from the accession of Pertinax (emperor for the first three months of AD 193) through to the death of British governor and usurper Clodius Albinus in AD 197.
- The Severan dynasty from the accession of Septimius Severus in AD 193 (died AD 311) through to the assassination of Severus Alexander in AD 235 (having become emperor in AD 222). This period saw continued campaigning in the north (for example the Severan campaigns in Scotland in AD 209 and AD 210) and east (where the initiation of the Sassanid Persian Empire from AD 224 saw the appearance for the first time of a regional superpower able to challenge the might of Rome).
- The 'Crisis of the 3rd Century' from the death of Severus Alexander through to the accession of Diocletian in AD 284. This was a time of great stress and ultimately change within and without the empire, including the military anarchy from the accession of Maximinus Thrax (emperor AD 235–238) through to that of Gallienus as sole emperor (emperor AD 260–268), multiple usurpations such as that of Postumus with the Gallic Empire (which lasted from AD 260 through to AD 274), and then the restoration of imperial unity and order under some of the great soldier emperors such as Claudius II Gothicus (emperor AD 268–270) and Aurelian (emperor AD 270–275). The period ends with the arrival of Diocletian who initiated his reformation, including new systems of government, beginning the Dominate period of Roman rule. See Chapter 8 for more detail here.

Transport in the Roman World

Lavan (2014, 1) and Bonifay (2014, 557) both argue that maritime transport (by sea, canal and river) was crucial to the smooth running of the Roman economy and had a major impact on the prosperity of a given region. Maritime transport was of course the method of choice for moving heavy goods over long distances in the pre-modern world, dating back to the origins of prehistoric long-range trading networks. In that regard, Manco (2015, 49) highlights the spread of Bell Beaker pottery culture along the coastlines and rivers of Europe from the 3rd millennium BC, while into the early classical period, Freeman (2010, 312) speaks of the use of rivers and the coast to transport extracted metals of all kinds in south-western Spain. This preference for maritime transport applies even today, specifically because of cost, given it was and is significantly cheaper than transport by land. The wider importance of transport costs is shown by Russell (2013a, 95), citing the example of the Baths of Caracalla in Rome, where 50% of the costs of construction were taken up by shipping and haulage. Therefore, any advantage regarding this cost would be taken, with the below table by Selkirk (1995, 144) particularly instructive in that regard:

Table 1: Comparative Energy Requirements for Modes of Transport in the Roman World. Selkirk, 1995, 144.

Vessel/ Animal/ Vehicle/	*Fuel Type*	*Distance able to carry 1 ton on 1 gallon*
Roman merchant ship	Food/cooking fuel	1,280 miles
Roman codicaria (towed river barge)	Food/cooking fuel	32 miles
Mule	Fodder	2.4 miles
Roman ox-wagon	Fodder	0.8 miles

Hard occupation-period data for this transport price differential can be seen in the Edict of Diocletian, this highlighting sea travel as the cheapest means of transporting goods, followed by inland waterways and finally (by some distance) roads. As an example, for the transport of Egyptian papyrus, the edict shows waterways to be 4.9 times more expensive than travel by sea, with roadways being up to 56 times more expensive than by sea (Campbell, 2011, 216). More recent examples of such economics can be seen in 16th century accounts from Corpus Christi College in Cambridge, which detail that it cost the same amount to move a load of stone 130km by water as it cost to move it 16km by land (Russell, 2013a, 96). Emphasising the point, Russell provides a further example, saying:

> As recently as 1962, limestone from Portland in Dorset was cheaper to purchase at Dublin (c.625km distant), to where it was transported by sea, than at inland Birmingham (c.210km distant).

A final example from Roman-occupied Britain also emphasises the importance of sea travel for mercantile transport. Lyne (1994, 540) shows that the Dorset-based Black-burnished ware 1 (BB1) and Thames Estuary-based Black-burnished ware 2 (BB2) industries were two of the main suppliers of pottery to the military garrisons in the north of Britain into the 3rd century AD, using maritime transport routes up the west and east coasts.

The role of the state in transport, largely through the military, is very visible in the highest profile example, the supply of grain to the citizens of Rome under the aegis of the *Cura Annonae* (care for the grain supply), the title given to those tasked with victualing the city. To give some idea of the scale of this commitment, it included the construction of the new harbour 3km from Ostia to help cope with the growing city's demand for increasing quantities of grain during the reign of Claudius (Erdkamp, 2013, 272). The imported grain arriving at this new port was itself often state-owned, originating from the numerous agricultural imperial estates across the provinces of the empire (increasingly from Egypt), and was transported on shipping coordinated and often owned – through the regional navies – by the state (Erdkamp, 2013, 272). The significance of these agrarian imperial estates is ably illustrated by the extensive wine-producing example at Vagnari to the east of the Apennine mountains in ancient Apulia. It was large enough to feature its own *vicus* associated settlement

(Carroll, 2016, 31). The role of the military in agricultural production is specifically discussed in Chapter 7.

The state's responsibility for key public amenities also extended to the transport network, and not just the trunk road network detailed in Chapter 6 below. As Campbell (2011, 91) explains, this also included the river and canal systems of the Empire, with the former dubbed *flumen publica*. In this case, while private individuals controlled the banks, the river itself was the property of the state.

A final example of the state's involvement in transport comes in the form of the *cursus publicus* state courier service discussed above in this chapter (Kolb, 2001, 95, and Burnham and Wacher, 1990, 5).

The Roman Economy

A discussion of the nature of the Roman economy is useful at this point to provide context for the later consideration of the use of the Roman military for non-conflict purposes given such uses were often economic in nature. To ensure an accessible narrative, this section is divided into four parts. The first part provides background into the theories and modelling of the Roman economy that have been considered over time including those most up to date. Next, I consider the imperial economy and the means utilised by the Roman state to ensure a province paid its way, crucial to the smooth running of the Empire. I then move on to review the provincial economy based on markets, free trade and patterns of consumption (Mattingly, 2006, 496), which I broadly refer to as the market economy (in no way implying this functioned in the manner of a modern manifestation of a market economy). Finally, I look specifically at one aspect of the imperial economy: imperial states. These are important to this work given the focus in Chapter 6 on the role of the Roman military in industry (particularly the *metalla*), and in Chapter 7, the role of the Roman military in agriculture.

Background

The world of Imperial Rome has often been cited as the archetypal 'empire', attracting interpretations of its strengths and weaknesses by archaeologists and historians from all parts of the political spectrum. At the heart of this debate is the nature of the Roman economy, given the challenge of explaining the juxtaposition of long-lasting empire with successful financial institution (if the economy of the Empire can be described in such terms). It is a vital consideration, as it not only helps to explain the fiscal aspects of maintaining an empire that enjoyed this longevity (though often in times of financial crisis), but also gives great insight into the lives of those who experienced it. With regard to the latter, a range of views are evident here, from sometimes benevolent to often negative. In terms of the former, Temin (2012, 2) argues that the quality of life for the average citizen during the Principate was better than at any time before the Industrial Revolution, while Rodgers and Dodge (2009, 7) speak of ripples of prosperity spreading out across the empire and taxation in the provinces often being less than that exacted by the Late Iron Age (LIA) predecessors of those conquered by Rome (though acknowledging that the Empire was run for the benefit of its rulers). At the other extreme Pollard (2000, 249), in his analysis of Roman Syria, speaks of an economy where the exploitation of the population through taxation, the immediate requirement to support the army (admittedly this was a border territory, a good analogy for Britain), and the removal of natural resources under imperial control (see Chapter 6) outweighed the benefits for the population, for example in terms of investment. Similarly, Faulkner takes this negative experience to the extreme in his contention that the Empire, economically and otherwise, was robbery with violence (2000, 120). All of these themes are considered below as I follow the narrative of thinking over the nature of the Roman economy, with a particular focus on how similar to the western pre-modern economy it was (the 'modernists' seeing more similarities, the 'primitivists' less), and how integrated the Roman market was in the broadest sense.

The nature of the Roman economy has long been considered by economists and historians of all political leanings, for example Adam Smith, Adam Ferguson, Max Weber and John Kautsky (Bang, 2008, 61). From the 1950s however a model developed by A. H. M. Jones (1953, 293) began to gain ground. This stressed the centrality of agriculture to the Roman economy, argued that most of the agrarian produce was consumed locally (with notable exceptions, for example the Egyptian grain supply to Rome itself, see references to Paul Erdkamp's work in this regard below), and emphasised the importance of taxes and rents over trade and industry in the success or otherwise of settlements large and small.

A further and seminal contribution to this debate was then made by Moses Finley in his 1973 work *The Ancient Economy*, which, taking the 'primitivist' position, argued that status was a key factor in the economies of the ancient world (Finley, 1999, 45). Developing the work of Weber, he argued that these economic systems (including that of Rome) were embedded in social standing, saying that the ancient world placed so much importance in this regard that there was a clear differentiation between the economic activities in which those in the upper reaches of society could participate and those below them. In this way, these economic systems of the distant past, he argued, were very different from those of today (at least in the West) where there is a general freedom (he contends) for all to participate in commercial and legal enterprises. He also highlighted the lack of the concept of 'economy' in the ancient world, placing its origins in the early modern world, and sophisticated accounting systems (Finley, 1999, 21).

An additional and significant contribution was then made by Keith Hopkins (1985, xiv–xv) who returned to Jones' theme, adding his view that the Roman economic model also allowed for economic growth and was therefore not static. He said this growth was particularly noticeable in the late 1st millennium BC and the first two centuries AD, with political change driving surplus production, and the engagement of a native population with *Romanitas* being either indigenously-led or stimulated by the passive encouragement of the empire (Laurence, 2012, 63).

Next for consideration is Millett's dramatic intervention in 1990 with *The Romanization of Britain*, a watershed in appreciating not only the Roman economy but also Roman Britain, with its principal and controversial focus on cultural change. His work had its earliest roots in Francis Haverfield's 1906 *The Romanization of Roman Britain*, it then being incubated through Finley's conception of the Roman economy, and the subsequent academic debates of the 1970s and 1980s regarding the nature of this economy (Laurence, 2012, 59, 60).

Using socio-economic and anthropological models to analyse a wide range of archaeological, epigraphical and historical data (though with an emphasis on excavations), his central contention of the Romanization process was that the integration of a province into the Roman Empire (in this case Britain) was a two-way social acculturation process, with complex patterns of interaction between the incoming world of Rome and the native population, and with the impact of the arrival of Rome being minimised. In this regard, he believed, there was a low level of centralised control from the centre, at least early in the occupation, he saying:

> The net effect of this was an early Imperial system of loosely decentralised administration which allowed overall control by Rome while leaving the low-level administration in the hands of the traditional aristocracies.

This certainly set him against the views of the likes of Hingley (1982, 17) who earlier argued in favour of the province of Britain as being an administered economy. Millett added that he saw Roman imperialism as an extension of a manifestation of the competitive elite in Rome itself, his referencing of status aligning him with Finley's earlier work regarding the Roman economy (though also incorporating the conception of long-distance trade based on ceramics data), and with imperial expansion being piecemeal rather than planned.

More recently Erdkamp (2005, 2) has used the grain market of the Roman Empire as a cipher through which to appreciate the wider Roman economy. It is particularly relevant to this work given Erdkamp's focus on market integration, pertinent to the *metalla* considered in the context of Roman military involvement in Chapter 6 in terms of their access to markets, transport and connectivity.

He bases his research largely on epigraphic and philological evidence given the lack of material sources to allow reliable statistical analysis. A 'modernist', he believes Roman society was not dissimilar to that of pre-modern Europe (for example using analogies with imperial Russia) and therefore looks for similarities there with the world of Rome. These include the dominance of agriculture (a common thread above), the high cost of transportation, and market integration. Erdkamp (2005, 14) specifically separates out wealthier farms from those of the peasantry, saying the latter less frequently participated in the capital market and often had the poorest land, this often being overworked. This led to a pattern of diminishing returns as more of the output was consumed by those working the land the harder they had to do so to produce this return (Erdkamp, 2005, 15). This stood in juxtaposition to the larger, wealthier farms which found it much easier to generate a larger surplus. Sticking with the peasant farmers, he adds that given the high instability in prices for their produce, and the back-breaking nature of their daily working lives, they most frequently aimed to produce just enough crops to subsist, with productivity significantly diminishing above this line. This would mitigate against the peasantry producing any significant surplus.

Erdkamp later looks at the evident dichotomy in the ability of the two levels of farming to distribute their surplus (such that it was for the peasantry), with the larger estates far more able to sell their produce in bulk, in so doing defraying their transportation costs (often through middlemen). Meanwhile the peasant farmers, with their far smaller surpluses, were much more likely to sell excess produce within their own communities (2005, 135).

He also looks at the relationship between the larger and smaller farms in the context of market integration (200, 143), illustrating this through the level to which the market could compensate against extreme changes in annual yields. In the pre-modern world, the measures to mitigate against such challenges were either storage or the transportation of surpluses to regions suffering shortages, the latter only possible universally if there was a high degree of market integration. He determines that this was actually lacking in the uniform sense, with the Mediterranean not being a macro-region economically but a series of bioclimatic micro-regions (Erdkamp, 2005, 146). In this context, long-range trade and shipping lanes did exist, especially between the large cities and their hinterlands, but not everywhere was so connected, with the majority of the smaller and medium-sized settlements far less integrated and being supplied from their own hinterlands (with most grain purchases here local in nature). Lavan (2014, 1) adds another factor here in terms of market integration, namely proximity to the coast. He says there was a differential in the experience of such integration between landlocked inland regions and those with a coastline. Using data from the distribution of ceramics as an example, he says (2014, 3):

> ...(inland) regions found it more difficult to participate in inter-regional trade (in the context of market integration) because of high transport costs involved in moving goods by river, or especially road, in comparison to those moved by sea.

Bonifay (2014, 557) expands on this idea, using Roman Africa as an example and basing his conclusions once again on ceramic data. He argues that Mediterranean patterns of consumption were only visible along the strip of coastline adjoining the sea, adding that in inland regions local production and markets substituted for more recognisable Mediterranean products. Again, the differential cost of transport is the key factor, and this is a major element defining the provincial (and indeed Imperial) economy.

Returning to Erdkamp, another dichotomy he identifies is again geographical, but this time on a macro-scale. Given the often-present lack of market integration, he argues (2005, 279) that the west and east of the Empire had different means of dealing with occasional harvest shocks. Where such integration was lacking, he says that in the west the shortfall was often taken up by local aristocrats keen to maintain the regional societal *status quo*. In the east however, permanent institutions were in place to deal with such crises, perhaps reflecting their longer exposure to post LIA classical culture.

Finally, as one clear example of substantial market integration, he cites the grain supply to Rome, where he estimates 30–40% of the Sicilian and Egyptian grain was taken as taxes in kind to feed the citizens of the imperial capital (2005, 222, see below for detail on methods of Roman taxation). In terms of how this was transported, his views have been informed by those of both Finley (1999, 128) and Rickman (1980, 4). The former argued that much of the grain importation from Sicily and Egypt to Rome was under government control, with private enterprise being less important. In this context, Russell (2013a, 353) has more recently suggested that, in the context of the improved spatial connectivity that was a manifestation of the imperial experience, state-orchestrated redistributive mechanisms played by far the biggest role in the distribution patterns for goods. Rickman however argued that much of the grain importation to Rome was through the State relying on grain dealers, shippers and warehouse owners, with private enterprise being more important than previously thought. Erdkamp takes a middle ground in this debate between Finley and Rickman, saying that while the private entrepreneurs were vital to facilitate the grain trade in the integrated market, the state closely supervised this through government-awarded contracts and incentives.

Bringing the discussion of the nature of Roman economy up to date, and taking a more 'primitivist' position, Bang (2008, 12) recently challenged its similarity to that of early modern Europe, saying it was more akin to those of large, tributary or pre-colonial Empires such as Mughal India, the Ottoman Empire and the Ming/Ch'ing dynasties in China. In this context, he says it had features which a modern economist would recognise as manifestations of a Smithsonian market economy, but underwritten by the structural weaknesses (from his perspective) inherent in the nature of empire, for example exploitation, patronage and predation (2008, 204). Gardner (2013, 6) broadly agrees with such bi-polar manifestations of the imperial economic experience. On the positive side, he talks of improved spatial connectivity (in the context of market integration, based on modern interpretations of globalisation), the most obvious examples being the extensive Roman road network throughout the empire and improved maritime trade. On the negative side, he talks of commodification and alienation, these in the context of a post-colonial or even Marxist interpretations of the empire. The most extreme example of both commodification and alienation would of course be slavery, with Mattingly (2006, 294) describing a thriving provincial slave trade in Britain and elsewhere. Interestingly, in his critique of Erdkamp's work on the Roman grain market, Lemak's (2006) only criticism is that this aspect of the Roman economy (and a major differentiator when compared to western pre-modern economies) is never properly addressed. Temin (2013, 121), in his appreciation of the

Roman market economy, himself says that while an appreciation of modern economics can be applied to economies of the past (including that of Rome), the issue of slavery requires special consideration.

Finally here, note that later developments with regard to the Roman economy, for example the imposition of the Severan *annona* and the Diocletian's more sweeping *annona militaris* are discussed at length in the concluding Chapter 8.

The Roman Imperial Economy: Making the province Pay

Roman provinces were always challenging to finance, though clearly simple subsistence was not actually their purpose, with each imperial procurator under great pressure to ensure it also contributed substantially to the coffers of the imperial *fiscus*. It had after all to be seen to be *pretium victoria* (worth the conquest). Mattingly (2006, 491), in his stark appreciation of the experience of Britain under the occupation of Rome, is very clear about the economic drivers of the Roman state in this regard, saying:

> The economy of Britain was profoundly affected by the desire of the Roman State to extract resources from the province and this was a constant of Roman Imperialism.

In terms of the imperial economy, and continuing to use Britain as an example, in the first instance this was quickly evident during and immediately after the campaigns of conquest. In that regard the brutal exploitation of the spoils of war by Rome to offset the expensive costs of conquest were the first signs of the presence of the empire. Here, Mattingly (2006, 494) identifies private possessions in the form of portable wealth as being primary targets of the armies of conquest, with the redistribution of the territories of the landed elites being another. Once the conquest was complete however and a territory settled into the provincial family, the primary demands on the Imperial economy would be as follows (Mattingly, 2006, 493):

- The army, in terms of pay, bonuses, discharge bounties, materials, equipment and supplies (noting in Britain's case the exponentially large scale of this military presence given the province was a border territory, see Chapter 2). To give context here, the total annual costs of the salary and discharge bounties for the army in the 2nd century was 150 million *denarii* annually (Mattingly, 2006, 493).
- The provincial government infrastructure, noting for example that the annual salary for the governor alone in Britain was up to 200,000 *denarii* (Mattingly, 2006, 493).
- Transport costs, often facilitated by the state (see above discussion referencing Finley, Rickman and Erkamp with regard to the Roman grain supply).
- Capital investment, including the costs of running imperial properties and public lands.
- Diplomatic subsidies, always a consideration in Britain given the unconquered far north.

These demands were clearly huge in terms of the burden they placed on the province, especially early in the occupation. In this regard, Mattingly (2006, 493) estimates that the overall cost of running the province of Britain would have been 'some tens of millions of *denarii*', and that outside of the spikes in military campaigning activity such as the Agricolan Campaigns of the late 1st century AD and the Severan campaigns of the early 3rd century AD (Elliott, 2016a, 129 and 153).

Reflecting his hard-line view of the exploitation of the provinces by the Roman state and imperial household, and continuing with Britain as his example, Mattingly (2006, 494) goes on to outline the various options available to the state through the imperial economy to ensure the province paid its way. These included:

- The property of the landed classes, always at risk of being appropriated and redistributed by the state when an opportunity presented itself, their individual fortunes being equally at risk of a sudden change in providence for the owner (with confiscated estates often being received by the emperor in the form of a legacy after such an event, see below).
- The landed property itself, also vulnerable to state exploitation through gains from legacies, disposals, land rentals and sales.
- Land controlled directly by the state, in its most extreme in the form of imperial estates, these being considered in depth below given their importance to this work.
- The exploitation of the wider population through regular taxation (see below), tribute demands, liturgies and labour requirements, military recruitment and slavery.
- With regard to rural populations, the use of exploitative tools such as rents, dues, requisitioning, price fixing, and once again, tax.
- The exploitation of natural resources, for example the *metalla* covered by this research. Again, this could come in a number of forms, up to and including being State run and in the most extreme form imperial estates (noting here the wide variety of imperial estate types, not just those associated with industry).
- Profit derived from the existence of harbours, markets (detailed below in the discussion regarding the provincial economy) and trade (which Temin says was specifically stimulated by the *Pax Romana*, 2012, 2), again through taxation (for example indirect taxation through harbor dues) and surcharges. Also included here are customs charges at the borders of the Empire, either from within-to-without the empire (or vice versa) or inter-provincial in nature. The *portoria* standard dues when traversing provincial boundaries were paid near to such borders, though some goods such as those supplied under army contracts were exempt.
- The system of military supply, incorporating a number of aspects of the above. In Britain as an example demand from this source had a marked affect on the economy of the province, involving peaks and troughs in the required output and often long distances for such goods to travel (for example from the Wealden iron working sites to the northern border).

A key theme running through all of the above means of financially exploiting a province for the betterment of the empire was taxation. For much of the Principate, this was based on a periodical census listing the resources of a given province which allowed two direct taxes to be levied. These were the *tributum soli* (based on land) and the *tributum capitis* (based on capitation). Such *tributa* direct taxes were ultimately paid to the procurator, with Mattingly (2006, 496) saying that tax-farmers (working under state contracts), imperial fiscal officials and local authorities often acted as middle-men to ensure the smooth running of the system. Meanwhile, *vectigalia* indirect taxes (such as the harbour dues referenced above) were collected by officials such as *publicani* contractors. While such methods of taxation were the rule, there was clearly regional and inter-provincial variation across the geography of the empire and the chronology of the Principate, with individuals and communities often seeking exceptions in some shape or form. Further, as detailed above, given the lack of market integration across much of the empire, it was often easier to collect taxes in kind, for example in the context of the grain supply to Rome from Sicily and Egypt (see references to Finley, Rickman and Erdkamp above).

The Roman Provincial Economy

Running parallel to the imperial economy was the provincial economy, as detailed above featuring regional markets, free trade and localised patterns of consumption (Mattingly, 2006, 496) and often difficult to distinguish from its imperial fellow economy. Its nature was heavily influenced by the pre-conquest economy of a given province, especially at the beginning of a territory being incorporated into the empire. Thus, in Britain, the market economy in Kent and the south-east was more sophisticated than elsewhere, not surprising given the existing links with northern Gaul (Blanning, 2014, 484).

Continuing the use of Britain as an example, from the point of conquest and the growth of the province it seems that the provincial economy grew extensively here, particularly during the years of the Principate, such that it catered for the top-down needs of the State (and so feeding into the imperial economy) but also for the downwards-up demand from a new consumer class feeding on new ideas and innovations. In this regard, Mattingly (2006, 497) says:

> If measured in simple terms across the period 50–350 (AD), there is plenty of evidence for the evolution of urban markets and the integration of rural territories with them, of an increase in coin use, of expanded manufacturing activity and increased consumption of a wide range of goods across a broad spectrum of sites (military, urban and rural).

Specifically on the issue of coinage, he adds (2006, 497) that this was initially part of the imperial economy given the need to pay the military and administration, only slowly becoming part of the provincial economy and not reaching a level with that used in the Imperial economy until the 2nd century AD. The availability of coinage was then disrupted during the 'Crisis of the 3rd Century' when supply was dislocated and poor quality forgeries entered circulation to compensate.

The key component of the market economy were the markets themselves (mostly located at urban centres) which would have been officially sanctioned by the State (showing again the ever-present proximity of the imperial economy). Such markets, which Temin (2012, 6) says knit the Roman economy together such that it could actually be termed a market economy (though again not in the manner of a modern conception of a market economy), acted as emporia for the distribution of manufactured products, many innovations of the occupation. A key issue here is the inability to identify whether demand for many of these goods would have derived from local communities, or manifestations of the Imperial economy such as the military and administration.

To conclude this sub-section, the experience of the provincial economy was often bi-polar in terms of market integration as detailed above, based on the geography of the territory, with Lavan (2014, 1) and Bonifay (2014, 557) outlining of the importance of being near the coast to get the full benefit of participating in an integrated market (in their example in a Mediterranean context). Evans (2013, 438) too develops this theme in his own consideration of the Roman economy, yet again using ceramic data to explain that the economy of a given area (in the case of his research Britain) always featured a balance between local, regional and inter-regional trade and economic engagement, with geography (through relative transport costs) being a constant factor affecting the balance.

Imperial Estates

Mattingly (2006, 494) says that the exploitation of natural resources as part of the imperial economy in a province was a matter of state control. Referencing particularly the *metalla* (but also noting agricultural activity in this regard, see Chapter 7), this would have been in the form of direct control, at its most extreme in the form of an imperial estate, or indirectly through the use of contractors or natives under production agreements and licenses (they reporting up the procuratorial chain of command as detailed below in Chapters 3 and 6), though with such contracted-out *metalla* enterprises often initiated under direct control by the military before being handed on (Mattingly, 2006, 495).

It was through the imperial estate model that the largest percentage of derived revenue could flow most ergonomically to the imperial coffers, with the least finding its way into the regional market economy. In that sense, it is one of the reasons archaeologists and historians have often cited a lack of display of disposable wealth at a local level, for example in the form of villas, as an indicator of the presence of an imperial estate. Similarly, Mattingly (2006, 495) says there is little evidence that individual *civitates* benefited from their proximity to such resources, another indicator of a significant state presence in the form of unusual land use patterns (see discussion below regarding both).

Given the importance of imperial estates to this work, especially in Chapters 6 and 7, here the imperial estate model as part of the imperial economy is examined in detail. This will include a definition of what an imperial estate was and their types, their management, the evidence used by the archaeologist and historian to identify them (especially when lacking written and epigraphic evidence), the rebuttals to such identification to provide balance, and finally a summary of all of the above to allow an imperial estate template to be developed which can be utilised in this research when considering the nature of occupation-period industrial enterprise in the south-east of Britain.

Crawford (1976, 36), in her detailed study of agricultural imperial estates, emphasised that such geographic economic entities were the personally owned landed wealth of the Roman emperors, the same being true of their industrial imperial estate counterparts (Crawford said the latter included the large scale *metalla*, brickworks and salt pans (1976, 36) though see below with regard to the latter). They were not the only such privately owned assets of the *princeps* however, others including gardens, palaces and hippodromes. They were the most important though, given the wealth they generated for the imperial *fiscus* to be utilised by the state, and while they might change in form or nature across the geography (there being imperial estates in most provinces, though with more extensive documentation for those in the east, Crawford, 1976, 36) and chronology of the Roman Empire, they remained broadly as described above, the landed wealth of the Roman emperors.

Such imperial estates came into the possession of the emperor in a variety of ways. Mattingly (2006, 455) says that imperially-owned (and indeed other state-owned) land was often the result of confiscation at the point of conquest from regional elites (Salway, 1981, 104 cited the royal estates of the Catuvellauni becoming the private possessions of the emperor after the AD 43 invasion) or later in terms of failed usurpation attempts and other revolts. They could also be the result of inheritances from the provincial elite, the imperial household being one of the largest provincial landholders. Crawford (1976, 38) gives an excellent example of the latter, based on written records, in the form of Emperor Hadrian's sister-in-law Matilda bequeathing extensive agricultural estates around Sitifis in Mauretania to the imperial household. Meanwhile, as detailed above, many commentators (Crawford, 1976, 36 as an example) have long argued that the *metalla* and other significant industrial enterprises naturally fell under the immediate aegis of the emperor as imperial estates.

In terms of how imperial estates were managed, below the administrative level of the procurator's office, options could have included the military where appropriate (often in terms of opening up the opportunity in the case of the *metalla*, Mattingly, 2006, 507, see Chapter 6 below), *vilici* (bailiffs, singular *vilicus*), chief tenants (in the form of head lease *conductores*, for example) or other tenurial arrangements, and to confuse matters any combination of such (this also applying to non-imperial state-owned land, adding an extra layer of confusion). Mattingly (2006, 455) is rather blunt in his interpretation of the role of such estate managers, saying in a British context:

Their function was to cream off surpluses from the British occupiers of such lands.

A good example of one such *vilicus* comes from the exceptionally large eastern/coastal Wealden iron working site at Beauport Park in the form of a reference on the bath house stonework entrance to such an official who ran the site (Brodribb *et al*, 1988, 261, see 3.1.3 below).

I now turn to the evidence used by archaeologist to identify imperial estates. These include:

- The written and epigraphic record. As an example, Crawford (1976, 37) highlights papyrus *P. Bouriant* 42 from Egypt dated AD 167, which features an administrative survey of 3,032ha of land, of which 39% were agricultural imperial estates, while the Beauport Park *vilicus* above provides another. Such evidence is clearly the firmest method of identifying such economic entities, though see the discussion in Chapter 6 below regarding the latter example. Other epigraphic examples are more contentious, for example that from the villa estate at Combe Down near Bath (RIB 179) referencing an imperial freedman named Naevius who carried out reconstruction work for the procurator, which, it has been argued, might indicate a possible imperial estate (Mattingly, 2006, 399). Crawford (1976, 36) speculated that such an imperial estate might be related to quarrying. One can perhaps add here the large quantities of *Classis Britannica* stamped tile often associated with a state presence at some of the key iron working sites in the eastern/coastal region of the Weald, including Beauport Park (Brodribb *et al*, 1988, 275, see Chapters 4 and 6 below).
- The lack of villa estates in a landscape featuring other activity, for example large-scale industry. Cleere and Crossley (1995, 68) have for example highlighted this in the context of the eastern/coastal iron working sites in the occupation-period Weald where such elite settlement is singularly lacking.
- Sticking with settlement, other atypical rural settlement patterns (Mattingly, 2006, 455). A good example of one such example is the interpretation of the stone tower and settlement at Stonea in the Fens, Cambridgeshire as a regional administrative centre (Potter and Jackson, 1982, 118) associated with an imperial estate. Here Malim (2005, 126) argues that this central multiple-storey stone building with its surrounding gridded street pattern (for largely non-stone built structures) is a better fit for the model of state-intervention than private enterprise. Artefacts recovered here have also been used to interpret the site's official function, for example writing tablets, a stylus and evidence of luxury food stuffs, as has the difficulty in supplying the stone along regional waterways to build the central structure on this upland 'island' site amid the peat fens. Further, Malim (2005, 126) specifically references the use of the military in facilitating the running of agricultural imperial estates such as that argued for at Stonea.
- Unusual archaeological data, for example ceramic evidence supporting the significant expansion of the farming activity around Stonea in the early 1st century

AD (Hartley and Hartley, 1970) which has been used to date the initiation of the imperial estate there (if such it is) to the visit of Hadrian to Britain in AD 122 (Salway, 1981, 190). Malim (2005, 129) later added the land itself may actually have come under Imperial control after the Boudiccan Revolt of AD 60/61, later being fully exploited from the time of Hadrian's visit and reaching its full potential by the time of Antoninus Pius.

- Unusual and unattributed developments in transport networks. Sticking with the Fens as an example, new and often raised roadways (the Fens Causeway being the best example, though noting this dates to the mid-late 1st century AD) and canals (both needing specialist surveying and engineering skills in their construction) are cited as examples of the Stonea location being an imperial estate (Malim, 2005, 126).
- Unusual developments in land usage. Again using Stonea as an example, significant land reclamation with drainage (which again would have required specialist skills in terms of surveying and engineering) and secondary land division have been referenced in this regard by Malim (2005, 126).
- Demand, in the case of Stonea from the Nene Valley to the west of Peterborough given the rapid population expansion there from the 2nd century AD and for the military in the north of the province, easily supplied from this location given the easy maritime access, a pull factor for the imperial estate's produce if indeed it was one (Malim, 2005, 128). One can perhaps add here demand for building stone in Roman London for the ragstone quarries of the upper Medway Valley through to the mid-3rd century AD (Elliott, 2016a, 102), this being fully detailed in Chapter 6.
- Using Stonea one final time as an example, other industrial activity associated with imperial estates. Here, this is salt manufacturing, as referenced by Malim (2005, 128), which Salway (1970, 10) originally argued was an imperial monopoly.

I now turn to the rebuttals of these various means of identifying imperial estates, given the fact that outside the very hard examples of written and epigraphical data the various models and methodologies of identifying these economic entities are a matter of judgment by the individual archaeologist and historian, even when backed by a substantial body of archaeological data.

In the first instance Mattingly (2006, 371) doesn't see the imperial estates as being so black and white in terms of their identification. Noting, as detailed above, that an absence of villas has often been used to identify an area as a potential imperial estate, he says:

> ...there are no good reasons for thinking that imperial estates would have been devoid of villas, since such properties were often contracted out to private individuals to run for profit. In North Africa, for instance, large imperial estates at the heart of the agricultural zone (such as those detailed in papyrus P. *Bouriant* 42) were studded with farms, villages and villas...The more probable candidates for imperial estates may in fact be found in areas of higher villa development, where rural culture and identity also stand in contrast to the average development.

A vessel of the Classis Britannica Roman regional navy in Britain as seen by one who viewed it first hand. The 'Rocklands ship' image found in Norfolk, graffiti on waste lead. The fleet played a major role in running industry in Roman Britain. James Beckerleg.

This is an important consideration in Chapters 6 and 7 regarding the *metalla* and Roman agriculture. Importantly, he then identifies the variety of candidates who might occupy such villas. These include representatives of the Roman emperors and the state, absentee landowners, the army (including the regional fleets such as the *Classis Britannica*, Elliott, 2016a, 108), members of the *civitates*, settler groups (for example discharged soldiers with investable capital), private individuals (from the home province and abroad), religious bodies and entrepreneurial bodies.

Mattingly also adds, in the context of atypical rural settlement patterns, that in the absence of hard epigraphic evidence it is difficult to detect large agricultural imperial estates on the ground given they possibly resemble other types of agricultural settlement (2006, 455).

Meanwhile Millett (1990a, 120) has also argued that there are a number of problems with the identification of land as an imperial estate. These include his belief that there is no reason to suppose that land owned by the emperor is archaeologically distinguishable today from other types of land use. Additionally, with regard to agricultural imperial estates, he says that if they were created from virgin territory, there would be more sign of a deliberately even distribution of land, for example by centuriation, and this is often lacking (he uses the Fens as his example). Meanwhile, regarding the issue of unusual land use, and again using the Fens as his example, he says there is no reason to believe that local populations would not have had the social organisation needed to reclaim and develop their own land. This is a theme taken up by Taylor (2000, 654) who argues that the canals and roads of the Fens weren't part of an imperial project but the result of localised improvements to an existing network.

Finally, Millett debunks Salway's earlier assertion (1970, 10) that salt production was an imperial monopoly in the province, thus undermining this argument in favour of the Fens – in this example – being an agricultural imperial estate.

I conclude this sub-section by reflecting on the above discussion regarding the nature of Roman imperial estates as part of the imperial economy to determine a usable model going forward in this work given their importance in Chapters 6 and 7. Clearly, outside of definitive written and epigraphic data to support such a geographic economic entity being identified as an imperial estate, classifying one as such is problematic. This is further complicated by the fact that the running of imperial estates themselves were often sub-contracted out, as were other state-run entities within the imperial economy, making a determination as to their nature even more confusing. Such identification must therefore be a question of individual consideration by the researcher, based on the available data. The issue can be helped however by utilising a general though heavily caveated model (noting the reservations of Mattingly, Millett and others above) which can be utilised as a concluding template after considering the data for each candidate in detail to act as a check list. This will help to present a viable if imperfect final consideration for each candidate (whether industrial or agricultural), the specific features I identify in this model being:

- A lack of non-worker related settlement, whether villa estates, non-villa settlements/native settlements or small towns, where one might expect to find them, or otherwise unusual settlement patterns.
- Unusual transport networks.
- Unusual land use patterns.
- An association with other industry.
- The presence of the Roman military in an unlikely setting.

Chapter 2

The Roman Military Machine

This chapter will examine the Roman military machine in detail to provide context when later examining their use in non-conflict duties. Such forces would have comprised both land and naval personnel, the former comprising the famous legionaries and auxilia, the latter the *milites* of the regional fleets. These are considered sequentially here, starting with the legions. The chapter closes with a brief consideration of the nature of Roman military identity, currently the subject of a lively academic debate and particularly relevant when looking at the civilian activities of the military given the potential for greater interaction here with civil society.

For the majority of the Principate, starting with the accession of Augustus, the legions in the west were stationed on the frontiers of the empire where D'Amato (2016, 6) says natural barriers such as the Rhine (in the case of north-western Europe) created a natural frontier, later to be fortified here as part of the famous *limes Germanicus*. The military units themselves were based within easy reach of these borders, for example again in the case of Germany at the four legionary headquarters of Xanten, Bonn, Mainz and Strasbourg (D'Amato, 2016, 7). This pattern was replicated across all of the northern and western borders of the Empire. That is not to say there were not a few permanently garrisoned camps positioned further back from the frontier, for example the fort at Arlaines in the Aisne Valley located 10km west of Soissones, but such bases in no way presented the defence-in-depth that was to be a feature of the later empire.

As detailed in Chapter 1, in the east this pattern of legionary deployment was slightly different, with the major military formations often deployed in or near the major urban centres (though noting these were closer to the imperial frontiers than many of their western counterparts). In both west and east however it was common for small detached units of troops to be sent elsewhere on a variety of duties, with the vexillation fortress at Vindolanda south of what later became the line of Hadrian's Wall providing some excellent examples in that regard. Here, one of the famous Vindolanda tablets (number 841), dated to the AD 90s, shows detached units guarding the provincial governor, being deployed at Corbridge (Roman *Coria*) and even being found further south in the provincial capital of London.

Broadly, these western and eastern patterns of deployment began to change from the time of Septimius Severus (Emperor AD 193–AD 211) and his early military reforms. This is perhaps best seen with his recruitment of *legios I, II* and *III Parthica*, with the second iconoclastically being based at Albanum, 34km from Rome (Elliott, 2016a, 156). Even here, rather than being a response to an external threat, this was a move designed to send a clear signal to the elites of Rome after the turbulence of his accession: behave – or else. It is also from this time that the 'defence-in-depth' deployment of major military formations began to gather pace, with Severus creating what was effectively the first Roman field army (in the form of a strategic reserve) from the Praetorian Guard, the Imperial Guard cavalry, *legio II Parthica* and one of the urban cohorts of Rome (P. Elliott, 2014, 29). This strategy of defence-in-depth came to dominate Roman military thinking as the Principate Empire ended and that of the Dominate began, through the military reforms of Diocletian (who created more new legions than any preceding emperor from the time of Augustus) and later Constantine (sole emperor AD 324–AD 337). This change was ultimately dramatic, with the formations of the late empire radically different from those of the Principate. Thus, by the later empire, the legionaries and auxilia had been replaced by troops where there was a clear distinction between the *comitatenses* field army troops and *limitanei* border troops.

Back to the Principate however, before moving on to examine the specific troop types that would have carried out non-conflict activities on behalf of the state, to provide context for what follows I briefly touch here on the size of the military presence in a given province, in this case Britain. This will give an appreciation of how such a presence would have impacted wider society, and of the resource the state was able to call upon when such troops and naval *milites* were not engaged in military activity.

The province (later provinces and then *diocese*, see Introduction) of Britain is a particularly good example given that this presence was exponentially large here throughout the occupation, it being a border territory. A simple examination of the map of Britain illustrates this, showing Britain as a salient probing north from the western *Limes* on the continent and featuring potential opponents on three sides – Germanic raiders to the east, Irish raiders to the west (a threat which increased throughout the occupation) and Caledonians (and later Picts) in the never-conquered north. Given this threat level it is no surprise that, at its height during the 2nd century AD, up to 55,000 troops were stationed in Britain (Mattingly, 2011, 219). This is an enormous number for this north-western archipelago of the empire, even more impressive when one considers that the population was only some 3.6 million (compared to 64 million in Britain today). In fact, Mattingly's figure of 55,000 for the military presence in the province represents up to 12% of the entire Roman establishment at that time in only 4% of the entire territory of the empire. As is detailed below, one can add to this total for land forces the 7,000 naval *milites* of the *Classis Britannica*. This whole would have put an enormous strain on the regional economy, especially the north and the west where the economic system was almost wholly given up to supporting the military presence there. It was therefore in the best interests of the State to ensure that these military personnel, when not being used for conflict purposes, were put to use creating wealth for the imperial *fiscus* in any reasonable way possible.

The Legionaries

The Roman military machine was a permanent and professional institution by the time of the death of Augustus in AD 14. At its core were the legions, of which the first emperor had inherited around 60 after the vicious civil war from which he had emerged as the victor. He reduced this to 28 and the total would hover around 30 for the rest of the Principate, with for example 29 existing at the time of the accession of Marcus Aurelius and his co-emperor Lucius Verus in AD 161 (Cowan, 2003b, 6).

In terms of numerical strength, by the late 1st century AD the Principate legion numbered some 5,500 men, organised into ten cohorts. Of these, the first cohort had five centuries of 160 men, while the rest had six centuries of 80 men each (Connolly, 1988, 217). Each such century of 80 was broken down into ten eight-man sections called *contubernia* who shared a tent when on campaign and two barrack block rooms when in camp, where they ate and lived together. Additionally, the total compliment of the legion was made up by 120 auxiliary cavalry (Goldsworthy, 2003, 50) who acted as dispatch riders and scouts, and also by support staff.

The numbering and naming of the legions was rather confusing, unusual for the Romans, reflecting their being raised by different Republican leaders (particularly during the civil wars of the late Republic, Connolly, 1988, 217) and emperors, and at different times. Thus, many shared the same number (which was always permanent, D'Amato, 2016, 8) but had different names. For example, there were five 'third' legions. The longevity of the numbering but clear differential with the naming suggests a strong sense of identity within these elite military units. As Goldsworthy (2003, 50) says:

> Legionaries were proud of their unit and contemptuous of others. The standards and the symbols on men's shields...made each unit unique.

The standards were particularly important symbols of *Romanitas* within the legion and a key reflection of legionary identity, with each legion having a variety of types. First and most important was the *aquila* eagle standard, by the time of the Principate made entirely of gold and which only left camp when the entire legion was on the move. Another standard, the *imago*, carried an image of the emperor, while *signa* standards were allocated to each individual century. Flag-based standards were also used, called *vexilla*, one of which showed the name of the legion while others of the same type were allocated to legionary detachments, hence their naming as *vexillations*. A full discussion of military identity, taking into account not only legionaries but also the auxilia and naval *milites*, can be found at the end of this chapter.

Legionaries could be volunteers or conscripted (under the *dilectus*, or levy) dependent on circumstances, though by the time of Marcus Aurelius they were increasingly enrolled as conscripts, usually on a regional basis as with *legios II Italica* and *legio III Italica concors* (Cowan, 2003b, 6). Those recruited by either means were exclusively Roman citizens for much of the Principate, originally all Italian at the end of the Republic though increasingly from Gaul and Spain as citizenship spread.

Connolly (1988, 217) says that the eastern legions often struggled in their recruiting however given the smaller base of citizens and therefore such citizenship was awarded to non-citizens on enrolment.

The term of service of the legionary in the Principate legion was initially 20 years as set by Augustus as part of his military reforms, the last four as a veteran in a unit within the legion dubbed the *vexillum veteranorum* (D'Amato, 2016, 8). Such veterans were excused fatigues and guard duty. The overall legionary length of service was extended by Augustus later in his reign to 25 years, with five as a veteran, a term of service which lasted until the end of the Principate. The increase was due to a shortage of recruits, though Connolly (1988, 218) added that the strain placed on the specially created treasury used to pay a gratuity (the *praemia*) to a retiring legionary was also a factor. Such gratuities were in the form of money (3,000 *denarii* in the late 1st century BC, this rising to 5,000 by the early 3rd century AD) or land, in the case of the latter often in *colonia* settlements or centuriated land parcels (see Chapters 4 and 7 below). The retired legionaries often settled close to their former legionary fortresses, these often developing into *coloniae* themselves as happened with Gloucester (Roman *Glevum*) in AD 97 and Lincoln (Roman *Lindum Colonia*) after AD 86. Payment of the retirement gratuity by land all but died out in the 2nd century AD however.

In terms of the legionaries' lot while in service, they were officially unable to marry until retirement (though they often contracted technically illegal marriages, Connolly, 1988, 218) until the reign of Septimius Severus who granted the soldiers their right to marry, this providing the illegal spouses and offspring legal rights for the first time (Elliott, 2016a, 156). For pay, from the late Republic legionaries received 225 *denarii* a year, increasing to 300 during the reign of Domitian and then 450 under Septimius Severus (AD 193–AD 211), the latter increase making up for a substantial period of time when steady inflation had seen the salaries of the legionaries decrease in real terms. Severus' son Caracalla (sole emperor AD 211–AD 217) increased legionary pay even more, by a further 50% (Herodian, 4.4.7), following his father's advice to keep the soldiery happy above all else. It should be noted however that the legionaries did not receive the entirety of this salary in cash, with the state deducting at source the costs of food, clothing and donatives for retirement. On the positive side, however, the troops were always keen on campaigning given the opportunity therein for booty to boost their regular earnings. Meanwhile, in an age before popular banking, in terms of how their overall wealth was stored Connolly (1988, 218) said that the legionaries handed their savings to their unit standard bearers, an additional duty which placed a huge amount of trust upon them.

Religion was a key element in the daily lives experienced by the legionaries of the Principate, playing a major role in their appreciation of belief and belonging. Given the legionary was a citizen of Rome, he was clearly obliged to honour the gods of the Roman pantheon, in particular Jupiter, Juno and Minerva given their association with the empire's capital. To these in terms of popularity, one can of course also add Mars, given his obvious association as the god of war, while worship of gods associated with the location of a given legion's place of origin (often a local deity assimilated into the Roman pantheon) was also common. Additionally, certain gods also had a specific association with the military, for example, the eastern deity Mithras who was popular with the Roman soldiery across the empire. Worship of all of these gods, and also the dates of the traditional festivals of Rome (together with the accession days and birthdays of emperors), helped structure the religious year for the Roman legionary. Meanwhile, a final element of traditional worship for the legionary was the unit standard, often a symbol of cult worship in its own right whose loss could lead to the unit being disbanded.

Next, though the focus of this book is on the non-conflict role of legionaries, I will briefly touch on the arms and armour of the Principate legionary to give context when reviewing their other activities. Such troops were the elite soldiers of the classical world, being specialist heavy infantry whose arms and armour were geared towards defeating their opponents through the shock of impact and discipline. The principal missile weapon of the front rankers was the *pilum*, a weighted javelin of which two were carried, one heavy and one light (Cowan, 2003b, 30). Each had a barbed head on a long, tapering iron shank whose weighted socket attaching it to the wooden shaft provided the driving force to hammer the weapon through enemy shields and armour, the weighting increasing after AD 80 to improve penetrative power (Warry, 1980). The lighter weapon was used as the legionaries approached the enemy while the heavier one was used immediately before impact; the long iron shafts were designed to bend after impact to disable the use of the opponent's shield. As the Principate progressed into the 3rd century, there is some evidence that these *pila* were replaced by a thrusting spear (perhaps reflecting more exposure to mounted opponents) and light javelins, but certainly the famous barbed *pilum* was predominant for most of our period of study.

Once the *pila* had been expended the legionary drew his sword, worn on the right-hand side for rank and file troopers until the Severan period. For much of the Principate, this was the famous *gladius*, a weapon originating in Spain as the *gladius Hispaniensis* (though note that *gladius* was a generic name for 'sword' from the mid-Republic onwards). Bishop (2016, 9) contextualises the impression it made on the Romans:

> Clearly, the Spanish short sword must have made a considerable impact upon the Romans for it to replace the *xiphos* (its predecessor) so thoroughly.

Rather than being the short stabbing sword of popular legend, the *gladius Hispaniensis* was actually a cut-and-thrust weapon of medium length, up to 69cm long and 5cm in width, with a tapering stabbing point. This developed during the reign of Augustus into the Mainz type *gladius*, which was broader and shorter, featuring a longer stabbing point. A further development, adopted towards the close of the 1st century AD, was the Pompeii-type *gladius*, slightly shorter than the Mainz type with a shorter, triangular stabbing point. All of these weapons used the same cut-and-thrust combat technique, which continued to dominate Roman fencing techniques even when the length of the swords began to increase again in the late 2nd century AD.

The weapons complement of the legionary was completed by the 30cm long *pugio* dagger, again of Spanish origin dating to the Republic, which continued in use throughout the Principate. Both *gladius* and *pugio* were suspended from two individual belts which crossed over front and back.

For a shield, the early-to-mid-Principate legionary was equipped with the curved, rectangular *scutum* (a development of the Republican example which was more oval in shape). Some 83cm wide and 102cm long, it comprised planed wooden strips laminated together in three layers. An *umbones* iron boss was attached to the centre where the shield was slightly thicker. The shield was completed with a calf-skin and felt facing, and given its sturdy nature (at up to 10kg in weight) it was held by a horizontal grip using a straightened arm. Rather than simply being used for protection, the *scutum* an offensive weapon in its own right, being used to smash into opponents to push them over. In defence, it was also a highly effective body shield, with the well-trained legionaries able to deploy it in the *testudo* formation where the interlocked shields provided full cover on all sides of a formation, including from above.

As the Principate progressed a change began to take place with the legionary shield with Cowan (2003b, 31) saying that by the mid-2nd century AD the traditional *scutum* was in the process of being replaced by a large flat (sometimes slightly dished) oval shield, still called a *scutum*. This new design replaced the triple laminate construction of the earlier *scutum* with simple plank construction and stitched on rawhide, strengthened with iron bars. The two specific types appear to have been used side by side for some time however, presumably in either different contexts or with different units, given examples of each have been found at the fortified frontier trading town of Dura-Europos in Syria, both dated to AD 256.

In terms of armour, the legionaries of the Principate wore a variety of types of full body armour. The most commonly depicted in contemporary culture and found in the archaeological record in the early-to-mid period is the famous *lorica segmentata*, constructed of articulated iron plates and hoops. As time progressed this complicated though highly effective armour was simplified for ease of use by the legionary, one example found at the *principia* (headquarters building) at the vexillation fortress of Newstead (Roman *Trimontium*) in 1905 featuring simple rivets to replace earlier bronze hinges, a single large girdle plate replacing the two previous ones and strong hooks replacing earlier and more complicated belt-buckle fastenings (Warry, 1980, 191). Such simplification of this armour continued through to its demise in the mid-3rd century AD.

Other types were also worn however, some with their roots in the Republic such as the *lorica hamata* long chainmail shirt. Weighing up to 15kg, this was the predominant legionary armour of the later Republic and early Principate, it continuing in use throughout our period of study and coming back into full favour in the 3rd century AD when it largely replaced the *lorica segmentata* (being notably easier to maintain). From this point, chainmail coats of various lengths (including with sleeves) became the principal armour of the Roman infantryman through to the end of the empire in the west in the later 5th century AD, and continued to dominate in the east.

A further variant of such body armour was *lorica squamata* scale mail (cheaper than chainmail but inferior in flexibility and protection, Cowan, 2003a, 32) while in the provinces even more exotic types were to be found, for example a suit of crocodile-skin armour found in a 3rd-century AD context in Manfalut, Egypt, and now housed in the British Museum. It is not clear in such cases however if the function of the armour was more religious than military, for example in this instance with a military crocodile cult.

Additionally, when fighting certain types of opponent (such as Dacians using the two-handed *falx* slashing weapon) extra armour was fitted including articulated iron *manicae* arm guards, thigh guards and greaves.

Specific troop types within the legions were also often differentially equipped with armour when compared to the rank and file to mark them apart, with officers frequently shown wearing iron and bronze muscled cuirasses and centurions and *aquilifer* standard bearers in chainmail (even when the majority of legionaries were wearing *lorica segmentata*).

Finally, in terms of military equipment, the helmet of the legionary also evolved throughout the Principate. The traditional Republic Roman Montefortino type, originally a Celtic design featuring a domed conical crown and neck guard, was still in use into the 1st century AD. However, by this time two new types began to appear, again reflecting a Celtic influence following Caesar's campaigns in Gaul and the ensuing incorporation of the territory into the empire. These were the Coolus type with a round cap of bronze and small neck guard (which disappeared in the middle of the 1st century AD), and the iron Port type (named after the site type location of Port bei Nidau in Switzerland) with a deep neck guard. This latter type developed into the classic 'imperial' Gallic helmet often associated with the Roman legionary of the 1st and 2nd centuries AD, featuring an even larger neck guard. A final 'imperial' type was that originating in Italy, hence it being called Italic, which Connolly (1988, 231) called a bronze compromise between the new designs of Celtic origin and the more traditional Roman types. All of these helmets featured prominent cheek guards (again of Celtic provenance) and often a reinforcing strip on the front of the cap to deflect downward sword slashes. Ear guards had been added by the AD 50s.

As the Principate progressed legionary helmets became increasingly substantial, the Italic 'imperial' type disappearing in the early 3rd century by which time all legionaries were being equipped with heavier, single bowl designs (Cowan, 2003a, 41). These were reinforced by cross-pieces and fitted with deep napes, which meant only a minimal T-shaped face opening. While suffering from a lack of ear holes and obscured peripheral vision, such helmets offered exceptional protection. They remained in use until the end of the Principate when they began to be replaced by *spagenhelmes* and ridge helmets that fall out of the main chronological focus of this book.

In terms of non-military kit, when on the march the legionary carried all of his unessential equipment on a T-shaped pole resting on his shoulders, with his *scutum* held in place on his back. Epigraphic evidence shows that helmets were normally strung from the neck across the front of the chest. In terms of the marching kit itself the legionary would normally have a *paenula*, a hooded woolen bad weather cloak made from thick wool which fastened with toggles or button on the centre of the chest (officers wore the shorter rectangular *sagum*, which fastened on the right shoulder using a broach). Additionally, a very important piece of kit for the legionary were his sandals (*caligae*), especially given the huge distance the soldier could expect to march during his military career. Connolly (1988, 234) said that a typical piece of the legionary footwear featured a leather upper made from a single leather piece sewn at the heel, this then being stitched to a multiple-layer hide sole shod with many iron studs. Each such sandal could weigh up to 1kg.

The legionary would also carry a cross-braced satchel for his personal effects, a water skin in a net bag, a *patera* bronze mess tin, a cooking pot and canvas bags for grain rations and spare clothing (Windrow and McBride, 1996, 26). Additionally, and of great relevance to this book, as will be seen later, every legionary in the Principate had to carry a saw, pickaxe, sickle, basket, chain, two stakes and a leather strap to enable him to carry out engineering and fortification activities (Connolly, 1988, 239). This was over-and-above the specialist engineers and troops within the legion, fully detailed in Chapter 4, with the overall marching load of the average legionary thus amounting to an impressive 30kg.

As for the command structure of a legion, from the early Principate under Augustus this was streamlined with a permanent commander being appointed for the first time, usually a senatorial-level *legatus legionis* (Goldsworthy, 2003, 50). Providing context, P. Elliott (2014, 25) says such individuals were usually in their 30s, following a fairly set career path as they worked their way up the senatorial ladder.

This preference for a senatorial background for the legionary legate declined as the Principate progressed, particularly from the time of the reign of Septimius Severus, who was keen to promote the ordinary soldiery. More and more legionary commanders from this time were equestrians and this was formalised in AD 261 when Gallienus issued a statute which from that time forbade senators from taking up the post.

The *legatus legionis'* second in command was also of senatorial-level, being called the *tribunus laticlavius*, a younger man gaining the experience needed to command their own legion in the future. The third in command of the legion was the equivalent of the regimental sergeant major, a seasoned centurion called the *praefectus castorum* (camp prefect) who was responsible for the administration and logistics of the legion. Below this level there were five younger equestrian-level tribunes called the *tribuni angusticlavii* who were allocated tasks and responsibilities as necessary rather than having a bespoke role.

The actual control of each cohort in the legion was the responsibility of the centurions (six to a normal cohort) who had specific titles reflecting their seniority, these based on the old manipular legions of the mid-Republic. These were, in ascending order:

- *hastatus posterior*
- *hastatus prior*
- *princeps posterior*
- *princeps prior*
- *pilus posterior*
- *pilus prior*

Meanwhile an army marches on its stomach and the legions of Rome were no different. In terms of diet, Vegetius (1995, 3.3) in his late 4th-century AD military manual says the troops should never be without corn, wine, vinegar and salt. This was the same for Roman troops of all periods, with bread, porridge, beans, vegetables and eggs forming the core diet of the Principate legionary. Meat would be eaten on feast days, with the wider diet supplemented by local produce and hunting. When on campaign, the daily staples were hard tack and wholewheat biscuits, together with bread baked at the end of the day's march after the marching camp had been built.

Finally regarding the Principate legions of Rome, the below table details all known such formations for reference in the following chapters of the book.

Table 2: The Roman Legions. After Goldsworthy, 2003, 51.

Legion	*When founded*	*Destroyed/disbanded*
legio I *Germanica*	Later republic	Disbanded AD 70 after Civilis Revolt
legio I *Adiatrix pia Fidelis*	Under Nero	
legio I *Italica*	Under Nero	
legio I *Macriana*	Under Nero	Civil war legion, disbanded AD 69/70
legio I *Flavia Minervia pia fidelis*	Under Domitian	
legio I *Parthica*	Under Septimius Severus	
legio II *Augusta*	Later Republic/under Augustus	
legio II *Adiatrix pia fidelis*	Under Nero	
legio II *Italica*	Under Marcus Aurelius	
legio II *Parthica*	Under Septimius Severus	
legio II *Traiana fortis*	Under Trajan	
legio III *Augusta pia fidelis*	Later Republic/under Augustus	
legio III *Cyrenaica*	Later Republic	
legio III *Gallica*	Under Caesar	
legio III *Italica concors*	Under Marcus Aurelius	
legio III *Parthica*	Under Septimius Severus	
legio IIII *Macedonica*	Under Caesar	Disbanded AD 70
legio IIII *Flavia felix*	Under Vespasian	
legio IIII *Scythica*	Under Mark Antony	
legio V *Alaudae*	Under Caesar	Destroyed under Domitian
legio V *Macedonica*	Later Republic	
legio VI *Ferrata fidelis constans*	Under Caesar	
legio VI *Victrix*	Later Republic	
legio VII *Claudia pia fidelis*	Under Caesar	
legio VII *Gemina*	Under Galba	
legio VIII *Augusta*	Later Republic	
legio IX *Hispana*	Later Republic	Possibly destroyed in the reign of Hadrian during the Bar Kochba rebellion in Judea
legio X *Fretensis*	Later Republic	
legio X *Gemina*	Under Caesar	
legio XI *Claudia pia fidelis*	Later Republic	
legio XII *Fulminata*	Under Caesar	

(Continued)

Table 2: The Roman Legions. After Goldsworthy, 2003, 51. (Continued)

Legion	*When founded*	*Destroyed/disbanded*
legio XIII *Gemina pia fidelis*	Later Republic	
legio XIV *Gemina Martia Victrix*	Later Republic	
legio XV *Apollinaris*	Under Augustus	
legio XV *Primigenia*	Under Caligula	Disbanded AD 70
legio XVI *Gallica*	Under Augustus	Disbanded AD 70
legio XVI *Flavia Firma*	Under Vespasian	
legio XVII	Under Augustus	Destroyed in AD 9 in Germany
legio XVIII	Under Augustus	Destroyed in AD 9 in Germany
legio XIX	Under Augustus	Destroyed in AD 9 in Germany
legio XX *Valeria Victrix*	Under Augustus	
legio XXI *Rapax*	Under Augustus	Possibly destroyed under Domitian
legio XXII *Deiotariana*	Under Augustus	Possibly destroyed under Hadrian
legio XXII *Primigenia pia fidelis*	Under Caligula	
legio XXX *Ulpia Victrix*	Under Trajan	

The Auxilia

The legions were only part of the military power Rome was able to deploy in both war and peace. A significant proportion of its martial might during the Principate was also made up by the auxiliary infantry and cavalry, troops recruited from non-Roman citizens, often those recently conquered in the new provinces as the empire expanded in the early to mid-Principate. Such auxilia often retained the military characteristics of their origin populations, for example the Batavian infantry from the great river systems of the modern Netherlands, who accompanied Aulus Plautius in the AD 43 Claudian invasion of Britain, and who were renowned for being able to swim in full armour while retaining their formation. This was a tactic they famously used during the river crossing battle, probably on the River Medway, detailed by Dio (60.19–60.23) during this invasion.

The auxilia originated in the armies of the Republic when allied formations of troops regularly supported the citizen armies of Rome. These fought in their own formations and under their own commanders however, and it wasn't until the accession of Augustus that they were professionalised as a regular component of the Roman military. The auxilia were certainly the junior partners to the legionaries (P. Elliott, 2014, 26), with their pay being 100 *denarii* for infantry from the later 1st century AD (compared to the 300 for legionaries) and 200 *denarii* for cavalry (though those based on the wing of a battle formation were paid 333 *denarii*). As with the legionaries above, all of these salaries were markedly increased under the Severan emperors. Terms of service for the auxilia were similar to those of the legionaries after the later reforms of Augustus – 25 years. Upon retirement, the trooper was given a small gratuity and, much more importantly, a citizenship diploma granting Roman citizenship to the soldier and his heirs.

Despite their lower status when compared to the legionaries, the auxilia were a formidable fighting force in their own right and it was very rare for a campaigning army to comprise only legionaries (in fact it was far more common for a force to comprise only auxilia). Further, even when legionary forces were present, it might often be only the auxilia who engaged in combat, for example at the Battle of Mons Graupius in AD 84 when Agricola finally confronted the Caledonians in a set battle to the south of the Moray Firth in the Grampians (Tacitus, xxxvi.1–2). Here, the governor deployed 11,000 auxiliary infantry together with auxiliary cavalry in an overall force of up to 30,000. The battle was famously won by a frontal uphill assault by Batavian and Tungrian (from Belgic Gaul) auxiliaries, with the legionaries looking on.

Auxilia infantry formations were based on a single *quingenary* cohort of 480 troops or a double-sized *milliary* cohort of 800. Auxiliary cavalry formations, which made up by far the largest mounted component of the Principate military formations, were organised into *quingenary* alae of 512 men or *milliary* alae of 768. Confusingly, auxilia units could also be fielded in units that featured both an infantry and a mounted component, though their organisation is less well understood (Goldsworthy, 2003, 58). One interpretation with regard to the latter is that such units had a full compliment of infantry, with 120 cavalry added to a *quingenary* unit and 240 to a *milliary* unit. Such infantry, mounted and combined units of these sizes were very flexible and could easily be moved around the Empire as needed in the same manner as *vexillations* of legionaries.

Auxilia infantry cohorts of both the smaller and larger sizes were divided into centuries of between 80 and 100 men under the command of a centurion, clearly replicating the similar structure in a legionary formation. These centurions, unlike the auxiliary troopers, were sometimes Roman citizens appointed from the legions (for example by the governor of a province or even the emperor). Others were drawn direct from the rank and file of the auxiliary unit. Above this level the command of the overall cohort was given over to aristocrats from the equestrian class, a *praefectus* for a *quingenary* unit and a *tribunus* for a *milliary* unit.

The majority of auxiliary troops were close order infantry who fought in a similar manner to the legionaries. They were armed with short, throwable spears called *lancea* rather than *pila* and with a sword similar to the legionary *gladius* (Connolly, 1988, 239). Auxilia are never depicted in *lorica segmentata*, they being most frequently shown wearing chainmail or scalemail hauberks shorter and less sophisticated that the equivalents worn by their legionary counterparts. Their helmets seem to have been cheaper bronze versions of those worn by the legionaries, while auxilia shields are most often shown as an oval and flat design (though not to the all-encompassing extent of the legionary *scutum*). The auxilia also provided the majority of the specialist troops of the Roman military formations, for example slingers, archers and javelinmen.

For most of the Principate auxilia cavalry seem to have been armed in a similar way to their infantry counterparts with chainmail shirts (shorter than those of the infantry to allow greater movement in the saddle, and weighing around 9kg), flat oval or hexagonal shields and spears. One point of difference was the use of a longer sword, the 70cm long *spatha* derived from the Celtic long sword (Connolly, 1988, 236). The armour and equipment of the auxiliary Roman cavalrymen did begin to change as the Principate progressed however, becoming increasingly either heavier (ultimately as the *equites cataphractarii* and *clibanarii* of the later Empire) or specialised, for example the javelin-armed *equites illyriciani* and bow-armed *equites sagittarii* skirmishing light cavalry.

The Regional Fleets

The military compliment of the Roman war machine was completed by the naval *milites* of the regional navies. These fleets originated once again with the Augustan reforms of the Roman military. Prior to this date the fleets of the Republic were more often than not *ad hoc* in nature, they being designed to fight symmetrical engagements against opponents such as Carthage, Macedon or civil war rivals in the Mediterranean. As with many other aspects of Roman military power however, the fleets were professionalised under Rome's first Emperor, and on a regional basis reflecting the Empire's expanding geographical reach. By the end of the 1st century AD there were ten such regional fleets in existence, each with a very specific area of territorial responsibility. These fleets are detailed below, with recent research by myself into the *Classis Britannica* giving some idea of their sizes, this particular regional fleet having over 900 ships and 7,000 personnel (Elliott, 2016a, 63). The below table is particularly instructive in that the size of the annual stipend for each fleet's commander also gives an indication of their seniority in the wider military framework of the empire.

Command of the fleets was also reformed under Augustus, he doing away with the single naval command structure of the late Republic which had been led by a single consular-level individual, perhaps with a *praetor* commander from the army beneath him. Instead, to provide greater flexibility, this arrangement was replaced with a devolved structure featuring an equestrian-level *praefectus classis* being

Table 3: Regional Fleets of the Roman Principate. Ellis Jones, 2012, 61.

Fleet	*Annual stipend (sesterces)*
Classis Ravennate	300,000
Classis Misinensis	200,000
Classis Britannica	100,000
Classis Germanica	100,000
Classis Pannonica	60,000
Classis Moesica	60,000
Classis Pontica	60,000
Classis Syriaca	60,000
Classis Nova Libica	60,000
Classis Alexandrina	60,000

appointed for each regional fleet. Reflecting the new post's importance in the imperial hierarchy, the commanders of the regional fleets were directly appointed by the emperor, reporting to a province's procurator rather than governor (though clearly falling under the latter's command for military operations, see Chapter 3 below). Birley (2005, 298) emphasises this importance, saying that in Britain through to the mid-3rd century AD the *praefectus classis Britannicae* was second only to the Procurator in terms of importance within the province's military and civilian chains of command.

As the Principate progressed the post of *praefectus classis* grew into a very senior position, with for example the commanders of the *Classis Ravennate* and *Classis Misinensis* having the same status as the head of the Praetorian Guard in Rome (Elliott, 2016a, 63). Initially senior former legionary or auxiliary officers, epigraphic evidence illustrates that it was common for the *praefectus classis* to switch between land-based military and *classis* command, and also between both of these and senior civilian posts. Later in the 1st century AD, as part of Claudius' (emperor AD 41–AD 54) rationalisation of the civil and military branches of the administration of the empire, the role of *praefectus classis* was opened up to allow freedmen of the imperial household to hold the post. This changed back following the 'Year of Four Emperors' in AD 69 when sea power played a key role in the eventual victory of Vespasian (emperor AD 69–AD 79), the post once again being reserved for members of the equestrian class.

As time progressed new titles began to be added to those of the *praefectus classis* to show their level of seniority (paralleling the stipend levels detailed above). In this context, the commanders of the Italy-based fleets received the title of *praetoria* as an addition to their *praefectus*, thus becoming the *praefectus classis praetorii Ravennate* and the *praefectus classis praetorii Misinensisin*. In the same way, the commanders of the Moesian and Pannonian regional navies gained the title of *flavia*, while the commanders of the Egyptian and German regional fleets gained the title *augusta*.

As part of his headquarters organisation, the *praefectus classis* had a specialist staff working beneath him to help manage his regional fleet. This featured his second-in-command, the *subpraefectus* (essentially an executive officer and aide-de-camp), together with a *cornicularius* acting as third in command and chief of staff. Other key members of the team included staff without a specific portfolio called *beneficiarii*, *actuarii* (clerks) and *scribae* (writers), and *dupliarii* (leading ratings) attached from the naval component of the fleet.

Below the headquarters staff the hierarchy of the regional navies relied on Hellenistic nomenclature, adapted following Rome's contact with Greek culture in the later Republic. Thus, the commander of a squadron of ships was called the *navarchus* (the most senior being called the *navarchus princepes*), with the captain of an individual vessel being called a *trierarchus* (this referencing the name's origins with the commander of a trireme). As the hierarchy progressed downwards land-based Roman military nomenclature was added, with the *trierarchus*' executive team including the ship's *gubernator* (the senior officer who was responsible for the steering oars), the *proretus* (a second lieutenant) and the *pausarius* (rowing master). Other junior officers on the staff of the *trierarchus'* included the *secutor* (master at arms), a number of *nauphylax* (officers of the watch) and specialists such as the *velarii* (with responsibility for the sails) and the *fabri* (the ships carpenter). A number of *scribae* completed the team.

The ships company itself, below the level of the executive team, was called a century, reflecting the preference of the Republican Roman navies for close action based on the expertise of their land-based counterparts. The company was commanded by a centurion, again a direct transference of terminology from the legions and auxilia, he being assisted by his own team which comprised an *optio* (second in command), a *suboptio* (junior assistant), a *bucinator* (bugler) or *cornice* (horn player), and finally an *armorum custus* (armourer).

The rest of the ship's compliment was comprised of marines (*sagitarri* archers, *ballistarii* artillery crew and *propugnatores* deck soldiers), *valarius* (sailors), and plenty of oarsmen (*remiges*, these being professionals rather than slaves), the whole company being styled *milites* (soldiers, the singular being *miles*) as opposed to *nautae* (sailors), again reflecting the original Republican preference for maritime close action.

At the beginning of the Principate service as a naval *milites* was less well regarded than serving in the legions or auxilia, although this did change over time as the regional navies began to make their presence felt. The initial recruits for the navies came from local communities with maritime experience in each fleet's area of responsibility. This recruiting base expanded as the Empire grew, and by the 2nd century recruits were being sourced from inland communities. These new naval *milites* were then trained on the job after joining a ship's crew. This was especially the case for the highly skilled rowers whose training began ashore in *icria* oaring system mock ups.

The terms of service for all of the ranks in the regional navies (up to the *trierarchus*) was 26 years, this then being rewarded with Roman citizenship. Only the *navarchus* could achieve citizenship within this 26-year service period. Perhaps reflecting recruitment issues, after AD 160 this term of service was increased to 28 years.

Each naval *milites* received three gold pieces or 75 *denarii* upon enlistment, with basic annual pay at the onset of the Principate for the lower ranks being 100 *denarii*, putting them on a similar level to the auxilia. Crew members with greater responsibilities were paid an additional amount on top of this, for example those being paid 1.5 times the normal salary being called *sesquiplicarii* and those being paid twice the amount being called *duplicarii*. Just as with the legionaries and auxilia, from this annual salary the naval *milites* would have had to deduct an amount to cover the cost of food, equipment and arms, together with a further amount to be paid into the squadron's savings bank for to provide a retirement fund.

The actual types of vessels operated by the fleets differed chronologically and geographically during the Principate, though by this period the ram and ballista-equipped *liburnian* bireme war galley had by and large replaced the giant polyremes of the Punic, Hellenistic and Roman civil war conflicts of the mid-late Republic. The regional fleets also utilized a variety of different *myoparo* and *scapha* cutters and skiffs, and transport vessels of all types.

The regional fleets of this period had specific military roles, including (Elliott, 2016a, 75):

- Blue-water sea control of the regional oceanic zone.
- Control of the coastal littoral zone in the region of responsibility.
- Intelligence gathering and patrolling.
- Transport and amphibious warfare.
- General maritime supply.
- Communications.

As is fully detailed in the following Chapters, the regional fleets also fulfilled a variety of civilian functions (again paralleling the experiences of the legions and auxilia). In this regard, Parfitt (2013, 45) is explicit, using the British regional navy as an example, he saying:

> The Classis Britannica seems to have (often) functioned...as some kind of army service corps, supporting the Government and provincial army, rather than (just) as a Navy in the modern sense.

Clothing for the naval *milites* differed between the regional fleets, reflecting differing climatic conditions. Taking the *Classis Britannica* as an example, an essential item of clothing in the northern waters at the edge of empire would have been the *birrus* hooded woolen cloak for which the province was famous. Other staples here would have been the *pilos* conical felt hat, a belted tunic with trousers, and either sandals or felt stockings with low-cut leather boots. The short *sagum* military cloak, as used by the officers of the legions, would have been worn when on formal duty.

For weaponry, the marines of the regional fleets were armed and equipped in a similar fashion to the land-based auxiliaries. The principal missile weapons, in addition to artillery, would have been the bow, javelins and darts. *Pila* armour-penetrating javelins as used by the legionaries would also have been used at close range, while for closer work the marines would have been armed with boarding pikes, the *hasta navalis* (naval spear), various types of the *gladius* and the *dolabra* boarding axe. Armour would again usually mirror that of the auxilia with a hip-length shirt of chain mail or scales, while in sculpture the *navarchus* and *trierarchus* are often depicted wearing a muscled cuirass. Helmets ranged from those of a standard military pattern made at state-run *fabricae* workshops to the simple *pilos* conical type. For a shield the marines used the auxiliary wood and leather oval design which, when at sea, would have been stowed along the sides of the *liburnae* over the oar ports.

Military Identity

Throughout this chapter, when considering the legionaries, auxilia and naval milites of the Roman military, reference has been made to military identity, and that is considered in more detail here. This is particularly important given the bearing this has when considering the use of the military for non-military purposes in subsequent chapters.

When compared with the other aspects of Roman society, the military was of course 'other', being separate and therefore able to be deployed for military or other purposes as required. There is now a lively debate however among Roman academia as to whether the military was a single, homogenous whole as often portrayed or whether it featured a variety of different types of identity.

Fortunately, there are a number of paradigms which allow us to study concepts such as multiple military identities. These include:

- Capability and specialisation. This is particularly relevant to this work given the heavy reliance on specialist units for engineering and construction as detailed in the following chapters.
- Chronology. At a simple level here, in the case of land forces we can examine differences in the composition of the armies of the Principate (with the legionaries and auxiliaries detailed above) and the *comitatenses, limitanei* and *foederates* of the later Dominate.
- Geography. This is particularly relevant to this work, with some arguing that a significant degree of regional variation in military identity existed across the Empire. This paradigm affects military identity on two levels, the first being with regard to the place of origin of each given military unit. In this case troops raised in a certain area would definitely maintain an association with it, just as with military units today. In a Roman context, this is visible at a macro level, for example with the *legio* IIII *Macedonica* or the *Classis Britannica*, and also at a micro level, an example being the *barcariorum Tigrisiensum* – Tigris boatmen – who operated from the fortified harbour at South Shields on the River Tyne in the later empire. Meanwhile, the second impact of geography on a given unit's military identity reflected its base of operations which, over time, clearly impacted self-appreciation, no matter how firmly this was originally rooted in their region of origin.

Clearly this debate over military identity continues to be of great interest to those studying the Roman military. For our purposes, however, the fact that the Roman state frequently used the military for non-conflict activity indicates that in a contemporary context the Roman state itself viewed the military as more homogenous than diverse and that is the interpretation used for this work.

Chapter 3

Command, Control and Administration

Having established the size and nature of the Roman military machine, this chapter will explore the channels of command through which this military force was utilised (from the emperor down through the provincial chain of command), both for military activity and also as agents of the State for other functions. It will then specifically examine the use of the military in some of its most important civilian roles as an instrument of state government, namely in helping to administer the empire across its entirety, policing, fire fighting, and finally in the facilitation of the Games.

Imperial Rule

As detailed in Chapter 1, from the time of Augustus, the Roman Empire was ruled by the *princeps*, with Vespasian the first to call himself *imperator*. Augustus himself specifically avoided such trappings of power, preferring to quietly remove the Republican checks and balances on power and to collect the levers of imperial control while still presenting himself as the champion and saviour of the Republic. These acquired levers of imperial control included:

- Taking over the regulation of the Senate, including the ability to convene its sessions and setting out the agenda for its meetings. Emperors also had control over who could be appointed to be a senator, this being based on property-qualifications and being of free birth as in the Republic (see definition of the senatorial class in the Introduction). The means used to make such senatorial appointments was by the granting of the *latus clavus* (broad stripe). Augustus also first instituted a system of pre-senatorial service, with 18-year-old candidates spending a year as a member of one of the four boards (the *vigintiviri*) through which the city of Rome was run.
- Seizing the authority to consecrate temples and oversee religious ceremonies (as the *Pontifex Maximus*, the leader of the college of priests), and similarly taking charge of the appointment of vestal virgins.
- Taking control of the Roman calendar.
- Assuming the legal authority of a tribune. In this capacity, the emperor enjoyed the powers of *consular imperium* (the power the command), *tribunicia postestas* (the power of coercion) and *sacrosanctity* (legal inviolability through sacred law).

- Becoming the supreme commander of the Roman military in all of its manifestations.
- Taking over many of the financial controls of the empire through the management of the imperial *fiscus*.
- Exercising regional authority through the appointment of governors, procurators and *praefectus classis* (see below).

With these powers, the emperor exercised authority through three main bodies. The first was the *Consilium Principus* (main council), created by Augustus to be his central legal and legislative advisory body. Effectively always in session, the *Consilium* was at the emperor's call whenever required to advise on legal matters and the drafting of legislation, in so doing further usurping the powers of the Senate. Hadrian later created a similar and parallel judicial advisory body to focus on purely legal matters.

The most important means of controlling the empire however was through the second body, the *fiscus* imperial treasury. Controlled by a *rationalis* (high ranking financial officer), this became the magnet for the wealth generated in each of the empire's provinces and was used to fund the emperor's activities, including the use of the military for both conflict and non-conflict roles.

The final body was the famous Praetorian Guard, again founded by Augustus and institutionalised by Tiberius under a praetorian prefect. It had a monopoly of force within the walls of Rome over and above that of the *cohortes urbanae* (urban cohorts) and allowed the emperor, if he so chose, to coerce the Senate and people of Rome to his will. It was, however, a destabilising centre of power within the city on occasion, often associated with the appointment of new emperors and later usurpations, leading to its major reform by Septimius Severus upon his accession in AD 193.

Provincial Rule

An imperial Roman province, until the Diocletianic reformation, had two different chains of command to ensure its smooth running as part of the wider imperial structure set out above. The first was of the staff working for the imperial governor, and the second the staff of the procurator. The governor himself was usually of senatorial-level (and an ex-consul) and tasked with ruling the province, he being the military leader and the chief administrator of Roman law. Meanwhile, it was the equestrian-rank procurator who was tasked with making the province pay, ensuring it was *pretium victoriae* (worth the conquest). He reported directly to the emperor and ensured the regular financial contributions of the province to the *fiscus*. This senior team was joined by the *praefectus classis* commander of the regional fleet and his staff, fully detailed above in Chapter 2, a role which increased in importance as the Principate progressed. The *praefectus classis* sat within the procurator's chain of command and, as I argue in previous work (Elliott, 2016a, 75), there was often a cross-over between the roles, a spectacular example being one Marcus Maenius who, when one references two epigraphic mentions of his career from Umbria and

Maryport, appears to have held both posts in Britain in the mid-2nd century at the same time.

The *cursus honorum* career path for senators and equestrians was reformed by Augustus early in his reign and was to stay the same for the majority of the Principate (Birley, 2005, 3). In the case of senators, this was generally as follows (though noting the want of individual emperors to occasionally make a break with the norm):

- *Quaestorship* (lowest ranked magistrate) – 24 years old.
- Tribunate of Plebs/*aedileship* (responsible for public buildings/festivals) – 25/26 years old.
- *Praetorship* (military commander or senior elected magistrate) – 29 years old.
- Consulship (effectively now an honorific title) – 41 years old.

Once at consul level, the senator could be considered for a Provincial governorship, he then appointing his own staff on arrival in his province. At the outset of the Principate arrangements for such staff were *ad hoc*, with the new governor appointing *amici* and members of his own household. In the mid-1st century AD military personnel (the *beneficiarii*, roughly translating as headquarters staff and based on the term *beneficium*, meaning personal favour) began to appear more regularly as members of the governor's staff, not surprising given his responsibility as the commander of the armed forces in the province (Dise, 1997, 274). They were still rare through to the end of the 1st century AD though, beginning to appear in greater numbers in epigraphy as the 2nd century progressed.

By the time of Trajan, the make-up of the governor's staff had to an extent been regularised in the form of the *officium consularis*. This was the body through which the governor would, from this point, formally control his province on behalf of the emperor (and the military located there). It comprised an *iuridicus* (legal expert, the role originating in the Flavian period), three legionary legates and three Senatorial-level military tribunes. The remaining military hierarchy was made up of equestrian-rank officers, with 15 legionary tribunes and up to 60 auxiliary commanders. Many of these military posts were in the capacity as *beneficiarii* as above, they by definition being excused normal duties.

Of equal importance to the governor, however, was the procurator, whose role it was to ensure the smooth running of the province's finances. A post once again having its origins in the reforms of Augustus, it was a position often viewed as a useful counterweight to the governor. The procurator was supported by a number of lesser *procuratores*, mostly other equestrians though with some freedmen. Such personnel would have been finance officers and registrars, along with other superintendents and specialists who were tasked with running major state-sponsored industrial activity such as the *metalla*. The procurator and his team had specific responsibility for the collection of taxes, including running industrial-scale mines and quarries, imperial estates and other state-run monopolies (see Chapter 6). It was here that many of the superintendents and specialists detailed above would have been based. Meanwhile, as already noted, the *praefectus classis* also reported to the procurator, emphasising the role of the regional fleets as something more akin to an army service corps.

Given the focus in this book on the Roman military in its non-conflict roles, the procurator's chain of command is clearly the most relevant to this work. There would have been some specific mechanisms that allowed him to call upon the non-naval (given the *praefectus classis* was already within his aegis) military assets of the governor when they weren't required in conflict-related roles, and serious state-level resources were required to facilitate making the province pay its way. To help in this regard, Hirt (2010, 199) argues that the governors often also appointed a *beneficiarii procuratoris* from his own military team to serve on the procurator's staff, acting as a go-between.

Later, after the Diocletianic reformation, the role of the procurator was replaced by a *vicarius* with responsibility for the new *diocese*, with the smaller provinces within these new units of government being run by a *praeses*-rank governor combining the roles of the original governor and procurator. With this reformation, a new constellation of civil servants supporting state activity was installed, which I explore in detail in Chapter 8.

The Roman Military as Administrators

Turning to the actual non-military tasks performed by the army and regional navies, clearly the provision of an administrative function in a given province would have been a priority.

What is clear from the above narrative regarding provincial rule across the Roman Empire is that, even when taking both the governor and procurator's staffs together, there would have been only 80 or fewer senior officials to run the province legally and financially (possibly a few more after the administrative reforms of Septimius Severus which saw an increase in the number of procuratorial staff and the first iteration of an *annona* service, but even then taken together still minimal in number). In a province such as Britain, with its population of 3.6 million (see Chapter 2 above), a comparison with today's civil service is insightful where over 25% of the population are in public sector jobs (almost 50% in some areas) out of a population of 64 million. It is in this regard that we can therefore see how essential the military were in this first major non-conflict role, as administrators to enable the Principate governors and procurators to run their provinces smoothly and ensure its regular and profitable contribution to the *fiscus*.

The military as administrators would have been at their most visible in a newly conquered territory. Mattingly (2006, 93) details that local military officers exercised very wide powers in such circumstances, including the ability to carry out summary justice, restricting the movement of the native population, carrying out forceable resettlement where it was thought necessary and restricting the ability to trade and indeed assemble. Defeated populations were also immediately liable to pay war indemnities or tribute, to provide animals to haul goods and also to provide forced labour. It is in such circumstances that we can see the roots of the Boudiccan Revolt in Britain in AD 60/61 (Moorhead and Stuttard, 2012, 73).

The conquered territories were also quickly surveyed by skilled military land surveyors to allow the quick assessment of the likely contribution to the imperial *fiscus*. In that regard, it is no surprise the procurators were normally among the first officials to enter the newly created province. Using Britain again as an example, the speediness of this is well illustrated by the fact that the first procurator, Publius Graecinius Laco, was at the outset of his term also the procurator in Gaul (Birley, 2005, 302). The emperor wanted his imperial coffers filled quickly.

The provinces often had a rather bi-polar feel to them in terms of administration, especially those in border territories. Again using Britain as the example, the north and west remained border territories for whole of the occupation, with unconquered Scotland – and later Ireland – being a constant source of agitation. In that regard the military administration of these parts of the province would remain hard-edged throughout the entirety of the period of Roman rule. Mattingly (2006, 290) specifically highlights 'the slow relaxation or continuation of military administration' here as one of the reasons behind differential economic growth in the north and west compared to elsewhere in the Britain. For the south and east of the province, however, fully functioning parts of the Roman Empire, the administration swiftly switched over to the standard pattern experienced elsewhere in the empire, though again with the military providing the personnel required.

Looking specifically at how the military were utilised to facilitate administration, in the first instance one can of course immediately look to the governor's own *officium consularis*, the principal tool used to both govern a province but also being capable of turning its hand to any administrative task required of it (Goldsworthy, 2003, 144). In his appreciation of the governor's staff during the Nervo-Trajanic and Antonine dynasties, Dise (1997, 274) makes it clear that it was common for troops under the governor's control to be deployed to his staff to help administer his province.

Provincial governors also often deployed *beneficiarii* from the military to command and facilitate the operation of way-stations (*stationes*) on the major trunk routes of the empire, including those utilised by the *cursus publicus* state courier service created by Augustus. Here they acted as the governor's local representative, fulfilling a variety for roles including enforcing the collection of taxes and their smooth transport to the imperial *fiscus* (see Chapter 8 regarding how this changed with the onset of the Severan *annona*, and particularly Diocletian's later *annona militaris*). Further, in the specific case of the separate *annona* grain supply to Rome, which dated to the Republic, Fuhrmann (2012, 129) highlights the use of *propugnatores* marines to ensure the safe movement of this vital grain supply from the harbours of Pozzuoli (Roman *Puteoli*) and Ostia to the capital. Meanwhile, in his correspondence with Trajan (emperor AD 98–AD 117), Pliny the Younger also gives insight into the utilisation of military personnel for such tasks involving the transport network, including escorting officials and directing traffic (as well as guarding prisons, Epistles, 10, 19f). With all of these examples there was clearly a cross over with the policing role of the Roman military detailed below, ensuring that the transport network remained free from interference by *grassaturae* (banditry activity, Fuhrmann, 2012, 102).

The specific roles played by military personnel in the more general administering of the empire was dependent on the nature of the community within which they were embedded. Clearly there was a difference in the experience of the military administrator between those deployed in the larger towns, small towns (such as Rochester, governing the *pagi* of what is now western Kent) and rural communities. Even within the larger towns, there was again a difference between those based in the *coloniae*, *municipia* and *civitas* capitals. In the former they would have had a closer relationship to the magistracy given the nature of such settlements with their settled veterans, while for *municipia* there would most likely have been a greater focus on enabling commerce. Meanwhile, for the latter the military administrators would have been key facilitators of the political and economic management of the various *civitates* in a province.

We are fortunate to have a number of very specific examples in the historical record and epigraphy of the military being deployed in such administrative roles at various types of settlement across the empire. One is provided by a Babatha, an early 2nd-century resident in the province of Arabia, whose private papers were found in Israeli caves at Khirbet Qumran. These papers detail her property assets as recorded in an official census in December AD 127, and indicate that her declaration was made to a cavalry commander named Priscus, who was acting in this administrative role of behalf of the Governor of the province.

Britain has similar examples, including an enigmatic one set amid the troubles on the northern border around AD 117 which eventually drew Hadrian to the province. This is with regard to a cavalry prefect named Titus Haterius Nepos who is detailed in a contemporary inscription carrying out a census in Annandale in Dumfries and Galloway. Such an act was clearly designed to put the mark of Rome on an unimpressed local population (Elliott, 2016a, 140). A further example of the military carrying out an administrative function is with regard to the agricultural imperial estate some have argued existed in the Fens in northern East Anglia and southern Lincolnshire during the occupation. Here Malim (2005, 126) suggests such a role for the military, most visible later in the occupation when military style belt fittings and crossbow-type brooches have been found in non-military contexts.

Others examples of the military as administrators come in the form of centurions such as T. Floridius Natalis of the *legio* VI *Victrix*, who performed the role of regional administrator at Ribchester, and C. Severius Emeritus of *legio* II *Augusta*, who performed a similar role in Bath. Here, he is recorded restoring a damaged shrine. Meanwhile the Vindolanda tablets mention a *centurio regionarius* based in Carlisle (Roman *Luguvalium*). Mattingly (2006, 187) also highlights the phenomena of *praefecti genti* (tribal prefects) drawn from the officer ranks of the military being found elsewhere in the empire, the most likely being found in the earlier *civitas* capitals as a newly conquered territory transitioned to being a full part of the Roman Empire.

The Roman Military Policing the Empire

Following on from the utilisation of the Roman military as the administrators of the empire, we can now consider their associated role in policing the empire.

This is most evident in the east where, for much of the Principate, the major legionary formations were often based in or near major urban centres such as Antioch and Alexandria (the two largest cities in the empire by a large margin). As an example, in the case of the latter, the two-legion garrison of the province of Egypt was based at the legionary fortress of Nikopolis close to the provincial capital, while the *Classis Alexandrina* regional fleet was based close to or in the city itself. Goldsworthy (2003, 143) argues that, given their huge populations, such cities often experienced turbulent unrest, with the military presence there being deployed to restore order with violent force.

Meanwhile, elsewhere in the empire, Fuhrmann (2012, 200) highlights that while the public perception of the *Pax Romana* was one where the military were dispersed to the far-flung borders of the empire, this was not actually the case and it was the norm for military units of various sizes to be deployed within the empire on various (usually non-conflict) duties, this over and above the larger embedded examples in the urban centres of the east detailed above. Whether reporting to the governor or local magistracy, we have direct evidence for these military personnel often being used in a policing function, for example with a document from Egypt dated AD 207 detailing that a centurion named Aurelius Julius Marcellinus was contacted by a woman called Aurelia Tisais who claimed her father and brother had been murdered on a hunting trip. Another document, dated AD 193, has a centurion named Ammonius Paternus being contacted by a man known as Syros with regard to the abuse of tax collection. Such cases give insight into the daily function of the military carrying out everyday policing, in these and other cases the centurions in question having the power to make arrests and then seek judgment through the legal system and local magistracy.

Outside of the day-to-day policing functions of the Roman military, the state also used them as a resource when sterner disciplinary action was required against specific communities. Fuhrmann (2012, 125) details one such example when the Emperor Tiberius (AD 14 to AD 37) sent a Roman cohort and troops from a client kingdom to deal with an unspecified scandalous incident in Pollentia in northern Italy. The troops surrounded the town and imprisoned most of the adult population who were the given life sentences in prison. A Praetorian cohort was similarly used by Nero (AD 54–AD 68) to stamp out insurrection in Puteoli in Campania in AD 58. The military was of course the force also deployed to deal with slave revolts, Tiberius for example dispatching a force to deal with such an incident in southern Italy in AD 24.

In cities which lacked such an embedded garrison as seen in the east, any available military deployed in a policing role were often joined by an urban gendarmerie, for example the famous six *cohorts urbanae* (urban cohorts, initially three) of Rome itself, formed by Augustus as a balance to the power of the Praetorian Guard (themselves deployed by a number of emperors to maintain order during times of crisis, see above). The importance of the *cohorts urbanae* is evident in the fact that they were commanded by an ex-consul in the form of the *praefectus urbi* (urban prefect). These were joined in the city by the *vigiles urbani* (watchmen of the city), principally firefighters (see below) but who also performed a night watchmen role.

The Roman Military as Firefighters

Firefighting was another public function of the military, D'Amato (2009, 14) highlighting the example of the two cohorts permanently stationed at both Pozzuoli and Ostia to guard against fire at the port facilities there. In other urban environments, for example Rome, the *vigiles urbani* described above were employed in this role (with Fuhrmann, 2012, 129, arguing it was actually such *vigiles* who were deployed at Pozzuoli and Ostia from the time of Claudius). The original such force was founded in the capital city by Augustus who formed 4,000 freedmen into seven cohorts for this role. Fuhrmann (2012, 117) describes them as military firemen, though perhaps they are again best thought of as another form of gendarmerie as with the *cohorts urbanae* given the night watchmen role outlined above. They were certainly a significant institution within Rome itself given they were commanded by an equestrian level *praefectus vigilum*.

The success of such fire-fighting forces is questionable however, using Roman London as an example, where occasional large conflagrations are known to have destroyed large parts of the provincial capital during the Roman occupation. One well known such event occurring during the reign of Hadrian.

The Military and the Games

Finally, the *milites* of the regional fleets were also deployed in a very specific civilian context to facilitate the smooth running of the games in the arenas of the Empire, particularly around the Mediterranean and in the east. This is with regard to their use in operating the *vela* (sail) awnings in arenas such as the Colosseum in Rome which provided vital shade against the hot sun. Fuhrmann (2012, 129) highlights the specific example of permanent detachments from the *Classis Ravennate* and *Classis Misinensis* being stationed in Rome for this purpose, clearly a prestige appointment for these naval *milites*. Such a role may occasionally have been slightly less savory however, with Commodus known to have called on these sailors to punish the crowd on occasion, emphasising that even when deployed within a civilian context the military were still 'other' when compared to the rest of society.

Chapter 4

The Roman Military as Engineers

The Roman military was also highly skilled in other areas too, with engineering and construction being the two subjects which most resonate with both the academic and public audience. One only has to look at the output of their expertise across the breadth of the empire, whether in the form of the famous Roman roads, canals and canalised rivers, bridges, aqueducts, fortifications, public buildings or indeed the wider built environment. Examples of each of these are considered in great detail in Chapter 5, which looks at the great construction projects of the empire facilitated by the Roman military. Here however, to set the scene, I consider the Roman soldier as an engineer (both in terms of managing such activities, and physically participating in them). The narrative of the chapter is specifically designed to provide the reader with an understanding of how the Roman military was able to undertake such impressive feats of engineering and construction, beginning with the engineering skills of the individual Roman soldier himself (whether legionary, auxiliary or naval *milites*). I then turn to the specialist engineers within the military units who, over and above the skills of the average soldier, provided the wider expertise needed for engineering projects of such ambition. This focus then tightens to look at specific skillsets, beginning with surveying techniques (a key feature of military *Romanitas*), before considering construction techniques. Finally, to provide context, the chapter closes with a review of Roman construction machinery and Roman construction materials. My aim here is for the reader to then be fully equipped to engage with the examples of military construction expertise detailed in Chapter 5.

The Roman Legionary as an Engineer

The professional soldiers themselves were skilled engineers in their own right, able to fully participate in the construction of not only their own fortifications but civilian structures of all kinds too (many detailed in Chapter 5 with reference to specific units). As Southern (2007, 103) says:

> Building work played an enormous part in the legionary's (and other troop types) working life. It was the legionaries who built the roads and bridges, the forts and fortresses in any province, and they are also attested to have worked on canals and river-widening projects.

Goldsworthy (2003, 48) argues that the legionaries would have willingly provided any required labour force in this regard, not surprising since for the majority of the late Republic and Principate these were highly motivated and disciplined troops, and the same could be said for other troop types too (though Goldsworthy, 2003, 146, later adds it was perhaps more common for legionaries to be involved in building work than others).

To enable them to participate in engineering and construction work, in addition to their panoply of fighting equipment, as detailed in Chapter 2 each legionary in the late Republican and Principate legions also had to carry a stake, saw, pickaxe, sickle, basket, chain and leather strap. Indeed, such was the load carried by the legionaries of this period that they were nicknamed *muli mariani* (Marius' mules) after the great military-reforming seven-times Republican consul. The carrying of such engineering and construction equipment was also true of the auxilia and the naval *milites* of the regional fleets, with D'Amato (2009, 15) detailing the remains of one such marine found at *Herculaneum* who was carrying not only his military equipment (for example sword and dagger on military belt) but also a wide selection of carpenter's tools. He has been identified as belonging to the *Classis Misinensis* on the west coast of Italy.

When larger construction projects were undertaken by the Roman military, either in terms of management or the physical work itself, it was common for manpower to be drawn from a variety of different units, for example the vexillations from *legio* II *Augusta*, *legio* VI *Victrix* and *legio* XX *Valeria Victrix* who all participated in the construction of Hadrian's Wall (an example considered in detail in Chapter 5 below). Here, each legion was given responsibility for a specific stretch of wall construction, with Goldsworthy (2003, 146) saying:

> The division of building works between the normal sub-units of the army appears to have been standard practice.

Such work entailed, for the most part, back-breaking hard physical labour outside of the planning/administrative process. Goldsworthy (2003, 147) also adds that it was common for the military to participate in the construction of roads across the empire (again see Chapter 5 below for specific detail), and here the physicality of this labour is evident, with Fields (2003, 27) highlighting the scale of the task faced by the legionaries and other troops. He cites work by the Royal School of Military Engineering who estimated it would have taken 40 man-hours to build 100m of roadway over grass, 450 over heathland and 600 through forest.

While Chapter 5 considers the great construction projects across the empire in which the Roman military participated, perhaps one of the best examples of their prowess in this area (given the quantity involved) is with regard to something much more mundane, namely marching camps. In normal circumstances, at the end of a marching day in enemy territory the Roman military of the late Republic and Principate would build a marching camp, largely through the labour of the legionaries (including specialist pioneers, see below) and auxilia (and sometimes the naval *milites* of the regional fleets). Constructed in a few hours after the day's march, the camps came in a variety of sizes based on the mass of the force that needed protection. A typology for permanent fortifications is detailed above in the Introduction, and their temporary equivalents highlighted here in general paralleled this, but at their extreme upper limit marching camps could be as large as those of up to 70 ha in size utilised by Septimius Severus in his Scottish campaigns in the early 3rd century. These massive fortified bases were able to house multiple legions, auxiliary formations and units of naval *milites.*

While temporary fortifications by nature, often being permanently abandoned after a day or two of use, marching camps nevertheless required substantial amounts of trained military labour in their construction. Almost always playing-card in shape, they generally featured a deep ditch between one and two metres wide, with the spoil then being used to create an internal rampart. Atop this ran a palisade created by the stakes the troops carried as part of their specialist engineering equipment (see above, with Oleson, in his appreciation of engineering and technology in the classical world, saying that a regular part of Roman military training was designed to enable this rapid raising of such fortifications, 2009, 702). This palisade was either a continuous wooden barrier or one created by the

Sequence of five defensive ditches at the Roman Flavian and Antonine fort site at Ardoch in Perth and Kinross, showing the scale in terms of depth and width of those used at marching camps, five such camps lying to the fort's immediate north. Simon Elliott.

Site (ploughed field in foreground) of the Roman Flavian and Antonine fort at Newstead (Roman Trimontium) in the Scottish Borders, with seven marching camp sites in the immediate vicinity. The largest, at an enormous 67 ha, dates to the Severan incursions in Scotland in AD 209 and AD 210. It lies to the south of the fort, across the greenery seen tracking left to right in the picture above the ploughed field. Simon Elliott.

stakes being lashed together to form large caltrops. Within this barrier would then be set out the camp for the night, effectively recreating the interior layout of a permanent Roman fortification. Cowan (2003a, 45) explains that after a night's rest (though noting that up to 20% of the soldiery would have been on guard duty at any one time), or longer if the formation stayed in one place for longer, the camp was then struck in swift order:

> In the early morning, camp was struck as quickly and in as orderly a way as it had been constructed. The first trumpet call signalled the striking of the tents; the second to ready the pack animals and destroy the camp; the third to fall into marching ranks.

Even though the camps were deliberately slighted to deny their use to any enemy after being abandoned, their substantial nature is clear in that even today one of the clearest ways to track the path of a Roman campaign in enemy territory (for example, in Scotland, the Agricolan Campaigns of the late 1st century AD and the Severan campaigns of the early 3rd century AD, Elliott, 2016a, 129 and 153) is to follow the lines of the marching camps in the archaeological record, their outlines often still being visible in the landscape today. In the case of the Severan campaigns this is well-defined enough to see the legionary spearheads separating as they headed north towards Stonehaven, then rejoining as they approached their furthest penetration into enemy territory.

Specialist Engineers Within the Military

The military formations of the later Republic and Principate Empire also included specialist pioneer military engineers, and also a large number of specialist craftsman, engineers and administrators who were attached to larger units, including highly experienced surveyors, architects and builders (Goldsworthy, 2003, 146).

In terms of the former, such pioneers fulfilled much the same role as their counterparts in subsequent regular military formations throughout history though perhaps today being more akin to modern combat engineers. For example, Cowan (2003a, 44) says that when on the march in enemy territory such specialists (together with assigned regular troops equipped for construction work as above) went ahead of the marching column to clear the path of the advance and, as the day's march neared its end, prepare for the building of the marching camp. I also recently argued that similar specialists from among the naval *milites* of the regional fleets built fortified assault harbours to speed the advance of legionary spearheads following coastal routes during Roman campaigns of conquest (Elliott, 2016a, 119).

However, it is with the specialists that this work is most interested, and to that end most units within the Roman military, whether legionaries, auxilia or naval *milites*, contained a very wide range of artisan skills and crafts. Paternus (Digest, 50.6.7) usefully details many such specialists in his list of legionary *immunes* (soldiers exempted from general duties because of their specialist skills), including ditch diggers, farriers, pilots, master builders, shipwrights, ballista makers, glaziers, arrow makers, bow makers, smiths, coppersmiths, helmet makers, wagon makers, roof-tile makers, water engineers, swordcutlers, trumpet makers, horn makers, plumbers, blacksmiths, masons, woodcutters, limeburners, charcoal burners, butchers, huntsmen, sacrificial animal keepers, grooms and tanners. This range of specialist skills, and the scale of their output or contribution, would have been greatest in the legionary and vexillation fortresses, for example being very visible at the fort at Vindolanda where references in the famous tablets speak of supplies of iron and lead and smithing in general, of *scutarrii* shieldmakers, and with archaeological data from spreads of tap slag, charcoal, ash and broken crucibles providing further clear evidence of extensive, self-contained metal-working and other related skills. These military workshops produced much of the weaponry and tools for their respective formations, over and above the large state-run *fabricae* detailed below in Chapter 6. The tablets also reference *sutores*, leather workers and cobblers, always in demand if only to maintain the tentage needed to keep the army in the field when on campaign (some 70 goatskins were required for each tent, 48 of which were needed by even the smallest auxiliary unit). Meanwhile, specifically in terms of construction and engineering, such specialist military personnel in the legions also included *agrimensor* land surveyors, *librator* land levellers and *mensor* quantity measurers (Garrison, 1998, 75). In the case of the military building aqueducts (see examples in Chapter 5) one can also add here *aqualegus* aqueduct inspectors.

These specialists of all types were an ever present within the military formations, and thus a resource always available for non-military activity, they coming even more sharply into focus in the context of those tasked with the smooth functioning of their unit, namely administrative specialists. To that end most military formations also included a range of clerical staff drawn from the ranks, responsible for roles including the keeping of grain store records and also managing the financial accounts of the troops (Southern, 2007, 103). Details of such *immunes librarii* can be found from across the empire, for example Septimius Licinius of the *legio* II *Parthica* who set up a commemoration to a daughter in Albano, Italy, and Marcus Uplius Firminus who similarly set up an inscription in Potaissa (modern day Torda), Dacia.

Roman Surveying Techniques

The Roman military were the supreme surveyors of the ancient world, putting the stamp of Rome in a very physical way everywhere they went. Highly skilled professionals, the military surveyors used a number of tools, instruments, and techniques (all detailed below) to plan the settlements, farmland, courses for roads and aqueducts and fortifications that were an every day part of the experience of living within the Roman Empire. This was particularly the case at the beginning of a territory becoming part of the Roman Empire, as set out by Poulter and Entwhistle in Chapter 5 below in the particular example of roadways (2016, 12) and also by Wilkinson (2009, 41). Mattingly is also very clear in his belief regarding the importance of surveying as part of the expression of *Romanitas*, military or otherwise, he saying (2006, 359):

> A fundamental tool of Imperial Government was accurate measurement of the extent and quality of landholdings and the Romans were skilled in this area.

Such was the sophistication of the surveying process that land marked out for settlement and, particularly, farmland was categorised into three types, these being divided and assigned land (centuriated, based on *centuriae* squares of around 706m per side), land measured out but only in outline and not assigned, and land not defined by measurement (*ager arcifinus*). This surveying expertise was particularly evident in Italy, southern Gaul, Africa and Spain where huge orthogonal (right angled) land surveys created a dense pattern of centuriated land to impose the rule of Rome across vast swatches of land, tracking the Roman Republic's campaigns of conquest in the later centuries BC.

The Roman expertise in surveying was an amalgam of the experience gained or acquired as the Republic, and later the empire, expanded and integrated new cultures, they then refining it to a fine art as advanced as anything until the advent of the modern era. Whether building roads of epic scale or creating new stone-built planned settlements (for example London, a Roman founding), the *agrimensores*, *libratores* and *mensores* used a panoply of advanced technical equipment which ensured the quality and accuracy of the work. Such specialist surveying equipment included:

- The *decempeda*, a graduated measuring rod of 10 Roman feet with iron or bronze caps at either end, which was the principal tool of the surveyor. An *agrimensor* would typically use two of these laid end-over-end (leapfrogging as it were) while laying out a routeway or wall course.
- The *groma*, comprising a vertical staff with a tapered end, featuring at the top horizontal cross-pieces which were mounted at right angles onto a bracket. Each of the cross-pieces had a plumb line with bob hanging vertically from each end (the cross pieces and plumb lines being called the *stellata*), the tool being used to survey straight lines and right angles. Another key tool of the *agrimensor*, the *groma* was particularly associated with laying out roadways and the distinctive grid patterns of planned Roman settlements and is thought to have originated in Egypt. To use the *groma* the *agrimensor* used the plumb bobs as guides to lay out a line of flags or stakes. Then, using the naked eye, the flags or stakes could be constantly realigned for the length of the route being surveyed to maintain a straight line as required, with the sun and stars, astrolabes, and armillary spheres (a model of objects in the sky) being used to help with accuracy.
- The *chorobates*, in effect a Roman spirit level, featuring a long wooden frame with vertical legs, plumb bobs, a water level in a channel carved in the top and sightlines to assist finding the true horizontal. The *chorobates* was used to find multiple different levels between two points, with the water level being used if conditions were too windy for the bobs to be used. To use the tool the surveyor would insert wedges beneath the legs until it was level and then use the sightlines and a graduated staff to calculate the angle of an incline through the use of basic trigonometry. The *chorobates* was particularly used for leveling ground before construction work began, though when such sophisticated equipment was not available a rudimentary spirit level in the form of an elongated basin with a mark at either end to signify a level could be substituted.
- The *dioptra*, a circular table fixed to a tripod calibrated with angles, originally invented in Greece. Through the use of four screws the *agrimensor* levelled the table, finessing this with the use of two water levels set at 90 degrees to each other. The operator then used a rotating bar set with sights which pivoted around the center of the table, allowing the user to observe distant objects, then by rotating the circular table allowing a calculation to be made regarding a second object. The *agrimensor* could also measure distances using the *dioptra*, taking two readings from different points a known distance apart and then using triangulation to calculate the exact distance. The *dioptra* was the forerunner of modern surveying equipment and was used when even greater accuracy was required than that provided by the *chorabates*, or when a gradient was too steep to use the *groma*.

- The *libra*, another means of measuring gradients, thought to be a set of scales incorporating a sighting tube. Once suspended, the *agrimensor* could use the tool to calibrate a measurement.
- The *hodometer*, another advanced tool for measuring distance which consisted of a small cart which the surveyor would push along. This featured a one-toothed gear which was attached to the cart wheel, this engaging another gear featuring 399 short teeth and one longer tooth. Once the cart had travelled a distance of one Roman mile, the long tooth pushed a pebble into a bowl, allowing the *agrimensor* to count the distance traveled at the end of each day of surveying a new route. This also allowed accurate milestones to be set up along major surveyed highways.

Hamey and Hamey (1981, 14) used the construction of the Aqua Anio Vetus aqueduct (built in the 3rd century BC to provide an additional water supply to Rome from the River Anio) as an example of Roman surveying techniques in action. This was 64km in length with a difference in height between the source and the aqueduct outfall of 220m, which gave an overall fall of one in 291. The key to the successful construction of the aqueduct, given it relied on gravity to provide the water supply, was to actually work out these details well in advance before building commenced, and to do that the *agrimensores*, *libratores* and *mensores* (helped no doubt by an *aqualegus* inspector) would have laid out as straight a route as possible using wooden stakes (though making use of the natural topography as necessary). They then used their *dioptra* several hundred times over the whole required distance (it having a fairly limited sighting distance) to record each individual reading's difference in height in wax tablets, these then being added together to provide the total height difference from the start to the finish of the structure. Once this height difference was known, and with the route already laid out, construction could commence.

Roman Construction Techniques

Whether considering Roman roads, canals and canalised rivers, bridges, aqueducts, fortifications, public buildings or the wider built environment, once the surveying had been completed the Roman military specialists initiated the construction process. This is evident across the entirety of the Empire and, as in many other areas of Roman culture including surveying above, was the result of the acquisition of many of the most important construction techniques from the ancient world as the Republic and later empire expanded first across Italy (particularly from the Etruscans) and then later throughout the Hellenistic east. Such techniques included the arch, vault and dome that were to underpin the ongoing development of construction techniques in the Roman empire (their widespread appearance being dubbed the Roman Architectural Revolution), taking it on a different path to the Greek world which had initially preferred the use of 'post-and-lintel' construction.

In terms of arch construction, a key Roman technique was the use of the *voussoir*, this being a wedge-shaped element allowing the arch to be built out using multiple such *voussoirs*. The centre stone at the apex of such an arch is called the keystone, while the two lowest *voussoirs* on each side are called springers and are found where the arch sits on its vertical support. The Romans developed such arch construction into a fine art, with Hamey and Hamey (1981, 38) saying:

> Placed side by side, (such) arches could form an arcade of almost any length, to carry a road or a water channel. If extra height was needed, one arcade could be built on top of another.

Progressing from the arch, the vaulting techniques employed by the Romans again used simple geometric forms, for example the semicircular barrel vault (formed by the extrusion of a single or pair of curves over a given distance), groin vault (created by the intersection at right angles of two barrel vaults, a Roman innovation) and the segmental vault. A fine example of these various vaulting techniques can be found in the Forum in Rome in the form of the Basilica of Maxentius and Constantine, completed in AD 312. Still imposing today, the building consists of a central 80m by 25m nave covered by three groin vaults which are suspended to a height of 39m, these being supported on four large piers and with the western end featuring an apse which once housed a colossal statue of Constantine. The lateral forces of the huge groin vaults are held in place by four flanking aisles measuring 23m by 17m, they

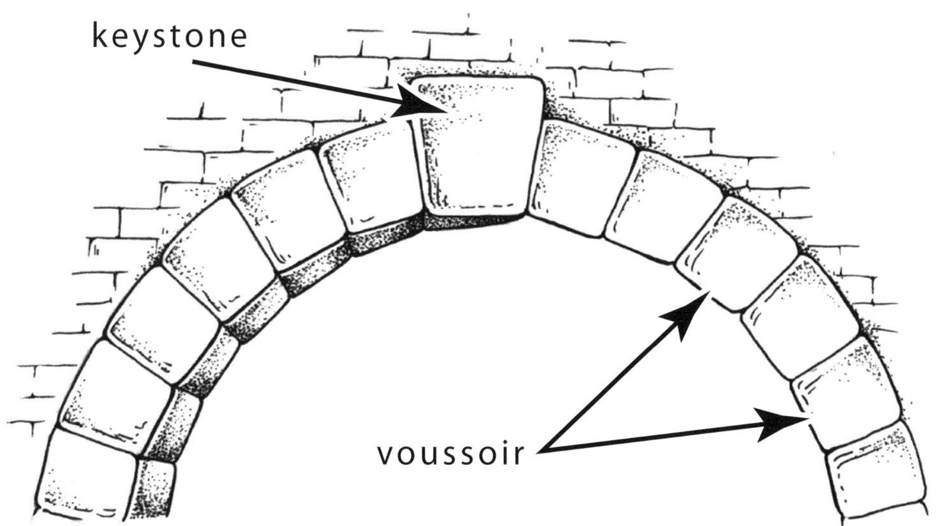

Stone built arch showing keystone and voussoirs.

themselves being spanned by three semi-circular barrel vaults running perpendicular to the nave, with narrow arcades running parallel underneath the barrel vaults.

The dome was a natural development of the vault that enabled the construction of high vaulted ceilings and also the roofing of large public spaces, for example public baths and basilicas. Good examples of the use of such architectural devices can be seen on an epic scale in Rome with Hadrian's Pantheon, the Baths of Diocletian and also the Baths of Caracalla.

The actual construction process for these grand stone-built structures is evident on closer inspection today, with projecting corbels showing where scaffolding was erected to facilitate the building process and (for arches) to carry the centring. Such corbels were often left in place afterwards, showing that the masons would typically build their piers (in the case of bridges and aqueducts) to just above the level of the springers after which carpenters would then construct the timber framework centring around which the *voussoirs* were set as the arch was built out, this staying in place until the final *voussoir* was set in place. Hamey and Hamey (1981, 35) say that it was most common for the centring to be built first at ground level to ensure accuracy, before then being rebuilt on the stonework above to allow the stone arch to be constructed.

Roman Construction Machinery

To carry out such a wide range of differing construction projects Roman engineers, military and otherwise, used a wide variety of equipment. At the most basic level, these included:

- Ropes, made in a variety of different ways to create elasticity, allowing them to be used not only for binding and pulling but also as a spring to conserve energy.
- Pulleys, used to gear force.
- Winches, mounted either horizontally or vertically. In the case of the former they could be utilised by turning the outward spokes of a horizontally-positioned wheel using men or oxen. For the vertically mounted types of winch the men (usually) could tread on the inside of the vertically-positioned wheel.

The application of these basic units in various combinations enabled the creation of the wide variety of machinery used by the Romans in their construction projects. Such machinery included mills of all sizes to grind the raw materials to make mortar, cranes and hoists to lift heavy materials to great heights, scaffolding as detailed earlier, trusses of ceramics or wood, and pile drivers to drive piles and stakes into the ground.

I detail one example here of such machinery to provide context for the various grand construction enterprises detailed in Chapter 5, namely the treadwheel crane (called the *Polyspaston* by the Romans) which used the vertically-mounted winch gearing detailed above. This wooden crane was human powered by individuals actually inside the treadwheel, with the ropes attached to a pulley system which turned onto a spindle through the rotation of the wheel, allowing the crane to hoist or lower very heavy loads. A fine example of such a crane is depicted on a tomb near the Porta Maggiore in Rome (Hamey and Hamey, 1981, 32), this substantial structure shown actually being built and featuring a two-sheave pulley. If the load needing to be lifted was larger than the capacity of the treadwheel crane, a wooden lifting tower was built, featuring a rectangular trestle designed so the material needing to be lifted could be carried upright through the middle of the structure using human or animal-powered capstans set on the ground around the tower.

One final point for consideration here is the Roman use of the lewis key/hole system, a device for allowing the cranes and towers detailed above to actually lift their heavy stone loads. The lewis system features a key (the lewis), and a specially shaped hole (the seating) in the stone to be lifted, which is dovetailed by a stonemason to be larger on the inside than the outside. The key folds into the hole, before being opened out to lock it into position against the internal dovetails. The load is then lifted, and once the block is set in place the key is slipped out by folding again. Lewis holes are a common feature on the large stone blocks of grand Roman construction projects and are often used by archaeologists and historians to date such buildings to the Roman period in the absence of other evidence (note, however, that they were also used in the Medieval period and later).

Roman Construction Materials

To conclude this chapter, I consider the actual materials used by the Roman military in their construction enterprises to inform the specific examples detailed in Chapter 5, also noting that in Chapter 6 I detail how the Roman military often ran the *metalla* extractive industries which extracted the raw materials so used. Here, I cover stone, mortar and concrete, bricks and tile and metal and wood (with regard to the latter, the focus is on physical asset building construction, though note it would also have been vital in other construction enterprises such as for naval vessels).

Stone

This was the most important Roman building material, often being used without any mortar, a testament to the fine skills of the Roman stonemason. Such skills were developed over the chronology of the Republic and Empire, techniques including the use of tapered sides on the back of squared blocks of building stone to ensure they fitted more tightly together along the joints on the face of a wall. Another device was the use of a technique called *anathyrosis* (door framing) whereby, in order to reduce the amount of time required to form a joint, the joining face of the block in question was smoothed only in the narrow contact band on the sides and top, with the interior of the face recessed. This was often used in the construction of walls and between the drums of columns. A further time saving device was to only smooth the outer face of a given wall once it had been built (particularly in the case of substantial walls which featured an outer and an inner face of worked stones with a rubble core (often set with mortar, see below).

The stone used in construction projects was often, though not always, sourced as locally as possible, and usually made use of the best available materials. An examination of the building stone used across the south and east of Britain during the Roman occupation illustrates these trends clearly, with many being used very locally, though Kentish ragstone from the upper Medway Valley was transported by river and sea far and wide across the region (see discussion of transport in the Roman world in Chapter 1, and detail on this important *metalla* industry more broadly in Chapter 6). Noting the many military contexts detailed in the examples below, the various types of such quarried stone made use of all of the geological formations in the region (broadly known as the Wealden Dome, formed by numerous layers and sub-layers of sedimentary rock dating to the Cretaceous and Tertiary periods, which was domed through the creation of the Alps – see Appendix A for context) and that imported from further afield, and included:

- Cement stone and *septaria* from the London clays of the north Kent coast (Allen and Fulford, 1999, 169), used as wall facing material in the south and west walls of the later 3rd century Saxon Shore fort at Richborough (Roman *Rutupiae*) and as part of the wall core filling at the early 3rd century Saxon Shore fort at Reculver (Roman *Regulbium*), and also exported north for use as a facing stone in the walls of the mid-2nd century East Anglian Saxon Shore fort at Walton Castle (Pearson, 2002b, 201).
- Thanet Sandstone, from the Thanet Beds, used in the north, west and south wall facings of the Saxon Shore fort at Richborough. The material would have been sourced from doggers found on the beaches at Pegwell Bay and further north at Herne Bay (Pearson, 2002b, 207).
- Locally quarried chalk from the North Downs and the east Kent coast around Deal (Lyne, 1994, 132). This was extensively used as a building material during the Roman occupation, particularly in eastern Kent, despite Pearson (2006, 123) describing it as a poor building material. Examples include its use with tufa, a variety of calcerous limestone, in alternating blocks in the walls of the early 2nd-century *Classis Britannica* fort in Dover (Philp, 1980, 20), in the bastions (possibly re-used) of the later 3rd-century Saxon Shore fort on the same site, and additionally its use alone in the Mithraeum/cellar at Wouldham/Burham (Taylor, 1932, 109) where three incised chalk building blocks were recovered, they now being stored in Maidstone Museum.
- Flint, sourced from the North Downs and from beach deposits (for example the storm beaches on Thanet, Pearson, 2002b, 198). This was used as a building material across the region during the occupation, often as a flint rubble core for major walls, examples being found at the Saxon Shore forts at Reculver and Richborough (Pearson, 2002a, 25). It was also extensively used as a facing stone set in a durable mortar, for example at the 2nd- to late 4th-century Crofton villa in Orpington

(Taylor, 1932, 110), the early 3rd-century 'Painted House' in Dover, the later Saxon Shore fort there (Philp, 1989, 31), and at a variety of sites in Canterbury (Wheeler, 1932, 61). Pearson (2006, 71) explains that expert stone working would have been required to make use of the flint as a facing stone.

- Ferruginous sandstone, quarried from the Folkestone Beds on the east Kent coast. This was used across the south-east, for example to form the decorative band in the north wall of the Saxon Shore fort at Richborough (Pearson, 2002b, 205) and being used as a capping stone on the late 2nd-century walls of London. Its notable red colour is derived from the iron-oxides which bind the grains of sand together.
- Ironstone, quarried locally as a building material along the foreshore of eastern Kent and being used as a material for building foundations and wall core filling at sites such as the late 1st century Villa 1 at East Cliff in Folkestone (Parfitt, 2013, 41). Ironstone, named after its very high iron-oxide content, is created either by the same ferruginous process as the sandstone above, or by chemical replacement.
- Greensand, of which various types were quarried from the layers of the Lower Greensand Formation during the occupation, particularly along the east Kent coast, and were widely exported as a building material across southern and eastern Britain. Prominent examples of its use locally include at the Kentish Saxon Shore forts at Reculver and Richborough (Pearson, 2002b, 202), and the late 1st-century bath house at Beauport Park (Brodribb *et al*, 1988, 232), while further afield it is also found exported for use in the East Anglian early 3rd-century Caister-on-Sea and later 3rd-century Bradwell-on-Sea Saxon Shore forts (Allen and Fulford, 1999, 169). Dark green greensands, very heavy in glauconite, are also found used as significant-sized ashlar blocks in the jambs of the city gates of Roman Canterbury (notably Worthgate, Ridigate and Queningate), and as the foundation of the west gateway at the Saxon Shore fort in Richborough. Meanwhile, very hard Folkestone Beds greensand blocks, rounded and thus indicating their origins on the beaches of the eastern Kentish coast, are found as a facing stone in some parts of the later 3rd-century walls of Roman Canterbury.
- Ragstone, a ubiquitous fine quality building stone from the Hythe Beds in the Lower Greensand Formation, distinct enough from other Lower Greensand materials to justify its own entry. The grey-green sandy and glauconitic limestone outcrops principally in the Upper Medway Valley above Maidstone (where the best quality stone is found), near Sevenoaks, and at the eastern extremity of the Greensand Ridge where the Hythe Beds outcrop in the cliffs near Folkestone and Hythe, though it is that extracted from the first location that was (by far) most widely used as a building stone across the built environment in the region during the Roman occupation. In that regard this stone's uses are too numerous to mention here (particularly with regard to Roman London) and so are specifically highlighted in the table at Appendix C, with the Upper Medway Valley ragstone *metalla* also considered in detail in Chapter 6 in the context of the military's involvement therein.

- Tufa, a calcerous limestone created by a secondary process involving the precipitation of carbonate minerals derived from ambient temperature bodies of water. It was used in a variety of forms as a building material during the occupation in Kent, predominantly in the east of the county, for example in many of the buildings and fortifications around Dover and Folkestone. Parfitt and Philp (1981, 176) and Allen and Fulford (1999, 169) all believe that much of the material was quarried in the valley of the River Dour (the original material deriving from the Hythe Beds), which flows through Dover. Specific examples of its use as a primary building stone include the walls of the *Classis Britannica* fort in Dover (Philp, 1981, 20), the bastions of its later Saxon Shore successor, the facing of the nearby *pharos*, the north wall of the Saxon Shore fort at Richborough, in the walls of the 3rd-century Saxon Shore fort at Lympne (only a small quantity and almost certainly re-used from an earlier structure), in the late 1st-century large aisled building located at Hogs Brook near Faversham (Wilkinson, 2005, 4), in the walls of the large villa at Eccles in all of its phases (Williams, 1971, 174) and indeed similarly at Villa 1 at East Cliff in Folkestone according to Parfitt (2013, 41). This Dour Valley tufa was also exported widely from Kent, for example providing dressed blocks for the East Anglian Saxon Shore fort at Walton Castle (Allen and Fulford, 1999, 169).
- Grey Wealden shale, of which finely cut high quality tiles have been found across Roman London and at the extensive 1st-century villa at Fishbourne in Sussex for use in *Opus Sectile* tiled flooring. The material was quarried either in the Weald or, less likely, in the Medway area from deposits sitting within the Wealden Beds.
- Ashdown sandstone from the Ashdown Formation in the Hastings Beds which Allen and Fulford (1999, 179) detail was quarried on the eastern/coastal edge of the Weald during the occupation, it being exported for use in the 3rd-century East Anglian Saxon Shore fort at Brancaster.
- Purbeck limestone, a fine quality fossiliferous limestone of which Lott and Cameron (2005, 2) say inlier beds were exploited in Kent and the south-east during the Roman occupation. They are found in the Purbeck Group, most famous for producing the very high quality stone quarried in Dorset and called Purbeck marble. Featuring large clasts within a very fine mud matrix, Purbeck limestone was well known for its ability to take a very fine polish (best seen in the Dorset Purbeck Marble variety), and also for ease of working. It was also in demand because of the variations in colour naturally available in the seams of the material. The best example of its use during the occupation in the south-east is at the Beauport Park bathhouse where it was used in the bathing complex itself (Brodribb *et al* 1988, 234).
- Other high quality building materials imported from greater distances given their excellence. Examples include the Tuscan Carrera marble used in the triumphal arch at Richborough, Ditrupa limestone from the Valois-Soissons region of Gaul found as small square blocks in the Saxon Shore fort at Reculver and in the North Wall of the Saxon Shore fort at Richborough (the latter possibly re-used from the arch

built there), the Bath Oolite columns found at Eccles (Williams, 1971, 181) and the Caen Stone imported from the Calvados region of Gaul which found its way into both Kentish buildings and those in London (Sowan, 1977, 1).

Mortar and Concrete

The first mortars in the ancient world were made from clays and mud, with the Egyptians adding gypsum. Such materials had an inferior performance in the presence of water and humidity, and by around 4,000 BC lime was being added, this being acquired by burning limestone in a kiln to remove the carbon from the calcium carbonite. With sand later becoming the base material in the mix, when the lime was combined with water (slaking) in the manufacturing process this created a far superior mortar which hardened with age. A typical ratio of sand to lime in the mortar mix would have ranged between three-quarters: one-quarter to two-thirds: one-third, dependent on the specific materials used including the type of water (fresh or salt). Such mortars of varying types were used extensively for a variety of purposes across the Roman Republic and Empire, with the best kinds including *pozzolana* volcanic ash in the mix, increasing its strength. Hamey and Hamey (1981, 42) highlight the mortar manufacturing process depicted on a tomb of one Trebius Justus, on the via Latina outside Rome, which shows workmen using *rutrum* broad-bladed hoes to mix their mortar in a large *mortarium* wooden trough (from which mortar derives its name).

Developing these mortars to the next level of complexity, the Roman Republic and Empire are particularly famous for the fine concrete utilised in all kinds of construction. Called *opus caementicium*, this concrete first emerged during the later Republic and was hydraulic-setting in nature, comprising of aggregate (materials added to the mortar, usually rock fragments using locally available materials) and mortar in a similar way to modern concrete, though it did differ in that the aggregate used was typically bigger than that used today. Gypsum and lime were added to assist the binding process, with the finest quality concretes including the *pozzolana* mentioned above which, in the context of concrete, helped prevent the spread of cracks, with some mixtures used also being able to be set underwater which helped facilitate bridge and waterside construction. The use of concrete in Roman construction led to the Roman Architectural Revolution (mentioned earlier), or 'Concrete Revolution', with the prime example of its use in epic construction being the dome of Hadrian's Pantheon (also detailed earlier), the world's oldest and largest unreinforced concrete dome.

Another cement-like building material used across the empire was *opus signinum*, made from the addition of very small, smashed pieces of building tile and brick being mixed with mortar, this often being used in flooring. Its use originated in North Africa in the 3rd century, being refined as it spread across the empire until it was being used for highly patterned pavements, sometimes set with fully formed tiles. The finding of *opus signinum* in an archaeological investigation is a key sign of *Romanitas* at a given site, and often points to it being an elite location.

Roman tile, mortar and wall plaster visible as construction materials in the Roman Imperial Baths, Trier on the Moselle. Simon Elliott

A number of techniques were used by the Romans when laying *opus caementicium* and *opus signinum*, a common one being to set down a layer of small stones between 30 and 60cm deep, followed by a layer of mortar, which was then lightly rammed to allow the cement to flow between the stones. After this, another layer of stones was positioned on top of the mortar layer, and so on. Wooden shuttering was used to hold the two sides in place, with more vigorous ramming employed if the mortar was being set between stone or brickwork facing.

Tiles and Bricks

The earliest tiles and bricks in the ancient world, as with mortar, were again made from locally available materials, often clays and muds. Even when left out to sun-bake for up to two years (a standard practice), these materials were still vulnerable to weathering from water and humidity and it is this that led directly to the kiln-based firing process in widespread use by the time of the Principate, seemingly initially for tiles (Hamey and Hamey, 1981, 43) and with bricks later following. One of the first large-scale structures built from fired-brick was the Theatre of Marcellus in Rome, completed in 13 BC.

The Romans perfected the tile and brick making process over the course of the 1st century AD, it ultimately being used ubiquitously as a building material across the empire in both public and private contexts. The principal vector for the spread of tile and brick use appears to have been the Roman military who utilised mobile kilns (operated by the specialists detailed above by Paternus) to manufacture such ceramics as the empire expanded.

Roman tiles came in a variety of types, for example box flue tiles which were hollow box-shaped tiles allowing hot air to travel from beneath hypocaust under floor heating systems through the walls in Roman buildings. Others were widely used to build up *pilae* hypocaust stacks or to provide bonding courses in stone built walls (see Chapter 6 below). Roman roof tiling in particular is a vital tool for the archaeologist when examining a potential Roman site, as it is a key sign of *Romanitas* (even given it originated in Greece). It featured *imbrex* and *tegula* (plurals *imbrices* and *tegulae*) overlapping roof tiles: the first, large, flat tiles with a flanged raised edge laid side-by-side flat on a roof, with the semi-cylindrical half-pipe shaped *imbrex* laid along the length of the two edges to create a water-proof seal running from the apex of the roof to its edge. The roofing area was often surrounded by *antefixae* decorated blocks to cover the ends of the tiles, with decorated *anthemia* used to cover each end row of *imbrex* tile.

Roman bricks were usually thinner than modern bricks, almost like large tiles. They came in a variety of shapes including square, rectangular, round and triangular, with the largest bricks measuring a metre in length, though the most common size seems to have been 45cm by 30cm.

McWhirr and Viner (1978, 360) summarised the manufacturing process for both tile and brick in the Roman world as follows:

- Clay excavated, usually in the autumn.
- Clay allowed to weather over the winter, being broken down by frost and rain.
- Clay prepared for manufacture, with aggregate sometimes being added and then the finished product being covered until needed.
- Tiles and brick made using a wooden frame, mold or former, when any modifications such as the flange on *tegulae* would be added.
- Tiles and brick left to harden, sometimes being stamped.
- Tiles and brick fired or burnt in a kiln or clamp and then stored. The iron oxides in the clay, and the conditions of firing, determined their colour.
- Tiles and brick transported to buyer and used.

Roman tile and bricks were often stamped with the mark of their maker, a well-known example from Roman Britain being located in Plaxtol, Kent. Here, a villa has an association with inscribed box flue tile stamped with '*parietalem cabriabanu farbicavi*' (translated as 'Cabriabanu made this wall tile'). The 4.2m by 4.2m up-draught kiln used by the tile-maker was found in 1999, with Cabriabanu being a Romano-Celtic entrepreneur who successfully used very locally sourced Gault clays to make and sell such tile in north-west Kent and up the Darent Valley into London. Davies (2009, 262) details that *Cabriabanu* tiles have been found at locations including the villas at Lullingstone and Darenth, and at Bishopsgate in London, showing the quality of his goods and his distribution network. The business had a particular specialisation in

Roman legionaries, in their capacity as trained engineers as set out in Chapter 4, constructing a fortification. Image from Trajan's Column, completed AD 113. By permission of Roger B. Ulrich.

the *voussoir* tiles designed for conveying hot air inside bath house arches, with 17 fragments with the *Cabriabanu* stamp having been found. Archaeomagnetometry has dated the kiln's period of use from AD 120 to AD 165.

Such stamps often referenced an official capacity however rather than an individual, with the stamps of procurators or military units commonly being found on all types of Roman tile and brick. An excellent example is detailed in Chapter 6, and concerns the naval tile and brick yards managed by the *Classis Britannica* regional navy in the eastern/coastal region of the Weald. While the industry is referenced in depth in that chapter, it is useful here to consider how the clays used here were sourced, as this illustrates similar activity across the entirety of the empire. The key point is the locality of the origins of the materials, as while Wealden clays are extensively used across the region, and we have the already referenced the Gault clays at Plaxtol, that specifically used by the *Classis Britannica* Wealden tile and brick industry was Fairlight clay from the Ashdown Formation of the Hastings Beds (Peacock, 1977, 237, see Chapter 6 below for detail).

Metal and Wood

Metals were also frequently used in Roman construction processes, particularly iron and lead, these being covered in detail in Chapter 6 below in the context of the Roman military running *metalla* mining and quarrying industries.

Wood was also clearly a vital resource in construction during the Roman Empire, as in many other aspects of life then and now. Visser (2009, 11) says that while much commentary regarding buildings in occupied Britain focuses on stone-built structures, the majority would have been at least partially timber-built, using posts, beams or planks. Hanson (1996, 3) adds that this was particularly the case earlier in the occupation. Goodburn (1991, 182) has carried out a detailed reconstruction of the techniques used, and their final form, for timber buildings in London based on the excavations at Cannon Street by the Museum of London. He says that the sequence of construction of such a building would have been as follows:

- Frame components on the building fitted together on site, using chalk or charcoal to label each piece.
- Base plates laid down, on clusters of supporting piles (as at the Walbrook site) if the ground was likely to be wet. These would be up to 6m long for an urban dwelling, matching in size the room to be located above.
- Partition plates laid down.
- Studs and corner posts set into the mortices in the base plate.
- Top plates laid on top of the corner posts.
- Diagonal brace elements fastened to the studs.
- Horizontal in-fill staves fitted into sloping recesses in the sides of the studs, with vertical rods or laths woven between them.
- Roof structure erected.
- Tie beams dovetailed over the top plates to prevent the walls from spreading under the weight of the roof. The tie beams would also have supported the feet of the principal roof rafters. Betts (pers. comm. 24 October 2012) says that the roofs of later buildings in London tended to be steeper, necessitating the use of a lighter tile when tiling was used.
- Daub, usually in a Roman context made of brick earth, applied to the infill. The studs and the baseplates would be left exposed on the inside of the building.
- Finally, the whole exterior would be clad in planks of up to 35cm in width and 3cm in thickness. In a London context, such cladding was usually of oak.

All of these findings were found replicated in the later excavation at the early 2nd-century Courage Brewery site in Southwark of a Roman timbered waterfront warehouse (Brigham *et al* 1995, 1). Specific examples such as these of where such timber has been used as a primary building material during the occupation in Britain, as elsewhere in the empire, are few and far between, but using the south-east as an example, one can be found at the Ickham Roman watermills site in eastern Kent. Here, the millhouse buildings and associated infrastructure were largely constructed of wood, a common practice with regard to millhouses in the north-western provinces of the empire as opposed to the Mediterranean where their counterparts were usually constructed of worked stone or brick (Bennett, Ridler and Sparey-Green, 2010, 63).

Another is the late 1st-century bakery at Springhead where flat foundations of flint, layered over with tiles, have been interpreted as the fittings for a half-timbered building (Williams, 1971, 175).

In terms of the sourcing of wood for construction and other uses this is considered in detail in Chapter 7 in the context of the Roman military and agriculture. However, to conclude this sub-section – and indeed chapter – we can consider one of our best phenomenological glimpses into occupied Britain in the context of Kentish woodland. This is in the form of an early 2nd-century transactional wooden tablet (originally covered in wax and found in the Walbrook Valley in London), which details the sale of two hectares of woodland in the land of the *Cantiaci* from one Titus Valerius Silvinus to Lucius Julius Bellicus for forty *denarii* (Tomlin, 1996, 209). It is unclear whereabouts in Kent the exact location of this parcel of woodland actually was, though if it were in the north then a reasonable assumption is that it would be agro-forestry as part of the wider agricultural landscape with the exploited wood resources being used for construction, while if in the Weald to the south then the likely exploitation would be through coppicing to support the iron industry there. Tomlin (1996, 210) suggests a third option, that it is a sacred site dating back to the origins of the *Cantiaci* prior to the occupation. Whatever the location and purpose, this case clearly illustrates the value of woodland and the worth attached to their legal registration.

Chapter 5

The Great Construction Projects

This chapter builds on the themes discussed in Chapter 4, and the detail set out there both with regard to the Roman military as engineers and such activity throughout the Roman Empire, to look at specific examples of Roman military engineering and construction prowess. As detailed at the outset of Chapter 4, specific examples considered in detail here are Roman roads, canals and canalised rivers, bridges, aqueducts, fortifications, public buildings and the built environment more broadly.

Roads

Road building was a central feature of the Roman experience, both politically and economically. In the first instance, the building of a substantial, metalled road network across a newly conquered landscape was the ultimate stamping of Roman authority on a new territory. Such was the scale of this type of enterprise that the presence of Roman road networks is felt even today, long after the Empire's decline. Long, straight roads along historical routes often mark the presence of the line of a roadway dating back to the empire, as do road names referencing stone and similar (at least in a British context).

Such roads often tracked the primary routes of conquest into a new province, and were built early. Using Britain as an example, Poulter and Entwhistle (2016, 12) say that surveying (by the army *agrimensores* with their *groma* and *decempeda*) during and immediately after conquest to take control of the landscape and its resources were a key part of the conquest experience, both for the invading Romans and the native inhabitants. This surveying, often using Pythagorean angles, created Long Distance Alignments over great distances, which meant that when road building began the most direct routes (for example from London to Chichester, later Roman *Noviomagus Reginorum*) were already understood. Therefore roads could be built quickly along the most ergonomical routes, facilitating the new province's ability to contribute to the Imperial *fiscus* as quickly as possible.

Jones and Mattingly (1990, 175) use Roman legal codices to identify three types of Roman road, these being:

- State-built roads, often principal trunk routes, implicitly associated with the military.
- Those built locally by regional government, often associated with *civitas* capitals and *coloniae.*
- Roads built by industry or smaller settlements for local convenience.

Though the military would have been used when available as a resource for building the latter two types of roadway, it is with the state-built road networks that we see their presence most clearly. They were always built by the military and initially for military purposes (the legionary being able to march an average of 36km a day) with, as Goldsworthy (2003, 146) explains, they:

> ...providing the military with improved communications for moving men and material as required.

Thus, in a British context, we see roads tracking the legionary lines of advance across the country, then further branching out as the economy of the new province grew (Elliott, 2016a, 66). Such major roads included Watling Street from Richborough through London to Chester (Roman *Castra Deva*), Ermine Street from London through Lincoln (Roman *Lindum*) to York, the Fosse Way from Lincoln to Exeter (Roman *Isca Dumnoniorum*) and Dere Street from York to the northern frontier. Such roadways across the empire are well known to those studying the world of Rome given they are often referenced in contemporary itineraries such as the *Antonine Itinerary*. At the opposite edge of the empire, we have a specific example of the military carrying out a road building and maintenance function, with an inscription on a milestone in the province of Arabia mentioning a road built by troops on behalf of the Governor Gaius Claudius Severus during the reign of Trajan (Southern, 2007, 103).

These good quality roadways enabled the rapid deployment of military personnel up to army group size across a province as required, also facilitating the rapid communications needed for imperial administration (hence many of the roadways in Britain radiating from or through London to the regions). These principal roadways were also used to a lesser extent for transporting goods, though as detailed in Chapter 1 maritime routeways were always the preferred option for bulky cargoes.

Metalled Roman roads of all three types were built to a standard pattern across the empire. The width of the military-constructed State-built roads varied between five (in Britain, the Fosse Way for example) and 10 metres (again in Britain, Watling Street), with a gauge of around seven metres. The roads were built on a wide strip of levelled land, up to 100m in width in extreme examples, sometimes with a shallow ditch at either edge to facilitate drainage. The carriageway itself (often with two lanes, as seen where Watling Street traversed the small town of Rochester immediately prior to crossing the River Medway, Chaplin, 1962, L) was built in the centre of the cleared strip of land using local materials, sand and gravel, with a convex form known as an *agger* which again facilitated drainage. The specific construction of the standard larger trunk road, particularly in the west, was as follows (bottom to top, Parry, 2005, 95):

- The *pavimentum* foundation of well rammed earth.
- The *statumen*, a base of flat squared stones between 200 and 300mm thick.
- The *rudus*, a layer of stone blocks set in lime mortar some 300–500mm thick.
- The *nucleus*, comprised of sand, broken tile and crushed stone set in *opus caementicium* concrete, around 300mm thick.
- The *summum dorsum* top layer, featuring cobbles or slabs up to 250mm in thickness.
- Sometimes a layer of packed gravel on top.

Either side of the *agger* lightly metalled footpaths were laid out, sometimes bounded by curbstones (placed on top of the *statumen* or *rudus*) and a further pair of ditches deeper than those at the edge of the strip of levelled land on which the whole was constructed.

These principal roadways were also maintained by the military, under the auspices of highways superintendents called *curatores viarum*, initially based in Rome itself but increasingly such administrators appearing in the provinces, on the staff of the procurators and with their cost being carried by local government.

In Britain, we have a specific example of a major Roman road built by the military which provides an excellent example of one of Jones and Mattingly's state-built roads and illustrates the use of such in a very specific military context. Though not one of the major routes often referenced in Britain, this road ran from Rochester, where Watling Street crossed the River Medway, south through what is now Maidstone, past the major military-controlled ragstone-quarrying industry there, to the huge (also military-controlled) iron working sites in the eastern/coastal area in the Weald just north of Hastings. Henceforth I refer to this road as the Wealden road. Broadly following the line of the modern A229 for much of its length (a testament to the longevity of major Roman metalled roads), this significant route dates to the later

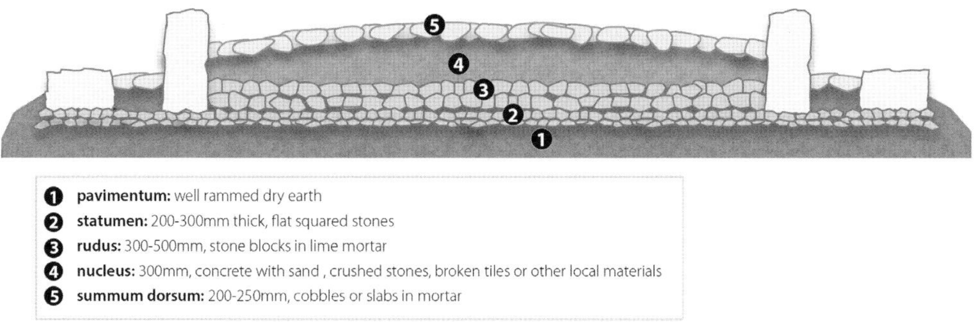

Cross section of well-made Roman road showing the different layers which gave these routeways such durability. Paul Baker.

1st century AD and served the specific administrative function of linking the north Kent coast with the military-run quarrying and iron working industrial sites fully detailed in Chapter 6. Particularly noteworthy is the difficulty of building this road, especially through the densely-wooded Weald with its heavy clay soils. Further, the ingenuity of the military road-builders is shown in that much of the road's metalling for the southern portion came from detritus from the iron working sites. Given the widely-accepted presence of the *Classis Britannica* in running the iron working sites and, as I argue in Chapter 6, the ragstone quarries of the Upper Medway Valley too, the regional navy seems the most likely candidate for the state to engage in the road's construction.

Rivers and Canals

As detailed in Chapter 1, transportation by water – sea, river or canal – was the preferred means of carrying heavy loads in the Roman Empire (and indeed the wider pre-modern world), predominantly due to the financial advantages it enjoyed over land transport. In that regard, the Romans made great use of the canalisation of rivers and the building of new, bespoke canals through the employment of their military engineering expertise. As Ellis Jones (2012, 86) writes:

> ...Roman military engineering was more than capable of improving and maintaining rivers...establishing an effective series of inland waterways.

These engineering skills had their origins in Rome's initial contact with the Hellenistic East, where its engineers refined their riverine and riparian management skills to enable the control of waterways, soon transferring techniques learned on the Nile, Tigris and Euphrates back to the Tiber in Italy and later into Spain and Gaul.

In terms of controlling existing river systems, canalisation was effected through the construction of riverine hydraulic infrastructure in the form of locks, weirs and dams, with the general aim of making a specified river system navigable above the tidal reach (though even more significant river management projects were also carried out, as detailed below). The tidal reach is the point at which the river ceases to be affected by tides that can naturally carry a vessel on its journey. Such tides are created by the gravitational attraction of the moon and, to a lesser extent, the sun, on the rotating earth. This then determines the tidal reach of a given river. For example, in Britain there are usually two high tides (every 12 hours and 25 minutes) and two low tides per day, creating what is known as a semi-diurnal regime. In addition to this twice-daily rise and fall, the positioning of the moon exerts a further influence to create the highest high tides and lowest low tides (spring tides with full and new moons), and the lowest high tides and highest low tides (neap tides), in a fortnightly cycle. Finally, a seasonal cycle can also have an impact, with the highest spring tides peaking during the spring and autumn equinoxes. The tidal range is the difference between high tide and low tide in this complex tidal regime, which differs around a given coast and up a river system based on regional littoral and riparian topography, and also water depth (bathymetry).

Once above the tidal reach, without the introduction of any riverine hydraulic infrastructure, the river effectively becomes a large stream and is largely unnavigable with regard to any significant military or industrial usage. Thus, the introduction of locks, weirs and dams to open up a river system is the key to making it a resource capable of supporting a regional economy. The Romans were the first to do this to a significant extent, again based on lessons learned as they expanded east.

A good example of such a controlled river system can be found at Rio Tinto in south-western Spain, where the Rio Guadiana and Rio Odiel were heavily used to support regional silver, copper and lead-mining activities (Jones, 1980, 148). Similar significant levels of hydraulic engineering skill have been revealed at the north-western Spanish gold-mining site at Las Médulas in the Eria Valley (Fernando-Lozano, Gutierrez-Alonso and Fernandez-Moran, 2015, 359). There, an extensive network of man-made hydraulic channels and reservoirs (some of the latter with a capacity of 5,000m^3 of water) were created through the diversion of regional rivers. Campbell (2011, 117) provides another good example of such riverine manipulation (this time of even greater scale and complexity), highlighting an inscription from *Axima/Forum Claudii Ceutronum* dated AD 163, which describes how Marcus Aurelius and Lucius Verus

> restored the roads through the territory of the Ceutrones, which had been torn up by the force of torrents, by shutting out the rivers and leading them back to their natural bed and placing embankments in numerous places.

Such canalisation of river systems by the Roman military is also evident in Britain. Ellis Jones (2012, 86) wrote:

> The Romano-British period saw the development of a coastal and riverine transport infrastructure that was not equaled until the advent of the Canal Age.

Manipulation through riverine hydraulic infrastructure in a British context was first – and somewhat controversially – suggested in 1983 by north-eastern archaeologist Raymond Selkirk in *The Piercebridge Formula*. His hypothesis, though never proven, suggested that the military deployed in the north of England were supplied mainly by waterways such as the Rivers Tyne and Tees, which were physically controlled by the authorities using locks and weirs. Such control, he argued, allowed the rivers to be navigable much further upstream than was naturally the case. His theories were challenged at the time and remain problematic today. The principal academic rebuttal is that of Anderson (1992, 212), who said that, because of the nature of the rivers in the region, with their troublesome shoals, strong tides, river cliffs and incised currents, navigation by ships, medium-sized boats and barges would have been difficult upriver of Wallsend, and impossible thereafter.

Even with this level of opposition to Selkirk's original theories, the fact that the Roman occupiers in Britain had the engineering capability to build such riverine infrastructure elsewhere in the province is not in doubt, given their use elsewhere in the empire. With that in mind, when finalising the synopsis for my UCL Archaeology MA dissertation, I decided to use Selkirk's contested ideas for the north-eastern river systems as a template to see if the River Medway where I live, with its gently sloping banks and broad flood plain, would be a better candidate for occupation-period riverine hydraulic infrastructure (dubbing the work 'The Medway Formula'). It had long been argued that the ragstone quarries which provided much of the material to build Roman London through to the mid-3rd century were located in the upper Medway Valley *above* the tidal reach (now at Allington, then at Snodland further downriver, Kaye, 2015, 232). Therefore, locks and weirs would be required to allow them access onto the river, which would have been the preferred route of transport for the quarried material. (This industry, and its association with the Roman military in the form of the *Classis Britannica* regional navy, is fully discussed and detailed in Chapter 6 below.) Such locks and weirs only appear in the River Medway in the historical record with the advent of the Medway Navigation Company in the mid- to late 18th century (earlier attempts in the 17th century by the Commissioners of Sewers on the Medway being less successful).

I initially based my efforts to find these Roman locks and weirs in the Medway Valley on the anecdotal considerations above, and analogies elsewhere in the empire. However, further research has since provided hard evidence of the existence of Roman riverine infrastructure here. This takes the form of newly found references in the historical record of riverine hydraulic infrastructure in the Upper Medway being removed during the 18th century. Specifically, *Mr Coles Observation of Nuisances on the Medway* goes into detail about stone weirs and shelves being removed from the river at East Farleigh, Barming and Teston (1630, 134). It is no coincidence that all of these locations are sites of historical river crossings on the Medway, implying that roads or tracks of ancient origin led to these points. Geographically, each site was also embedded within a landscape of industrial and settlement activity during the Roman occupation, for example the villa at East Farleigh, the villa and ford at Barming, the villa at Teston and two of the ragstone quarries detailed in Chapter 6. Most recently, the location of a likely Roman transport ship containing worked stone together with the remains of the wharf against which it founded has been found in close proximity to one of the removed weirs detailed above (at East Farleigh), adding to the sense that complex river management and manipulation was taking place here during the Roman occupation. This is again detailed in Chapter 6.

Finally, turning to canals themselves rather than canalised river system, examples built by the Roman military proliferate across the empire. A good example is provided by the 37km long Corbulo Canal (*Fossa Corbulonis*) in the Netherlands, a major hydraulic undertaking which linked the *municipum Cananefatium* (later *Forum Hadriani*, modern Vooburg) with the Rhine at Leiden to the north and the Meuse (or Maas) estuary to the south. It was initiated after AD 47 under G. D. Corbulo using regionally available troops (Campbell, 2011, 223; Driesson and Besselsen, 2014, 14), to supply the newly created frontier *Limes* in Germany and the Netherlands. Another such example is the three-mile long canal with bridges constructed near Antioch in AD 75, this time by 75 vexillations from four regional legions together with 20 auxiliary cohorts. In Britain, we once again have an excellent example of such infrastructure in the form of the Car Dyke canal in East Anglia. Here, in addition to the construction of the canal, recent research has identified at regular intervals along its 122km length gravel causeways submerged to a depth of 1m, which feature timber pile foundations. These were clearly laid during the canal's construction by the Roman military to facilitate crossing points for key local trackways.

Bridges

Bridges were also a potent and ubiquitous sign of the power of Rome, with every major river across the empire, excepting the Euphrates and Nile, being bridged. Such bridge building was a very significant undertaking and the vast majority were constructed either by or under the supervision of the military.

Some bridges were associated with military campaigning (usually of wood), while others were utilised to facilitate commerce and trade (often of stone, at least in part). In the case of the former, Caesar's construction of two substantial wooden bridges over the Rhine in 55 BC and 53 BC to facilitate his campaign against the Germans (Gallic Wars, 4.17.2–10) provide excellent insight into the techniques employed in their building.

The first was built downstream of Koblenz between Andernach and Neuwied, with double timber pilings (each of 45cm thickness) being rammed into the river bed every 60cm by using a large winched stone as a hammer. The upstream and downstream pilings were deliberately slanted inwards and then secured using a beam, with numerous such units being linked up to form the supports for the bridge, across which a wooden roadway was laid. Further pilings were then set upstream to act as a protective barrier for the bridge against damage from anything flowing – deliberately or otherwise – downstream, with guard towers being built at either end to secure the crossing point (the Romans typically going to great lengths to protect either end of a marine crossing of any kind). The bridge was up to 400m in length and 9m wide – effectively a dual carriageway – and was built in a few days. The second bridge was built at Urmitz, near Neuwied, two years later (the first having been demolished after a season of campaigning north of the Rhine), again in a matter of days, to the same design, enabling a season of campaigning north of the river. These bridges served as the model for future Roman campaigning bridges, the grandest subsequent example being the wooden structure constructed over the Danube by Trajan, facilitating his Dacian campaigns in the early 2nd century. This enormous bridge was 672m in length and featured 21 spans, each of 32m in length.

In the case of bridges built for commerce and trade, one can look to the Pont Sant'Angelo in Rome, still used as a footbridge to this day despite the fact it was constructed in AD 134. This is a classic example of how the Romans perfected the use of the stone arch –in this case the *voissoir* ring in semicircular form (Parry, 2005, 72) – as a construction technique. Originally called the Pons Aelius after the family name of the Emperor Hadrian, it was built to link his mausoleum (now the Castel Sant' Angelo) to the city itself. Though rebuilt in the 15th century AD, at least five of its seven arches are original, with spans of 19m. This structure was an enormous undertaking during the Principate, both in terms of manpower and capital, with locally available legionary and auxiliary vexillations and urban cohorts all being utilised for its construction.

Yet another spectacular example of a stone-built bridge, this time in the provinces (there being many such structures across the empire), can be found in Spain in the form of the majestic Alcantara Bridge over the Tagus, built in AD 104. This has six spans of up to 29m in length built on 9m tick bridge piers, with the road surface soaring 50m above the bed of the river.

To construct bridges of the latter stone-built type in particular required meticulous planning and preparation. The usual Roman bridge design featured stone-built bridge piers, over which ran a wooden (or, in the grander examples, stone) roadway. The piers were the most important feature of the permanent bridges and were constructed using a wooden cofferdam on the river bed. This is a water-tight box made of wooden piles driven into the river bed and bound together with chains and planks to create (usually) a double wall slightly larger than the required foundations. Water was then removed using waterwheels and water screws (classically, the archimedean screw) to create a water-free environment on the riverbed, within which the engineers would build the foundations and then bridge pier. The process is described in detail by Vitruvius (5.12.5). The foundations themselves would have been made from *opus caementicium* if the river bed was found to be solid, or from piles of wood (Vetruvius suggests olive, alder and charred oak) if not. The bridge piers would then be constructed from locally available stone, with abutments at either end, topped by the famous Roman arches across which the road surface was then laid.

A particularly fine British example of a Roman bridge built in this way was that at Rochester, which combined stone-built bridge piers with a wide wooden roadway. Though long assumed to have existed by antiquarians given it was the principal Watling Street crossing-point over the River Medway, the first factual evidence of this stone-built bridge's existence came to light in 1851, when construction of the current cast-iron bridge at Rochester (Brooks, 3, 1994) commenced. When work began on the western Strood pier, the engineers revealed immediately the remains of one of the Roman ragstone bridge piers (at TQ 7404 6895), together with the remnants of the cofferdam built to construct it in exactly the manner outlined above. Hughes (1851, 365) detailed at the time finding:

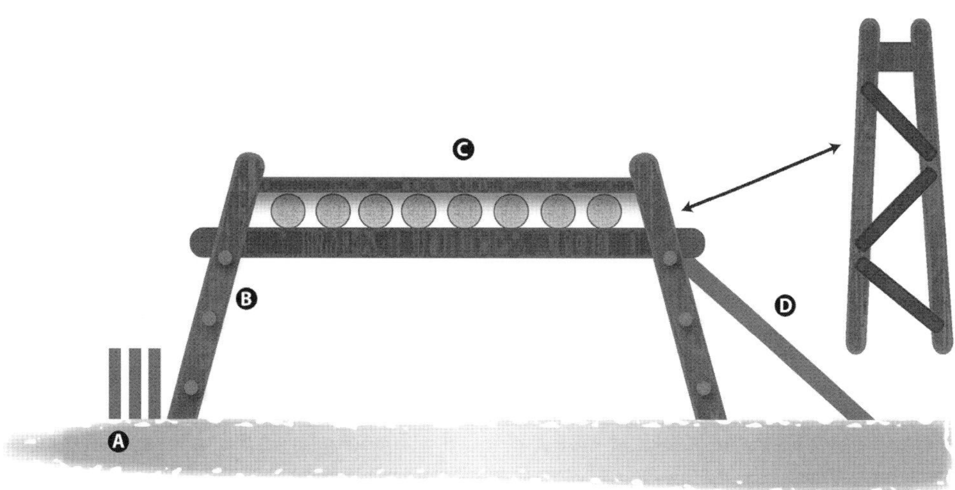

Stylised cross section of military wood-built Roman bridge, featuring (left to right): A) protective pilings set in the river bed upstream to prevent damage from debris (deliberate or otherwise) in the river. B) Pilings slanted inwards from bottom to top to act as bridge piers to carry a road surface (and in cross section at right). C) Roadway surface laid across beams set between opposite wooden bridge piers. D) Pilings set against wooden bridge piers downstream to act as bracing. Paul Baker.

> ...a mass of Kentish ragstone, of the nature of rubble without mortar...found to a depth varying from 4m to 8m below the present bed of the river. Pieces of timber of considerable dimensions, and which had been used as piles, or framing (for a cofferdam), occurred in this bed of rubble stone, penetrating a foot or two into the gravel, which proved to be 2m to 2.5m thick. This timber was oak, elm and beech – all except that last perfectly sound and tough...some fragments of iron proved that the piles had been shod with that material.

Brooks (1994, 3) argues that this structure was in fact the second occupation-period bridge at Rochester, the first being wood built along the lines of that described by Caesar when crossing the Rhine. While there is no hard data to support this theory, this pattern of an initial wooden bridge being replaced by a later stone built structure was not unusual elsewhere in the empire. What we do know, based on the above bridge pier details, is that the stone bridge, once constructed, was indeed substantial at some 183m in length. Though shorter than the London bridge crossing of the Thames, this is longer than that of the Ouse at York. The Roman stone bridge was built to last too; the then bridge engineer John J. Jobson wrote in 1921 (140) that he had seen documents indicating that this stone-built structure lasted until AD 960, when it was pulled down, having ultimately become unsafe. Jobson (1921, 141) also cites other documents he had seen, dating to AD 1115, which showed that the Roman stone-built bridge featured nine stone-built bridge piers, two abutments and two openings (with draw-bridges) for the transit of high masted vessels. Clearly the task of building the Rochester bridge was one undertaken by the military, as they were the only asset available with sufficient expertise to do so. This is underlined by the strategic importance of this route from the east Kent coast (and the Roman Imperial Gateway at Richborough) to the provincial capital of London.

Water Provision

Along with roads and bridges, aqueducts are also considered a key manifestation of the presence of Rome. While fresh water provision through artificial channels had long been a sign of the presence of advanced engineering capability, it was Rome that brought this to a fine art form.

The state would have been involved in the construction and subsequent maintenance of aqueducts from the outset, as the latter were controlled directly by the emperor. Campbell (2011, 91) wrote:

> The Emperors were masters of the aqueducts, through control of their finance and administration and the power to take initiatives. This included money for aqueduct repairs.

The importance of aqueducts in the Roman Empire is best illustrated by the fact that, among his many other reforms, Augustus created a specific position with responsibility for their provision and maintenance in Rome: the *Cura Aquarum*. The first to hold the post was Marcus Agrippa, though the best-known is Sextus Julius Frontinus, one of the early warrior governors of the province of Britannia. He later wrote his famous *De Aquis Urbis Romae* when in post in Rome, which is the standard contemporary work on the aqueducts of Rome and the most detailed evaluation we have of a Roman water supply network.

Planning for the construction of aqueducts was just as meticulous as that for stone-built bridges. The route prior to construction was laid out by the (often military) *librator* using his *groma, dioptra, chorobates* and *decempeda*. Garrison (1998, 75) says that the engineer would have specifically used the *dioptra* to run the traverse from the town in question to the source of the water. The required gradient, which varied across differing types of terrain, was then measured out using the *decempeda* and other leveling rods and chains. The differing gradients along the length of surviving examples of Roman aqueducts are well illustrated by the surviving sections of the Aqua Anio Vetus running from the River Anio to Rome (built between 272 BC and 269 BC), which ranges from 1:250 to 1:1000.

Once the route was laid, the construction techniques used to build the aqueducts were similar to those used in the building of bridges, with piers and arches being utilised to often dramatic effect. The main difference was the replacement of the roadway with a *specus* (water channel), usually enclosed and the size of a doorway (Hamey and Hamey, 1994, 9).

Aqueduct located outside the colonia of Caesarea Maritima on the coast of Judea, dating to the reign of Hadrian who heavily modified the Herodian original structure. Inscriptions show that a wide variety of military vexillations were used for building the structure and then its maintenance. Image courtesy of Dr Steven Tibble.

We have direct evidence that the Roman military was used as a resource by the state with regard to aqueducts. This takes the form of the fine example outside the *colonia* of *Caesarea Maritima* on the coast of Judea, dating to the reign of Hadrian, who heavily modified the original Herodian structure there. Here, inscriptions show that vexillations from the *legio* II *Traiana fortis* (one in number), *legio* VI *Ferrata fidelis constans* (two), *legio* X *Fretensis* (five) and legio XXII *Deiotariana* (one) were employed in building and maintaining the structure.

Water provision wasn't just limited to the building and maintenance of aqueducts. Indeed, the military were involved in a number of other major engineering projects in this regard. An excellent example relates to one Nonius Datus, a veteran of *legio* III *Cyrenaica*, who, from epigraphic evidence at Lambaesis in North Africa, is known to have been involved in the civilian project to bore a tunnel through a mountain range to provide a reliable water flow to a neighbouring town in Mauretania. Auxilia and naval *milites* from the regional fleet were also used on this project, military engineering expertise not to be seen again until the modern era.

Fortifications

Among the many examples of construction and engineering carried out by the Roman military, the most visible are of course the proliferation of fortifications which still remain across the territory of the empire.

The best example in a British context is Hadrian's Wall, the 117km-long fortified northern border of Roman Britain for much of the occupation. This ran west-to-east from Bowness-on-Solway (site of the Roman fort of *Maia*) on the Irish Sea to Wallsend (Roman *Segedunum*) on the River Tyne.

Construction of the wall, which began in AD 122 (Fields, 2003, 9), was an acknowledgment that the imperial expansion of the early years of the Principate had come to an end. In Britain, this manifested itself in the ultimate failure of Governor Agricola to physically conquer Scotland in the late 1st century AD (Elliott, 2016a, 125) despite his victory over the Caledonians in the Grampians south of the Moray Firth, at the Battle of Mons Graupius in AD 83 (as referenced earlier). After this time, with the north of the islands unconquered, this northern border became increasingly problematic and required the frequent attention of the British garrison.

Why Rome never fully conquered the far north of the islands of Britain has long been a point of heated discussion. James (2011, 144) makes a convincing argument that Rome's failure was due the 'open hand alongside sword' strategy behind much of the Empire's early growth failing in this instance. Such a strategy required an elite

Roman fort at Birdoswald on Hadrian's Wall, built by the Roman military. Francis Tusa.

sophisticated enough in newly-conquered territories to accept the imperial project once conquest had taken place. James believes that despite the various attempts to conquer Scotland, for much of the occupation (especially early on), this elite was singularly lacking. Therefore, outside of the simple desire for conquest, the economic imperative to invest heavily in controlling the far north was missing. This failure to physically incorporate Scotland into the empire therefore created friction on both sides of the border, which ultimately led to the building of the wall.

Construction was initiated by Hadrian when he personally came to Britain in AD 122 to survey the situation following significant trouble on the northern border at the beginning of his reign (he becoming Emperor in AD 117), which had led to great loss of life and severe disruption to the province (Elliott, 2016a, 139). He arrived with his friend Aulus Platorius Nepos, then governor of Germania Inferior, whom the emperor quickly appointed as the new governor in Britain. After a swift review of the province, the emperor decided on the Solway Firth–Tyne line as the physical frontier for demarking *Romanitas* from *barbaricum*, this already featuring the Stanegate, an important strategic and early Roman road in Britain running west-to-east from Carlisle (Roman *Luguvalium*) to Corbridge (*Coria*). This road already featured a number a forts pre-dating Hadrian, for example the auxiliary fort at *Vindolanda* (near modern Bardon Mill, Northumberland).

Hadrian's Wall was threaded with watchtowers and milecastles, commonly two of the former between each of the latter. The western part was initially constructed from compacted turf blocks, later replaced with stone. It was this section that was built first, and quickly (hence the original turf), perhaps giving some insight into the direction of the principal threat during Hadrian's visit. The eastern section was constructed as new from stone. The chosen line was north of the Stanegate and featured a north-facing fore-ditch. A large *vallum* was then constructed to the wall's immediate south. This featured a broad flat-bottomed ditch up to 2.96m deep, 5.4–5.9m wide at the top and 2.1m wide at the bottom, with a mound 5.92m wide on either side. Representing a substantial engineering achievement in its own right, it was designed to give protection to the rear of the main fortification, perhaps indicating concerns over the loyalty of the local Brigantian population following the earlier trouble along the border.

It is in the construction of the wall and its associated infrastructure, which took at least six years to complete, that we see a very clear picture of the use of the Roman military in such a major construction project. Breeze and Dobson (2000, 66) say that three British-based legions were used in the construction: *legio* II *Augusta* (normally located at Caerleon), *legio* XX *Valeria Victrix* (from Chester) and *legio* VI *Victrix* (from York, this legion having travelled to Britain with the Emperor and Nepos). Units of the *Classis Britannica* regional fleet also helped construct elements of the wall and its associated infrastructure, for example the granaries at the cavalry fort at Benwell (Elliott, 2016a, 107), and also possibly at Halton Chesters and Rudchester (Breeze and Dobson, 2000, 66). At least one and possibly more units of auxilia may also have been involved in the building of the wall, particularly the *vallum* (Breeze and Dobson, 2000, 67). The local populations either side of the wall would also have been at risk of forcible recruitment into service as indentured workers to support the building operation (Elliott, 2016a, 125). In this regard, Field (2003, 32) highlights research showing that, for every ten military personnel used for the construction work, some 90 additional individuals would have been needed to help supply and transport the raw materials (though even in this case Breeze and Dobson, 2000, 67, say the legions may have supplied some of their own workers given they already had their own carters and muleteers).

Evidence for the deployment of the legions to build the wall comes in the form of numerous examples of epigraphy. One of the best known comes from milecastle number 38 at Hotbank (RIB 1638), which records the names of Hadrian and Nepos and was set up by legionaries of *legio II Augusta*. Similarly, we know of the deployment of *milites* of the *Classis Britannica* at Benwell through epigraphy (RIB 1340), again referencing Hadrian and Nepos, here on an inscription set up in the portico of the granary. Benwell also provides great insight into how closely the units of the military worked together, as other inscriptions at the same fort indicate the presence (again) of *legio* II *Augusta* (RIB 1341, and others). Clearly, the building work was a matter of pride for the military units.

As mentioned above, the western section of Hadrian's Wall was constructed first and from turf, with a building season for the legionaries of seven months in each of the years of construction, from April to October (in normal weather conditions). This was because the turf would have been too weak in the winter months for effective use. The same regime would later have applied to the stone built western section, and the subsequent replacement of the turf wall in the east by stone, since the mortar used (for example, in the wall core filling mixed with rubble) would have been vulnerable to the severe frosts of the far north of the empire. By way of analogy, Frontinus in his *De aquis Urbis Romae* (2.123) says that work on major construction projects should be restricted to April through October because of the potential effects of frost on setting mortar (and that in the Mediterranean in his examples).

The scale of the engineering and construction endeavour faced by the legionaries and others in building Hadrian's Wall is highlighted by the experimental archaeology project carried out by the Royal Engineers in 1966 at Lunt Roman fort in Coventry. Here, it was estimated that to build a 283m circuit, featuring a rampart revetted with turf up to a height of 3.6m, and with a base-width of 5.4m, some 138,000 turf blocks would have been needed. This, alongside a double ditch, would have taken a labour force of up to 300 men, working 10 hours a day in good conditions, up to 12 days to finish.

Further insight is provided by the replica stone wall section of Hadrian's Wall built at *Vindolanda*. Some 14m in length, this needed 400 tonnes of stone, with another 400 tonnes needed for the turret attached to one end. It also required 3,637 litres of water to mix the lime mortar each day. Building this section also highlighted the proliferation of tasks performed by the legionaries and others when building Hadrian's Wall. These included:

- Quarrying the facing stone.
- Cutting and dressing the stone.
- Collecting stone rubble for the wall core filling.
- Making lime mortar in enormous quantities (hence the need for such large amounts of water, also facilitated by the construction team).
- Gathering timber for scaffolding, which the team then had to erect.
- Transporting these materials to the construction site itself.
- Actually building the wall, including excavating the foundations.
- Excavating associated infrastructure, including defensive ditches and the rear-facing *vallum*, which given the boulder clay soils would have been the most arduous task associated with building the wall.
- Administering all of the above.

In terms of the military personnel utilised for these tasks, and in a late Roman context, Paternus' (Digest, 50.6.7) list of the legionary specialists who would have been available for use in such major construction projects is detailed in Chapter 4, but I relist them here for completeness: surveyors, ditch-diggers, architects, glaziers, roof-tile makers, plumbers, stonecutters, lime-burners, wood-cutters and plumbers. Vegetius (1995, 2.11) similarly lists such specialists, while Breeze and Dobson (2000, 67) say it would have been predominantly the legionaries/naval *milites* themselves who would have done the work rather than simply overseeing it, reflecting the engineering skills associated with the Roman soldiery.

The work of the legionaries and others when building the wall would have been overseen by each legions *praefectus castorum*, the third most senior officer in the legion who had responsibility for all construction work. The wall was constructed in sections up to 10km in length, each the responsibility of a specific military unit (individual centuries then being allocated sub-sections within this length), with the watchtowers and milecastles built first. Centurions kept a keen eye on the quality of the work, using their *decempedae* (Vegetius, 1995, 3.8) as measuring tools, and as each section was finished the workers frequently set up the commemorative inscriptions detailed above, which have proved so valuable in tracing who built (and later maintained) each section of wall.

The quarried stone for the stone-built sections of the wall (sandstones and limestones, 3.7 million tonnes for the facing alone) was sourced from local quarries, for example Combcrag Wood in Cumbria. Here, eight inscriptions have been identified from specific individuals showing that this site was used throughout the Roman occupation to build and then later maintain the nearby sections of wall.

In terms of the physical construction of the wall, the foundations were created by setting stone slabs (basalt was often used in addition to the sandstone and limestone detailed above) in puddled clay. One or two courses of facing stones were then positioned (both on the inner and outer faces, with drains added at the base if required), with a rubble/clay/lime mortar core then added, before the next one or two courses were built. As the wall got higher, the timber scaffolding was then used to facilitate the ongoing construction. Once the wall section was complete, a lime-wash render was added to coat the surface. The lime for the mortar and render was created by burning limestone at high temperatures in lime kilns. This was a lengthy process that required specialist skills on the part of the legionaries. Vitruvius (2.5.1) said that for a good mortar mix, the required ratio was between 2 and 3 parts sand to one part lime depending on the quality of the sand (as detailed in Chapter 4). Fields (2003, 28) adds that the water for the mortar would have been sourced from local rivers and streams. Timber for the scaffolding would similarly have been sourced locally, as the region was at that time heavily wooded, so this resource was again readily to hand. In this regard, long-lasting timbers, such as oak, would have been chosen when available.

Detail of the construction techniques used in the wall circuit of the Roman civitas capital of Venta Silurum (Caerwent) in south eastern Wales, showing finely worked facing stones and rubble core. Simon Elliott.

Other materials needed to construct the wall would have been transported substantially longer distances. For example, iron from the Weald (principally from major coastal manufactories in Kent and East Sussex, Cleere and Crossley, 1995, 57) would have been transported up the east coast by sea and then along the River Tyne; lead from the south-west and Wales (Jones and Mattingly, 1990, 179) would similarly have used maritime transport, in this case up the west coast. Both materials are well referenced in the famous wooden tablets from Vindolanda in the context of smithing and metal working.

It is with respect to this long-distance transport of materials for use in building and maintaining the wall that we again obtain insight into the military's participation, in this case the *Classis Britannica*. One of its key roles through to its demise in the mid-3rd century AD would have been transport and supply operations, as it was originally conceived with these roles in mind; its original 900 ships were built and crewed to facilitate the Claudian invasion in AD 43. From that time onwards, the regional fleet contributed significantly to the maritime supply network around the British Isles, across the North Sea and the English Channel. This would have been particularly the case during the construction of Hadrian's Wall, in the context of the ongoing maintenance of this significant military presence in the north of this outermost extremity of the empire. In the context of the east coast route by which iron was transported from the Weald (the principal iron manufacturing sites there also operated by the *Classis Britannica*, Elliott, 2016a, 89, see Chapter 6 below), Selkirk (1983, 72) controversially argued that once the materials arrived on the Tyne, the transport vessels used riverine hydraulic infrastructure installed by the military in the form of locks and weirs (yet another example of Roman military engineering, see above) to allow goods to be transported up to the region of the wall.

Two interpretative models are particularly useful when reviewing the Roman maritime trade network around Britain in the context of Hadrian's Wall, and the role of the military therein. The first is provided by Morris (2010, 1), who says that from the LIA to the end of the Roman occupation there existed three specific regional maritime exchange systems that allowed the transfer of materials and peoples (a process he calls 'connectivity') and their interaction with each other, dependent to a large extent on economic and political conditions. These three systems were:

- The Atlantic System, from the Atlantic coasts of Britain and Europe to the western end of the English Channel.
- The eastern English Channel and southern part of the North Sea System.
- The eastern North Sea System, linking settlement from Scandinavia to the mouth of the Rhine.

Evans (2013, 433) has more recently argued for a two trade-route model around the occupation-period British Isles, on the west and east coasts. He says both were driven by the need to supply the military presence in the north as detailed above, with the west coast route having the passage between Brittany/Normandy and Poole Harbour as its principal English Channel crossing-point. Goods would then have been transported up the west coast from here, the loads of fish sauce, spices, olive oil and Samian ware pottery making their way north through ports at locations such as the legionary fortresses at Caerleon (Guest and Young, 2009, 97), Chester (Mason, 2001, 43) and Bowness (Mason, 2003, 116). Meanwhile, Evans argues that the east coast route featured London, which had strong links with Gaul and the Rhineland, as its principal emporium. Again, the archaeological data supporting such an interpretation includes evidence of fish sauce, spices, olive oil and Samian ware, together with Rhenish fine wares and Noyon mortaria (Dannell and Mees, 2015, 80). Evans once again argues that the imported goods were then transported north, in this case along the east coast.

Reflecting the significantly increased military presence in the north of Britain during the building of Hadrian's Wall, Allen and Fulford (1999, 178) say that coastal trade from these southern emporia northwards increased markedly during the Hadrianic period, only declining from the middle of the 3rd century. They continue that the epigraphic evidence detailed above for units of the *Classis Britannica* helping build the wall is also evidence for the important role the fleet played as part of the east coast trade route.

Moving on to other instances of the military playing a key role in major construction projects, the *limes* from the Wash to the Solent (and also on the coast of northern Gaul) known as the forts of the Saxon Shore provide some fine examples from the late Principate (Fields, 2006, 4). There is an ongoing and lively debate about the nature of these forts, which were built at various times throughout the 3rd century AD. While some argue they fulfilled an administrative/headquartering/harbouring role, to my mind they speak to the appearance of an existential military threat, almost certainly the initiation of North German raiding across the North Sea and English Channel as the century progressed (Elliott, 2016a, 167). Therefore, I argue they were military in nature. This is evidenced by the fact that the first three, built between AD 220 and AD 230 at Brancaster (Roman *Branodunum*) on the northern coast of Norfolk, Caister-on-Sea (thought to be Roman *Gariannonum*) further along the coast, and Reculver on the north Kent coast of Kent, cover key seaway approaches to the province. These three forts are different in design from the earlier *Classis Britannica* forts in Britain (which would also have been built by the Roman military) and were extensive at 3ha in size. Square in plan, they featured very substantial perimeter walls, again emphasising their military nature. As the century progressed further forts in the chain were built, even more substantial in nature, at sites such as Richborough, Dover, Lympne, Pevensey, and Portchester, each incorporating the latest military construction technology at the time of its building. This created the *limes*, which ultimately protected the littoral of the south and east of Britain and northern Gaul, the latest forts almost certainly constructed by Carausius and later Allectus (Pearson, 2002a, 45) after the Principate to protect their breakaway North Sea Empire in the late 3rd century. In the latter case the military threat was therefore actually from the Roman Empire itself rather than Germanic raiders.

Fields (2006, 19) says that the construction techniques used for all of the Saxon Shore forts were broadly the same, despite the differentials in building date and design, this being understandably similar to the techniques used by the military building Hadrian's Wall. A foundation trench was dug first, between 0.7 and 1.7m in width, into which foundation materials such as chalk, flint and clay were laid. *Opus caementicium* concrete was also used in this regard at Brancaster and Pevensey, while timber piles were also used to provide additional stability at Richborough, Lympne

Where is Brancaster Saxon Shore fort? Site of this key link in the later Roman shore defences of Britain on the levelled off plateau at centre, with the eastern side of the protective ditch in the foreground. All of the stone has been robbed out for local use. Simon Elliott.

and Pevensey. The superstructure of the fortification was then built from just below ground level, using a plinth of large blocks which were stepped out on one or both faces of the wall as the first stage. As with Hadrian's Wall, the structure was then built upwards in stages, with the inner and outer wall constructed and in-filled before the next stage was built, and so on. One point of difference with the northern wall, however, was the use of regular layers of tiles (say, a layer of six stones followed by a layer of three tiles) in many of the forts for additional bonding and levelling, though these were lacking at Brancaster, Caister-by-Sea and Reculver (those used at Lympne are evidently reused roof tiles from earlier settlement there).

Materials used for the Saxon Shore forts were dependent on regional availability (not necessarily the most local), though many such as Richborough made extensive use of reused materials from earlier structures (Fields, 2006, 33). In terms of newly quarried materials used in the construction of the forts, Pearson (2002a, 83) helpfully shows the scale of commitment involved by highlighting that for the fort at Bradwell, where such building materials included:

- Locally sourced Septarian cementstone.
- Kentish ragstone from the Medway Valley.
- Lincolnshire limestone.
- Tufa from the Dour Valley in Kent.
- Imported Niedermendig lava from the Rhineland.

The Saxon Shore fort at Richborough in Kent, largely built of reused materials from earlier structures on the site and almost certainly built by the Roman military. John Lambshead.

These materials, unless sourced very locally, would have been transported to their place of use by sea and river as detailed in Chapter 1, often some distance for the more in-demand varieties of stone. One of these was Kentish ragstone (as detailed earlier, a fine limestone, easily workable, which also weathers well, found sitting in the Hythe Beds of the Greensand Ridge in the Wealden Anticlinorium), which, in the case of the fort at Reculver, was carried 50km further than any other material used. Greensand, of Folkestone origin, travelled even further, for example 175km to Caistor-by-Sea in northern Norfolk (Allen and Fulford, 1999, 177), while the Niedermendig lava used at Bradwell clearly travelled even further.

Table 4: Building the Saxon Shore Forts. After Pearson, 2002a, 85.

Location	*Boat loads*	*Local cart loads*
Brancaster	560	0
Caister-on-Sea	520	0
Burgh Castle	620	0
Walton Castle	470	0
Bradwell	870	0
Reculver	530	0
Richborough	960	0
Dover	0	13,540
Lympne	220	21,980
Pevensey	1,580	660
Portchester	240	15,530
Total	**6,570**	**51,710**

Burgh Castle, the southernmost of the two Saxon shore forts (the other, to the north, is Caistor-by-Sea) which guarded either side of the Great Estuary, the now largely silted up waterway which during the occupation gave maritime access to regional civitas capital Venta Icenorum (Caistor St Edmund). Simon Elliott.

The sheer scale of these enterprises on the part of the Roman military is illustrated by the above table, which shows the estimated number of boat and cart journeys required to build some of the forts (excluding the additional reuse of materials from earlier structures).

Exploiting these huge quantities of building materials required a major commitment in terms of manpower to build the forts, with Pearson (1999, 102) suggesting that 100,000 man days would have been needed to build the fort at Pevensey alone. This brings us to naturally reflect on who actually built the Saxon Shore forts, and yet again the principal participants were the Roman military, epigraphy specifically identifying some of the builders. This includes the *Cohors* I *Aquitanorum* auxiliary infantry and *Equites Dalmatae* auxiliary cavalry units based at Brancaster (Gurney, 2002, 10), the *Equites Stablesiani* auxiliary cavalry unit at Burgh Castle and the *Cohors* I *Baestasiorum* auxiliary unit at Reculver, all identified by stamped tiles and their incorporation in itineraries. Interestingly, the *Cohors* I *Aquitanorum* have also been identified as the builders of the small fort at Brough-on-Noe (Roman *Navio*) in Derbyshire, again showing the ubiquity with which the military were utilised in construction projects. Pearson (2002a, 90) argues that the *Classis Britannica* would also have been naturally utilised in the construction of the earlier Saxon Shore forts, particularly in the transport role given the extensive use of marine transport.

Staying in Britannia, the Severan land walls of London also present an excellent example of the military facilitating a major construction programme. This fortification was constructed in the late AD 190s after the defeat of the usurpation of British Governor Clodius Albinus when Severus sent military inspectors to stabilise the province. The 3.2km circuit was estimated by Merrifield (1965, 48) to comprise 35,000m^3 of ragstone quarried in the Upper Medway Valley, with Hall and Merrifield (1986, 28) later saying the wall comprised over one million squared and dressed ragstone blocks (for the inner and an outer facing), with a rubble ragstone core set with mortar. Based on the 100,000 man days Pearson (1999, 102) argues were required to build the much shorter 760m wall circuit at Pevensey (as above), I believe 420,000 man days would have been required for the land walls of London.

The quarried ragstone for this wall was transported from the quarries down the River Medway and up the River Thames, an impressive round trip of trip of 254km, including an overnight stop either way somewhere near the Hoo Peninsula or Sheerness. To carry the amount of material required would have needed 1,750 voyages of medium-sized cargo vessels such as the Blackfriars 1 type excavated in the early 1960s at the confluence of the Thames and its tributary the River Fleet. Though this wreck dates to earlier in the occupation, when excavated it was found to be carrying 26 tonnes of Kentish ragstone (Marsden, 1994, 83). This indicates a continuity of the industrial quarrying and transport operation starting early in the occupation through to the mid-3rd century, when it evidently stopped. In Chapter 6 below, I fully detail this huge quarrying operation, which also provided the material to construct much of London's contemporary built environment. In the same chapter, I also make the case that it was the *Classis Britannica* regional navy that facilitated this industry, and I believe they would also have been the principal resource used by the governor and procurator (newly appointed by Severus) to build the land wall, though I note that for a time after the revolt of Albinus some of the resources of the northern regional fleets may all have come under the same joint command structure (Elliott, 2016a, 25). Vexillations from the remaining British legions would also been used, given the scale of this task. We have less visibility regarding who built the late 3rd century river walls and bastions in London, as after the end of the *Classis Britannica* and the Upper Medway Valley ragstone quarrying industry, they were constructed not from finely worked stone but reused material from demolished public buildings and mausolea. The haste with which they were evidently thrown up seems to anecdotally point to the presence of the military again, perhaps in the context of the Carausian/Allectan Revolt. This falls outside of the scope of the Principate, however.

On an even grander scale, and looking farther afield to the heart of the later empire, the Roman walls of the capital city itself also show the military being deployed to facilitate key construction projects. The original 10m-high Servian walls date to the early 4th century BC and were built as a response to the sacking of the city by the Gauls in 390 BC. These walls were specifically *not* built by the military, due to the nature of the armed forces of Rome at this early date, with masons from Sicily being employed instead to construct to 11km circuit with its 21 gates, encompassing an area of 426ha. These walls lasted through the later Republic and the majority of the Principate, though inevitably the city outgrew their protection. As the 'Crisis of the 3rd Century' progressed, attention focused once more on the defences of Rome, and in AD 271 a vast new circuit was built, this time by the military: the Aurelian Walls, named after the emperor in whose reign their construction began. This circuit was 19km in length and incorporated state of the art military technology in the form of 383 towers and bastions, 18 main gates and numerous posterns. Completed in AD 282 in the reign of Probus, this circuit enclosed an area of 1,372ha.

Meanwhile, dating to the Dominate period of Roman governance rather than the Principate but still worthy of note, the walls of the capital of the later Eastern Empire are also worthy of consideration, as they were built by the military. The original walls of Constantinople were built in AD 328 and stretched from the Sea of Marmara to the Golden Horn, though it is the later wall of the Emperor Theodosius II (AD 408–AD 450) that most clearly shows the Roman military engaged in monumental construction. Initiated in AD 408, this new structure was built 2.5km to the west of the earlier wall and was much grander in ambition than its predecessor, arguably keeping Constantinople safe for the next 1045 years until it finally fell to the Ottoman Turks' cannons in 1453.

Stretching 5.7km, again from the from the Sea of Marmara to the Golden Horn, though much longer in length than the earlier wall, the Theodosian Wall contained 10 main gateways (five public and five military) together with a number of smaller posterns (smaller, often concealed gates). The most advanced military fortification of

The Aurelian Walls of Rome, a superb example of Roman military engineering and construction. David Campbell Bannerman.

its day – even more so that the Aurelian Walls of Rome – the wall embodied the concept of defence in depth and featured an outer moat some 19m wide and 7m deep, a 19m wide terrace called the *parateichion* (designed to provide a field of from the walls), an outer wall over 8.5m high, a second terrace called the *peribolos* which was 16m wide, and finally the inner and main wall, which rose to 12m in height. Both of the walls featured towers, in the case of the inner wall 96 of them evenly spaced every 55m, enabling covering fire over the outer wall into the *parateichion* from their 20m height. Both walls, and the lining for the moat, were constructed in the same manner, with layers of dressed stone blocks interbedded once more with the ubiquitous Roman tile layers for leveling and bonding. A single sea wall was also constructed at the same time, lesser in stature than the land walls but again of similar construction, to close the circuit around the city.

It is with the administration of the construction process for the Theodosian Walls that we see the military in action most clearly. In the first instance, the emperor appointed his most senior military officer, the eastern Praetorian prefect Anthemius, to oversee the work. This was completed in AD 413, with Anthemius using the regional field army and the city's garrison to carry out the physical building work. Such military

Roman amphitheatre at Trier on the Moselle, very likely built under the management of the Roman military who may also have carried out the physical construction work. Simon Elliott.

Roman amphitheatre in Nimes, southern France. In the Mediterranean climate, here the naval milites of the regional fleet would have worked the vela (sail) awnings to provide vital shade. Mitesh Patel.

Roman amphitheatre at the legionary fortress of Caerleon, home of the legio II Augusta whose specialists and legionaries would have built it. Simon Elliott.

organisation was also needed to maintain the wall; Theodosius II later ordered his urban prefect Kyros of Florus to engage the military in mobilising the city's 'racing factions' (organised supporters of the various chariot racing teams) to rebuild the walls after an earthquake caused extensive damage in AD 447, leaving Constantinople vulnerable to Attila's marauding Huns.

Public Buildings and Built Environment

Once again, the military was the first port of call for the construction of public buildings across the Roman Empire, especially during the Principate, when such structures were a key manifestation of the Roman urban environment. As an example, research by the Museum of London Archaeology (MOLA) into the rebuilding of London after the Boudiccan Revolt of AD 60/61 shows the Roman military taking such a lead. Some of the first structures built after this traumatic event were a timber and earth fort (clearly designed to reassert control of the geographical area of the city), roads, a water-lifting machine and a new quayside. New public buildings quickly followed, vital to enable the city to thrive again, and the fact that the city had been so comprehensively destroyed during the revolt indicates a comparative lack of a civilian population for this brief period. Therefore, the only asset available for all of these infrastructure projects was the military. Then, as the new city rapidly grew again from the ashes, its stone-built infrastructure began to proliferate once more, with, for example, the forum and basilica becoming the largest stone-built structure north of the Alps. A significant percentage of the construction from this time through to the mid-3rd century made use of Kentish ragstone from the Upper Medway Valley, for example the forum and basilica, the governor's palace, the second (stone-built) phase of the amphitheatre, numerous bath houses (for example at Huggins Hill) and many private dwellings. Once again, I argue below in Chapter 6 that it was the *Classis Britannica* that ran the quarrying industry, and was the principal resource used in much of the construction.

Numerous other examples of the military participating in the construction of public buildings are to be found from across the empire. For example, vexillations from the *legio* IIII *Scythia*, *legio* XVI *Flavia Firma* and *legio* III *Cyrenaica* are known – from inscriptions – to have been utilised in the construction of the mithraeum temple and an amphitheatre at Dura-Europos in Syria. This was a pattern repeated throughout the Empire during the entirety of the Principate, to a greater or lesser extent in each given city and town depending on their nature, and most commonly in the *coloniae* built for veterans.

Chapter 6

The Roman Military and Industry

While acknowledging the importance of agriculture in the Roman economy, industry nevertheless played a highly significant and integrated role, and is indeed central to the core theme of this work regarding the military in one of their key non-conflict roles, namely facilitating industrial enterprises across the Roman Empire. This particularly applies to large scale projects, and most often those involving the *metalla* extractive industries, frequently in the form of industrial imperial estates. In this chapter I will firstly consider Roman industry in general, a subject little considered in depth in most appreciations of the Roman Empire and economy, though important enough for me to argue elsewhere (Elliott, 2014b, 49) that in the case of Britain it amounted to a first industrial revolution. Next, I look at the role of the Roman military with regard to industry, before finally considering two very specific case studies of Roman *metalla* in the south-east of Britain during the occupation. The latter aim to determine their provenance for being military-run imperial estates (they were certainly part of the imperial economy under direct state control, see Chapter 1 for definitions) to provide a guide to analysing other such sites and the role of the Roman military therein – in short, providing a template for the use of others in this regard going forward. These latter two case studies, focusing on the iron industry in the Weald and the ragstone quarries of the Upper Medway Valley, are features of my PhD research and appear in detail in print here for the first time.

Roman Industry

Of course, industry did exist as an economic phenomenon before the advent of the Roman Empire. Taking Britain once again as our example, here in the Late Iron Age, this included the minting of coins, pottery production, quern stone production, mining and metal production. Technological innovation also occurred, for example with the adoption of the potter's wheel, the rotary quern and the lathe. However, with the arrival of the Romans something truly revolutionary happened, certainly in terms of scale, engineering innovation, the presence of manufacturing, and the growth of consumerism in response to the availability of newly mass produced goods (Gardner, 2013, 7). These new industries did not exist in isolation either, but were features in a complex international economic system, and were supported by an equally complex maritime and road-based transport infrastructure. This allows us to consider such activity as being part of a much wider industrious landscape, reviewed as a whole here across the entirety of the empire.

The sheer scale of industrial activity in the Roman Empire cannot be understated, with for example evidence visible through widely recognised data showing a high concentration of pollutants from Roman industry (particularly lead and copper emissions) found in Greenland ice cores. Here, the only other major pre-later 18th century peak occurs during the 11th century and relates to industrial activities by the Sung Chinese on the other side of the globe (Borsos *et al*, 2003, 5).

The Roman economy featured industries both great and small. These ranged from huge state-controlled mining and quarrying enterprises to manufactories producing a wide variety of products (for example weapons of uniform quality and size, *garum* fish sauce and fine quality Samian ware pottery), through to local milling and food production enterprises. With the arrival of the Romans in Britain (using this province as our ongoing example here), this industrial suite became a feature of the British experience of *Romanitas*.

In a specifically British context, we can look at a variety of examples of this new industrial experience. These included huge iron-producing enterprises and industrial-scale quarrying, both considered in detail in the case studies below. Other industries that thrived during the occupation included pottery production, with a wide variety of styles from differing modes of production catering for requirements high and low, a key indication of the arrival and ensuing spread of *Romanitas* in the islands. In this regard de la Bédoyère (2000, 9) states that Roman style pottery found its way into all areas of daily life, as can be seen by works of synthesis on Roman pottery types such as Tyer's atlas or the work of Willis on Samian ware (Tyers 1996; Willis 2005; 2011).

With regard to the Roman pottery industry, Peacock (1982, 8) usefully produced a model of methods of pottery production applicable not only with regard to this industry in Britain and indeed across the empire, but also transferable in terms of appreciating scale for all Roman industry. He broke this activity down into a hierarchy of seven different modes (domestic or imported):

- Household production (the least visible in the available data).
- Household industry (e.g. Dorset BB1 pottery).
- Individual workshops (e.g. Severn Valley ware).
- Nucleated workshops (urban examples including those in Colchester, and rural ones the Alice Holt potteries).
- Manufactories (e.g. imported Samian ware).
- Estate production (e.g. amphora manufacture for estate goods).
- Military or official workshop production (e.g. Holt in Cheshire).

For manufactories, Peacock did draw one link with the present that would sit comfortably with a modern economist: the evident connection at such sites between capital and labour. At the other end of this spectrum between past and present commonality, he identified the latter two modes of production (estate production and military/official production) as ones which do not sit comfortably in his wider hierarchy, let alone in a modern context. Interestingly, he also precluded factories in a Roman context (an eighth mode type, above the manufactory level) as a mode of production, given the arguable failure to exploit mechanical power to any extent (1982, 10), though he did cite the complex of water powered flower-mills at Barbegal near Arles in southern France as an example that might buck this trend. One could perhaps add other examples in this latter regard, for example the *fabricae* state-run workshops covered in more detail below.

To this native Romano-British industry we can add mill and quern stone manufacturing (for example in and around Folkestone) and the associated milling industy, and a modest indigenous glass-production industry, with the major known glass-production facilities located on the south side of the forum in London and at Caistor-by-Norwich (Roman *Venta Icenorum*, Jones and Mattingly, 1990, 216). Most recently, Howell *et al* (2013, 10) have also highlighted further significant glass production in Roman London at the Bow Bells House site south of Cheapside. Meanwhile, occupied Britain also featured a regionally focused mosaic manufacturing industry, which seems to have particularly thrived in the 4th century, after the time of the Principate. There seem to have been six specific mosaic schools in this later period (Table 5).

Table 5: Roman Mosaic Schools in Britain. After Smith, 1984, 357, and Jones and Mattingly, 1990, 224.

Location	*Date*
The Central Southern School based around Chichester, Winchester and Silchester.	c. AD 300–325
The Corinian 'Orpheus School', Cirencester	c. AD 300–320
The Corinian 'Saltire School', Cirencester	c. AD 320–340/350
The Durnovarian School, Dorchester	c. AD 340/350–370+
Petuarian School, possibly based in Brough-on-Humber	c. AD 340–350
The Durobrivan School, Water Newton	c. AD 350/365–370/380

Britain was also home to a thriving textile industry. In particular, the province was known within the Empire for two specific textile products. These were a type of the *birrus* rain-proofed hooded cloak, and a form of fine quality *tapetia* woollen rug (Wild, 2002, 1). In the AD 301 Edict of Diocletian, the British version of the latter is actually listed as the best available across the empire. For its cloth fibres, this industry made use of sheep's wool and flax, with the occasional addition of hemp and animal hair. Silk is also present, though as an import. Some of the cloth would also have been dyed, with around 20% of the woollen products found at the northern border fort of Vindolanda showing evidence of dyestuff (Wild, 2002, 1). The dyes identified here were either imports such as Madder (*rubia tinctorum L*), which gave a red colour, or local lichens, which gave a purple colour.

Table 6: Mints across the Roman Empire. After Moorhead, 2014, 32.

Alexandria	47
Amiens	193
Antioch	108
Aquileia	474
Arles	4,300
'C mint' (Carausius and Allectus)	417
Carthage	11
Constantinople	50
Cyzicus	65
Gallic mints (Gallic empire)	1,949
Heraclea	48
London	2,987
Lyon	4,012
Milan	10
Nicodemia	37
Ostia	15
Ravenna	15
Rome	11,701
Rouen	6
Serdica	6
Sirmium	19
Siscia	712
Spain	45
Tarraco	5
Thessalonica	110
Ticinium	143
Trier	10,616
Tripolis	5
Viminacium	1
Total	**38,441**

Brewing was also a major industry in occupied Britain, with Kent providing an excellent example of the industrial scale of brewing operations during the Roman presence. Carruthers (2014, 143) explains:

> In the Ebbsfleet Valley at Northfleet villa, brewing appears to have been taking place on an...industrial scale... Malting ovens, a barn and three brewing tanks with the largest holding up to 16,000 pints (9,092 litres) were excavated.

Meanwhile salt (vital as a preservative and a flavouring for food) was also the subject of industrial activity in occupied Britain. Roman salterns of significant size have been located around the Wash (a continuation of a strong LIA tradition), the East Anglian coast and Thames estuary, along the south coast, and around Bridgewater in Somerset. Further, brine springs associated with salt production have been located at Northwich, Middlewich, Henhull and Whitchurch along or near the Rivers Weaver and Dane, and around Droitwich in Worcestershire (Woodiwiss, 1992,183). Even a type of fish sauce such as *garum* may have been produced in occupied Britain, with Biddulph (2013, 20) suggesting Stanford Wharf in Essex as a possible location, while Locker (2007, 151) suggests a site excavated at Peninsula House in London as another based on the remains of vast quantities of young herrings and sprats found there, in association with shards from amphora used to transport fish sauce.

Last but not least, an occupation-period coin minting industry is also evident in Britain. Contemporary copies of Roman coins were produced here in very large numbers in the Claudian and Neronian period (AD 41–64), Severan Period (AD 193–235), the Barbarous Radiate period (AD 275–285) and in the 4th century from AD 330 to 348 and AD 355 to AD 364. Meanwhile the principal official mint for purely indigenous coins was first founded in London in AD 286 by the usurper Carausius, with coins produced here from AD 286 to AD 324, and AD 383 to AD 388 (Moorhead, 2014, 32). Of the 29 major Roman mints from across the empire in the Portable Antiquities Scheme (PAS) database of Roman coins found in Britain, the 2,987 coins made in London make this mint the fifth largest represented, as one can see from the preceding table (impressive when those with higher representations are Rome, Trier, Arles and Lyon). Additionally, Carausius set up a second mint (dubbed the C mint), which manufactured further coinage, of which 417 are recorded in the PAS database. There were clearly far more coins being minted and in circulation in Britain during the occupation than both before or indeed after.

The Role of the Roman Military in Industry

As detailed throughout this work, in an age before the advent of a civil service, nationalised industries and a free market able to fund large scale capital expenditure projects, the military was the go to resource for the Roman state (in any of its manifestations) to facilitate a variety of activities, and this included large scale industry as part of the Imperial economy detailed in Chapter 1.

There are many examples, including in the first instance running the major *fabricae* state-owned manufactories across the empire that provided mass-produced equipment for the Roman military and administration. Esmonde Cleary (2013, 93) details the scale and sophistication of these operations, for example that at Autun in eastern France, which specialised in making ballista, armour and shields, and that at Reims in northern France specialising in sword manufacture. The state, often through the services of the military, also controlled the official mints that produced coinage for use across the empire (Moorhead, 2012, 8). An even more pronounced example of the military controlling industry however comes in the form of the major tile and brick tile manufactories which produced many of the building ceramics detailed in Chapter 4. One of the best-known examples, with a very specific link to the Roman military in the form of stamps of the *Classis Britannica* regional navy, is found in the Weald in south-eastern Britain. Sitting side-by-side with its occupation-period iron-producing counterpart (in the eastern/coastal part of the Weald), this first came to light in 1778 when the Revd. John Lyon found the first Roman tile so stamped in Dover. From such modest beginnings, subsequent archaeological investigation has built out our knowledge of this immense industrial enterprise and I go into detail about it here to provide context for other military-run industries of this scale.

Mills (2013, 453) says there is no evidence of tile and brick manufacture in quantity in Britain before the occupation, with the industry in the Weald beginning very soon after the AD 43 Claudian invasion, perhaps as early as AD 50, though on an initially small scale for local use. As with other industrial activity that commenced in short order after the invasion, there was clearly a degree of foreknowledge regarding the available extractive materials here. Mills (2013, 461) notes that the military and settling veterans were the principal vector for the introduction of tile use in Britain. The first municipal or official stamps on tile and brick in Britain appear in AD 90, in a legionary context. Betts (1987, 28) argued that this late appearance of official stamping shows that the very early tile manufacturing industry in the Weald and elsewhere in Britain would have been local in nature rather than extra-regional. The first *Classis Britannica*-stamped tile appears in a late 1st century AD/early 2nd century AD context, while Peacock (1977, 245) believed that Wealden tile and brick manufacture may have actually begun in the late 1st century AD to facilitate the building of regional state infrastructure such as the twin *pharos* lighthouses at Dover. This industry peaked in the later 2nd century AD, as did the iron industry (see below). By this time, the eastern/coastally-produced *Classis Britannica* stamped tiles were ubiquitous around the entire east Kentish coast, and indeed further afield (see distribution table at Appendix C), as buildings featuring this mark were often associated with a state-related function. In terms of utility, Brodribb (1979, 141) asserts that the official stamp of the regional navy was used on the state-produced tiles for prestige reasons and to ensure their quality. In that regard, it is noteworthy that the stamps always appear on the upper sides of *tegulae, imbrices* and floor tiles (the stamp also appearing on bonding, hypocaust *pilae* and box-flue tiles) rather than their underside, and would thus have been externally visible. Hirt (2010, 197) argues that the naval *milites* would have physically participated in the manufacture of tiles in the same way they would have carried out stone quarrying and wood cutting (see Chapter 4), in addition to managing the operation. Whether this activity was part of an imperial estate or not is considered below.

Two specific types of tile with *Classis Britannica* stamps were identified by Peacock (1977, 236) in his extensive survey of the eastern/coastal Wealden occupation-period tile and brick industry, which is still the benchmark used to this day, and is based upon their material composition, styled Fabric 1 and Fabric 2. The Fabric 1 type is a uniform buff colour with scattered quartz sand-grains, identical to unstamped tiles found extensively around Boulogne. Peacock believed they were manufactured in a brickyard in the vicinity of the *Classis Britannica* headquarters there from material quarried locally, and were used regionally, with very limited export taking place. Until recently, the only tiles of this fabric found elsewhere were an example from Dover and another single tile from the central Wealden port and iron-working site at Kitchenham Farm. However, recent research has dramatically increased the number found at the latter location, with 29 out of 31 additional pieces of *Classis Britannica* tile of this origin recently coming to light. A total of 98 stamps of the *Classis Britannica* have been found on partial or complete Fabric 1 tiles.

The Fabric 2 tiles are very different to those of the Fabric 1 type and represent those manufactured by the *Classis Britannica* in the eastern/coastal Weald. Peacock (1977, 237) described them thus:

> Fabric 2 is of a distinctive reddish-pink colour relieved to a degree by streaks, lenses and swirls of creamy white clay. The most prominent and abundant inclusions are of black or red-brown ore, usually as near-spherical particles about 1mm across: but irregular rounded fragments up to 3mm or more across are usually present. Sub-angular fragments of white, finely laminated siltstone (up to 10mm) are another feature and a few pieces are almost invariably present in a cross-section 20cm long. In contrast to Fabric 1, quartz is not visible in the fractured cross-section, but sand- or grit-size fabrics are occasionally seen on or near the surface, where they result from dusting to prevent the clay sticking to the mold during manufacture.

As detailed in Chapter 4, Peacock (1977, 237) believed that the material used for these tiles was Fairlight clay, which sits within the Ashdown Formation in the Hasting Beds. This material appears a very good match for that used in the Roman tiles, and Peacock notes that, while such tiles were used across a wide variety of sites across the region, the area where the vast majority were found was in fact around Fairlight (located in the eastern/coastal region). He specifically believed that the principal naval tile and brick yards used were located near where the Fairlight clay actually outcrops at Fairlight Head, or from deposits beneath the alluvium of Romney Marsh between Rye and Dungeness. In the first case, he argued there is a good chance that the principal tile and brick works have been lost through coastal erosion, while in the second he believed the evidence would have been covered over by recent alluvium deposition in Romney Marsh.

While predominantly found in the eastern/coastal region of the Weald, the use of the Fabric 2 tile was widespread, as is evident in the distribution table in Appendix C. Peacock (1977, 237), believed that of the two regions manufacturing *Classis Britannica* tiles, that making the Fabric 2 tiles was by far the most important: over 2,800 partial or complete tiles of Fabric 2 type featuring *Classis Britannica* stamps have been found to date. In terms of the longevity of this industry, data from across all the sites where *Classis Britannica* tile has been found supports the theory that it continued to thrive while the iron industry in the region was still running at full capacity, then declined after the mid-3rd century AD. It was certainly still in operation at the beginning of the 3rd century, when newly manufactured Wealden *Classis Britannica*-stamped box-flue tiles were being used to build the 'Painted House' *mansio* in Dover (Philp, 1989, 101).

Moving onto other examples of the Roman military facilitating industrial activity, that perhaps best known is with regard to the *metalla* mining and quarrying industries across the Empire. This included the larger mining and quarrying enterprises, with Hirt (2010, 106), Cleere and Crossley (1995, 66), de la Bédoyère (1992, 100) and Jones and Mattingly (1990, 192) all arguing that the majority of such operations exploiting natural resources were under state control (often through the military in some capacity, see case studies below), to ensure the continuity of supply of the mined and quarried materials and thus the flow of wealth to the imperial *fiscus*. It was invariably the troops who, at the very least, initiated each significant *metalla* mining operation. This was clearly common, a fine example being the award of triumphal honours by Claudius to Curtius Rufus, governor of Upper Germany, for allowing his troops to carry out silver mining. Mattingly (2006, 507) adds another example of the military being involved in mining, this time for lead. This metal was a vital part of the Roman economy, for use in its own right and also a source of silver for coin production (in this latter case the silver being extracted from argentiferous lead by the process of cupellation, Jones and Mattingly, 1990, 185). The exploitation of lead during the occupation in Britain is a useful tool for the archaeologist and historian given it was produced in ingots (known as 'pigs'), which were often stamped and dated, thus giving insight into their origins both geographically and chronologically. We know the legions were producing lead early in the occupation as a 'pig' originating in the Mendips has been found at St Valury-sur-Somme in France with the stamp of the Britain-based *legio* II *Augusta*, dated to AD 49, while three other examples found in Britain from this period indicate that the export route for lead from this source was through Southampton Water (Jones and Mattingly, 1990, 184).

Salway (1981, 634) argued that the early exploitation of lead in Britain was so important that it was a key factor in the earlier prioritisation of the south-west for conquest in Vespasian's famous campaigns in the mid-late 40s AD when *legate* of the *legio* II (Elliott, 2016a, 119). In this region, at sites such as Charterhouse-on-Mendip, lead production soon reached industrial proportions (the lead here having a particularly high silver content), to be quickly joined by other areas such as Wales and Northumberland. In fact, the industry was so successful that by the AD 70s Britain had surpassed Spain as the leading province supplying the metal, to the extent that the state directly intervened. As Salway (1981, 635) explained:

> By Flavian times the much greater ease with which the surface deposits of Britain could be worked than the mines of Spain...had proved a serious embarrassment to the Imperial Government and production was limited by law, presumably for political reasons such as the protection of interests in other provinces.

Once successfully initiated by the military, the lead mining and manufacturing claims seem to have been quickly let to either *metalla* contractors, companies of *socii* investors or ambitious entrepreneurs (Mattingly, 2006, 507, though such letting was not always the case with the *metalla*, see discussion in Chapter 1), out of state control and a useful counterpoint to the different experience of state involvement detailed below for the iron manufacturing *metalla* in the Weald and ragstone quarrying *metalla* in the Upper Medway Valley. We have a specific example of one of these entrepreneurs taking over a lead mining *metalla* concession, the freedman C. Nipius Ascanius. His private stamp has been found on a Mendips 'pig' dated AD 59, and he is later found acquiring lead deposits in the early AD 60s in the Clwyd region in Wales, before this district was actually pacified (Salway, 1981, 634).

The limit on lead production seems to have been lifted later in the occupation, with Todd (1996, 47) using data based on pottery analysis to show that lead mining continued to thrive in the Mendips until at least the 3rd century. The lifting of the limit may actually have occurred during the reign of Hadrian (Salway, 1981, 635) when lead mining in Derbyshire began, the emperor's name appearing on 'pigs' from this source which indicates the state was again initiating production, though the industry here may not have been as successful as that of the south-west given the comparatively poorer silver content. The same was true of lead mining operations in Shropshire and Yorkshire. Lead manufacturing did continue into the later period though, to facilitate demand for pewter in addition to its more traditional uses, and once again official stamps on 'pigs' indicate state involvement.

Meanwhile, another strong example of the military being involved in the *metalla* is with regard to iron ore and the associated iron manufacturing industry. Again, Britain presents a first-class example, this being the iron manufacturing industry in the Weald which sat alongside the tile and brick working industries there detailed above. Here, iron manufacturing from the LIA through to the mid-3rd century is visible on two scales: a localised one aligned with London (specifically its metal working centre in Southwark) in the central Weald, and a far larger-scale operation at various sites in the eastern/coastal Weald. It is the latter that concerns us here, with the *Classis Britannica* being well-referenced as being the procurator's agent in running an extensive industry whose demise coincided with the disappearance of the regional navy in the mid-3rd century as detailed in Chapter 2. Principal locations included Beauport Park (where the Wealden road terminated), Bardown, Chitcombe and Footlands, while ports along the coast would have provided the means of exporting the manufactured iron both regionally and abroad. These sites have been identified by the huge quantities of tiles stamped with the *Classis Britannica*'s mark. This and other evidence including numismatic data are considered in the following case study to determine whether it was run by the military and indeed formed a bespoke imperial estate, possibly also incorporating the tile and brick industry.

From mining, we can then move on to military involvement in quarrying *metalla*. Known British examples include the various types of freestone quarrying for pre-Flavian memorials around fortresses such as Colchester, Gloucester, Lincoln and Alchester. The manifestation of the State in these cases were the legions and auxiliaries themselves, with Hayward (2009, 112) reflecting the commentary in Chapter 4 regarding the military as engineers in saying:

> The army would have had the necessary specialists, manpower, equipment and organization at this time to survey, quarry and supply two metre long blocks (of freestone for monuments).

One can of course add here as a further example the 11 known quarries used to provide worked material, usually local sandstones, for the construction of Hadrian's Wall (Breeze and Dobson, 2000, 31). Here, in a number of cases, inscriptions in the quarries themselves identify the military units actually carrying out the stone extraction, these detailed in Chapter 6. A further example might be that set out in Chapter 1 regarding Combe Down near Bath where epigraphy referencing the imperial freedman Naevius has been interpreted as evidence of an imperial estate related to quarrying (Crawford, 1976, 36).

Meanwhile another example of the military participating in quarrying *metalla* comes in the form of the tufa used extensively as a building material on the east Kent coast, this also being exported more widely. Parfitt and Philp (1981, 176) and Allen and Fulford (1999, 169) argue that the quarries which supplied this stone were located along the River Dour near to Dover. Given the intense activity of the regional fleet in this region, I believe a strong case can be made that it was actually the *Classis Britannica* – as the state representative – that facilitated this industry.

One final, but exponentially important, consideration regarding the Roman military and British quarrying *metalla* is the ragstone industry in the Upper Medway Valley, which is a significant focus of my own PhD research (Elliott, 2016b, 103). I have identified five quarries at Allington, Boughton Monchelsea, Dean Street, Quarry Wood at West Farleigh and Teston, which from the outset of the occupation (the first use of the stone from this location is the first *forum* in London, dating to around AD 50) through to the mid-3rd century enjoyed a prolific output. The scale of this is evident from their combined quarry area, an astonishing 723,430m^2 (see Case Study 2 below for the areas of each individual quarry). These quarries are all above the tidal reach of the River Medway, then at Snodland, as argued by Kaye (2015b, 232), from where boatloads of the stone would have undertaken a 254km round-trip to take their loads of ragstone to London, with the stone also being used throughout the region (see Upper Medway Valley ragstone distribution map at Appendix B, and discussion in Chapter 1 regarding transport in the Roman world). I consider in the second case study below the evidence for this industry being run by the military in the form of the *Classis Britannica*, and whether it can be described as an imperial estate.

Meanwhile, looking further afield, there are many other clear examples of the military facilitating quarrying *metalla* elsewhere in the empire. These include the Mons Claudianus granodiorite mine in the Eastern Egyptian desert, where epigraphic evidence provided by letters, passes and receipts shows at least 20 centurions seconded there from the local legions and, topically for this work given the focus of the military in non-conflict related activities, the *Classis Alexandrina* Egyptian regional navy. Another example is the *Classis Germanica* quarrying along the River Rhine and its tributaries. Epigraphic evidence of this comes from numerous naval inscriptions in the Trass quarries on the left bank of the Brohol Valley, and from similar evidence that vexillations of this fleet quarried tufa for the Trajanic colonia Dee Ulpia at Vetara.

I now turn to the two case studies outlined above to show the interpretive pathway used to determine the association of a given industry with the Roman military, and indeed whether or not it was an imperial estate.

Case Study 1: The Eastern/Coastal Wealden Iron-Manufacturing *Metalla*

Many archaeologists and historians have long hypothesised that the state/Roman military in the form of the *Classis Britannica* managed the iron manufacturing industry in the Weald during the Roman occupation. Modern research in this regard has focused specifically on the eastern/coastal area where the largest sites were located and with its close association (presumably) with maritime trade. Some commentators have taken this view of a state presence even further, making the case for the region being an official imperial estate, as detailed in the Chapter 1 review of the Roman economy. There is certainly a large amount of archaeological data to support such views which I set out below.

Adherents to the view that the regional navy managed the Wealden iron industry include Brodribb (1979, 141), Pearson (2002a, 50), Hodgkinson (2008, 33) and Harrington and Welch (2014, 109), while those going further in supporting the imperial estate theory include Marsden (1994, 83) and Cleere and Crossley (1995, 68, based on Cleere's original work, 1977, 18). Mattingly himself, important in helping with the definition of an imperial estate in Chapter 1, says that a minimalist reading of the available data shows the Weald as under some kind of imperial control during the occupation (2006, 387). As those with an interest in the Weald in the Roman period will attest, these individuals effectively represent the entire canon of those whose research has shaped our modern appreciation of Roman activity in the region (with the notable exception of Millett, see below).

Background

The Weald was one of the three principal iron-producing areas in Britain during the occupation, the other two being the Forest of Dean and the East Midlands (Mattingly, 2006, 509). Both of the latter superceded the Weald in terms of importance after the middle of the 3rd century (Cleere and Crossley, 1995, 72). Iron was also produced on a lesser scale elsewhere in Britain, for example in East Yorkshire (the industry there having its roots in the LIA, Halkon, 2011, 148), Exmoor in the south-west and, later in the occupation, the Thames Valley.

Easily accessible raw materials were at the heart of the location of the Wealden iron industry, for example the region's siderite iron ore, which had an average iron ore content of 40% (Jones and Mattingly, 1990, 192). The heavily wooded Weald was also a ready source of the large amounts of timber needed to produce the vast quantities of charcoal required for the iron manufacturing process, with oak, beech, hazel and ash all being utilised in this regard. Hodgkinson (2013) adds that a readily available source of water was also important in the location of individual sites:

> A lot of the early iron-working sites are found in stream valleys. This provided water to support all aspects of the operation, with the added bonus that it also facilitated prospecting along the banks of the streams.

The iron industry in the Weald had its origins in the Late Iron Aga, and its success in that regard was a key factor in attracting Roman interest from the outset of the occupation (Hodgkinson, 2008, 30). Data from sites such as Beauport Park (Brodribb *et al*, 1988, 232) show that from these comparatively modest beginnings the iron manufacturing industry expanded rapidly from that point. Hodgkinson (2008, 2) concurs with this chronology, saying:

> iron making in the pre-Roman and Roman Weald should be regarded as a continuum that was unbroken, but intensified, by the Roman occupation.

Hodgkinson (2008, 32) says that there was considerable variation in the layout of Roman iron working sites. For example, the standard *chaîne opératoire* process for iron production at the smaller sites would typically find them based in a stream valley with the ore being dug from mines at the top of the valley slopes, then moving downhill to be roasted, then moving further downhill for smelting and forging before the waste was dumped into the valley bottom. As Hodgkinson (2013) notes regarding these smaller sites, 'everything moved downhill.' In contrast, the larger sites (especially in the eastern/coastal region) would have been much more akin to Peacock's (1982, 8) manufactory-scale mode of production in the pottery industry. This would have been in terms of their large size, engagement with regional transport infrastructure and the level of industrial organisation evident – in the case of the latter, with a clear symbiosis between capital and labour.

The siderite iron ore extraction operations would have been in the form of shallow quarries or bowl-shaped opencast pits, with the largest iron ore mining sites being located at Bardown and Beauport Park (the latter being the largest, Cleere and Crossley, 1995, 15). Hodgkinson (2008, 13) does emphasise however that iron ore would have been sporadically available across the whole of the Weald, and in many cases would have been mined very close to the iron working sites themselves, for example at Footlands Farm (Cleere and Crossley, 1995, 303). This is in contrast to the later occupation period iron manufacturing industry in the Forest of Dean, where the centrally mined ore appears to have been shipped across the region using the River Severn as the main arterial routeway (Allen, 2010, 41).

In the Weald, once extracted the ore was then roasted to create ferrous oxides from the carbonate, this being easier to smelt. Furnaces came in a variety of types and were generally larger than any of their chronological successors until the later Middle Ages at the earliest (Dark and Dark, 1997), with Hodgkinson (2008, 2) saying:

> both tapping and non-tapping furnaces were used, (with) both domed and shaft furnaces (being) found in the region during the same period.

The Roman iron-workers would have used the 'Direct Process' when producing their iron, with the iron produced in the furnace being available for forging immediately. The iron was obtained from these furnaces by creating temperatures of around 1,100°C, the slag then being removed and discarded, thus providing the principal evidence of the occupation-period iron industry, along with other waste products including charcoal refuse, ore refuse and furnace debris. From the estimated 75,000–100,000 tonnes of slag and waste estimated to have been produced in this way during the occupation in the Weald, we can determine that between 10,000 and 15,000 tonnes of iron were produced here, mostly in the eastern/coastal region where the military presence is hypothesised.

Cleere and Crossley (1995, 78) explain that to maintain this intense output some 15ha of woodland would have been needed to provide the annually required charcoal, with Hodgkinson (2013) believing coppicing would have been mandatory to maintain this level of woodland exploitation (see Chapter 6). Each site was extensively exploited for the locally available raw materials, and once these (particularly the iron ore) were exhausted satellite sites would have been established to make use of the existing supporting infrastructure, with the workers still likely to have been based at the original site (Cleere and Crossley, 1995, 72). A good example can be found at Bardown, where the main site fell out of use by the end of the 2nd century, but where satellites (including the location of the High Weald coin hoard, see below) continued well into the 3rd century.

Cleere and Crossley (1995, 81) believe that the iron produced by this intensive industry would have been used for four categories of goods, these being:

- Tools and implements.
- Weapons.
- Construction ironwork (nails, carpenters' dogs, clamps and similar).
- Miscellaneous (horseshoes, boat fittings, barrel hoops and similar).

Additionally, the iron slag which was a by-product of the manufacturing process was also used in compacted form as metalling for Roman roadways in the region. As an example of the scale of this use, Hodgkinson (1999, 68) says:

> Of the Roman road that runs north from Lewes, Sussex, across Ashdown Forest (and) towards Edenbridge, Kent, as much as 30km may be surfaced with slag.

Post-LIA iron production seems to have begun early in many of the eastern/coastal sites such as Beauport Park (Brodribb *et al*, 1988, 232), and also at a few of the more westerly inland sites such as Great Cansiron (Tebbutt, 1971, 11), peaking across the Weald in the middle of the 2nd century by which time some 114 sites were or had been operational as iron working or iron-industry supporting locations. Changes in this prime example of the exploitation of natural resources in the region become evident however from the beginning the 3rd century, with Jones and Mattingly (1990, 193) saying:

> The major workings at Bardown and Crowhurst Park appear to have run down while satellite sites developed around them. In the mid-3rd century mining seems to have ceased altogether in the Bardown/Holbeanwood complex and in the Battle area around Beauport Park. Therefore, the major production period for this industry...probably had a life span of approximately two centuries or a little more.

More recent analysis of each of these sites shows this still to be an accurate assessment, for example by Hodgkinson regarding Bardown (2012, 1). Cleere (1977, 18) also emphasised the abruptness of the end of iron production at these key sites in the middle of the 3rd century, while Cunliffe (1988, 86) added that the maritime infrastructure around Romney Marsh built to support the iron industry also disappeared in the 3rd century. More recently Booth (2001, 3) has similarly shown that activity of all kinds, including iron production, declined dramatically at the roadside settlement of Westhawk Farm in the same timeframe.

Some iron working does appear to have continued in the Weald after the middle of the 3rd century, mainly at a local level at the westerly sites which were less associated with the *Classis Britannica* (see evidential data set out below). Cleere and Crossley (1995, 81) estimate that annual production figures for iron across the entirety of the Weald between AD 350 and AD 400 would have been 50 tonnes, compared to a peak of 750 tonnes between AD 150 and AD 250 when the changes described above become visible. Hodgkinson (2008, 34) says that any evidence at all of iron manufacturing, even at a limited level, disappears totally with the end of the occupation. For a long time afterwards, there is no evidence of iron working at all in the Weald, and when it does reappear in a 9th-century Saxon context at Millbrook in Ashdown Forest, the technology in use is actually more primitive than that used in the LIA prior to the Roman occupation (Hodgkinson, 2008, 35).

Cleere and Crossley (1995, 81) make the case that one of the reasons for this evident decline of the occupation Wealden iron industry in the 3rd century was the silting up of the region's rivers, which had provided the crucial access to the coast, especially with regard to the major sites in the eastern/coastal region. Given the location of the latter sites near the coast, they were also highly exposed to attack by Germanic pirates (Harrington and Welch, 2014, 109), with the appearance of four Saxon Shore forts between Dover and Portchester testifying to the level of this threat. Rudling (2013) suggests that over-exploitation of the Wealden forests for timber would also have been a factor in the decline of the industry given the intensity of iron manufacturing at its height (particularly in the eastern/coastal region), while another factor was the decline in the demand for iron using the east coast maritime route, for example in London or by the military in the north. With regard to the latter, it certainly coincides with the post-Severan campaigns period in Scotland after which Southern (2013, 251) argues an unusual period of comparative peace followed which lasted for around four decades. She says in this regard that the 'slash and burn' policy of these campaigns led to severe de-population in the region, which took several generations of peaceful co-existence to overcome. Meanwhile, the additional synergy between the decline of the iron industry and the disappearance of the *Classis Britannica* (particularly in the eastern/coastal region) is discussed further below.

Evidence for Military Presence/Imperial Estate Interpretation

The most frequently used existing data detailed by the commentators referenced at the beginning of this case study linking the Wealden iron industry to the state and the regional navy is tile and brick stamped with a *Classis Britannica* mark (Brodribb *et al*, 1988, 275). This appears in large numbers across the eastern/coastal iron working sites at Beauport Park, Bardown and Little Farningham, and the associated port at Bodiam (see distribution table at Appendix C). In a specific example Brodribb (1979, 141) detailed that of the 41 complete *tegula* found in his excavations at Beauport Park in the 1960s and 1970s, all but one featured a *Classis Britannica* stamp. It is worth noting here that of the 3.35 tonnes of tile actually found on the site during these excavations (the vast majority of them only partial survivals), nearly all featured full or partial *Classis Britannica* marks (some 1,320 at the time, though this has since risen to 1,600, again see distribution table at Appendix C). To further emphasise the scale of this occurrence, Brodribb (1979, 141) said that given that the overall size of the site examined was 114m^2, and the fact that the total number of *Classis Britannica* stamps found at the time was 1,320, this represented 11 such stamps per square metre. Such use of *Classis Britannica*-stamped tile to identify the nature of an occupation-period site has other regional parallels, with Philp (1981, 100) using the very dense concentration of over 1,000 such tiles at the original Roman fort at Dover as evidence that it was directly associated with the regional navy. One dissenting voice here with regard to using such tile to interpret the nature of occupation-period sites is that of Millett (2007, 178), who says of the Wealden occupation-period iron industry:

> The suggestion (based on tile evidence)...that a substantial part of the industry (here) was under the direct control of the fleet and that rights over iron were owned by the Roman State is entirely speculative.

In his opinion the only exception here might be Beauport Park given the very large number of *Classis Britannica* tiles found here by Brodribb and others (Brodribb, 1979, 141, and Brodribb *et al*, 1988, 275).

There is further physical evidence however of a military presence in the eastern/coastal region of the Weald, this being in the form of three pieces of additional epigraphy. In the first instance Brodribb *et al* (1988, 269) recorded their finding at Beauport Park of a wooden tile comb featuring the, to date, unique imprint of the letters CLBR, identifying this as a marked tool of the *Classis Britannica*. Next, at the same site, they (1988, 261) also detail the location of an inscription on stonework above the bath house entrance which references the *vilicus* mentioned in Chapter 1 in the discussion there on imperial estates (Brodribb *et al*, 1988, 261). This is a most interesting term, originating as with procurator in a domestic context (a *vilicus* originally being an agricultural estate bailiff), which by the time of the occupation was being used in a variety of official ways. One such was as a *vilicus officinae* tasked with managing an industrial enterprise, for example a mine or quarry, with Hirt (2010, 288) detailing just such an individual carrying out this role at the state-run Carrara marble yards in Rome, and in the same context Brodribb *et al* (1988, 241) referencing a similar individual running the state-managed iron-ore mines located in the Sana Valley in Bosnia. While Millett (2007, 179) contests the state-association of the *vilicus* detailed in the Beauport Park example, to my mind it very clearly indicates the State representative who was responsible for the site during his time there. The final piece of epigraphy is in the form of an iron die found in London which features a stamp declaring its provenance as *m(etalla) p(rovinciae) B(ritanniae)*, referring to its origins in a provincial iron manufacturing facility (Birley, 2005, 300). Sadly, no direct link can be made with this and the Wealden iron industry, though it is easily the nearest major area of such official activity.

In terms of other material culture from the major sites in the eastern/coastal zone which have been used to suggest a state/*Classis Britannica*/imperial estate presence, Henig (Brodribb *et al*, 1988, 260) argued that an *intaglio* featuring a representation of victory found in the bath house excavations at Beauport Park also suggests the regional fleet being in attendance. Further, Hodgkinson (2012, 1) argues that a fine medallion of Antoninus Pius found in 2006 at Bardown is evidence of a significant state presence there, he saying that this token of prestige would have been the property of a high ranking official.

Fine quality intaglio showing a Roman merchant vessel, bow sail and main sail fully set. The Pharos in the background could be that at Dover. Ships such as this would have been a common sight around the coasts of Britain during the occupation, facilitating all kinds and trade and industry and often being operated by the military. From Caistor-by-Norwich, © Norwich Castle Museum and Art Gallery.

Next, we can move on to numismatic evidence, in the form of the 2008 High Weald coin hoard found at an occupation-period satellite iron working site near Bardown (the exact location being publicly undisclosed).

This contained 2,891 radiates dating from AD 215 through to AD 268 (with all emperors from Caracalla to the Gallic Emperor Postumous being represented apart from Severus Alexander and Maximus). The hoard is important because it is the only one found in the Weald itself rather than on the periphery (though noting here the comparative lack of archaeological investigation in this region). A mercantile origin for many of these coins can be inferred by the wide geographic range of mints from where they originated. These include Rome, Antioch, Milan and Lyons. The hoard also contains a comparatively high number of rare coins, for example a radiate of Gordian III's wife Sabinia Tranquillina and coins documenting the Secular Games of Philip I. These rare coins, together with the small number of highly debased radiates and the hoard's location near the occupation iron-working site at Bardown with its known *Classis Britannica* association, may therefore indicate it had a high-status origin with a military-association.

Those who have argued in favour of the *Classis Britannica*/imperial estate interpretation for the occupation-period eastern/coastal Wealden iron industry also cite other evidence. For example, Cleere and Crossley (1995, 62) detail the transport infrastructure of the occupation period eastern/coastal Weald. They argue that the north–south alignments for the key regional Roman roads, particularly the Wealden road from Rochester to Beauport Park, implies that they were built specifically to facilitate official communications for the *Classis Britannica* with the Medway Valley and the north Kent coast. The location of port facilities at sites such as Bodiam to facilitate (it is presumed) the transport of manufactured iron out of the region also indicates the involvement of the *Classis Britannica* according to Hodgkinson (2008, 34, though one could argue it is likely the port also handled other exports such as wool and wood). The unusual settlement pattern of the occupied Weald, with little elite settlement in the centre and with most of the villas on the periphery, also supports an imperial estate interpretation according to Cleere and Crossley (1995, 58), with the seeming lack of reinvestment of wealth (certainly in terms of conspicuous consumption outside of the limited amount of ubiquitous Samian ware) being striking. Though some of the value may have been used to develop infrastructure (for example roads and port facilities), the lack of evidence more broadly of a desire to overtly display *Romanitas* is very noticeable. Using Westhawk Farm as an example, Willis (2012, 434) says that this could point to the presence of absentee owners in the form of the State (and specifically in my interpretation, military), he adding:

> It is possible that wealth, like the iron products, went elsewhere, reinforcing a suggestion that the community and its enterprises were subject to a controlling military and Imperial force.

He says this contrasts with the evident existence of community wealth at the site both before and after this evident period of state interest at Westhawk Farm. Cleere and Crossley (1995, 58) also highlight the rapidity of the expansion of iron manufacturing at the eastern/coastal sites from the mid-1st century as evidence of a state presence (1995, 62).

Analogy is also useful here. For example, while there is comparatively little epigraphy outside the examples cited above from the Weald to link the region to a *Classis Britannica*/imperial estate association (even taking into account that stone inscriptions are generally less common in Britain than elsewhere in the empire, with comparatively smaller assemblages of finds), other useful examples in both Britain and across the rest of the empire are detailed earlier in this chapter (e.g. the Mons Claudianus granodiorite mine in the Eastern Egyptian desert and the *Classis Germanica* quarrying along the River Rhine and its tributaries).

Finally, in terms of anecdote, Hodgkinson (2008, 34) has directly linked the disappearance of the regional navy after AD 249 with the similar decline of the vast majority of the iron working sites in the eastern/coastal Weald in the same time period (particularly the larger sites).

Determination

As can be seen above there is a compelling body of data and opinion-based evidence to suggest a *Classis Britannica* interpretation for the management and more of the eastern/coastal region of the Wealden iron industry during the occupation. Further, if one sets the above evidence against that set out for imperial estate interpretations in Chapter 1, the case in this regard is also strong, with positive answers for all five evidential questions set out there: lack of settlement (especially villas), unusual transport networks, unusual land use patterns (with little evidence of extensive agriculture excepting the exploitation of woodland for the iron industry), an association with other industry (that manufacturing tile and brick here, clearly I believe run by the *Classis Britannica*) and the presence of the Roman military in the form of the regional fleet.

Therefore, while the case is not 100% proven (for example through the location of epigraphy specifically mentioning the *procurator metallorum*), I believe that there is enough evidence for a very strong case to be made that the extractive industries exploiting natural resources in this eastern/coastal Wealden *metalla* were being managed by the state through the services of the *Classis Britannica* as an imperial estate.

Case Study 2: The Upper Medway Valley Ragstone-Quarrying *Metalla*

As with the iron-industry in the occupation-period Weald, a number of commentators have argued that the state, often through the military, also played a major role in the Upper Medway Valley ragstone quarrying industry. These include Jones and Mattingly (1990, 219), Milne (2000, 131) and Pearson (2002a, 44). Marsden (1994, 83) goes further, saying:

> Since ragstone was being quarried in the Maidstone area in huge quantities from the mid 1st to the 3rd centuries for public buildings in South East England, many constructed by

The upper Medway Valley in full bloom in late summer. During the later occupation, after the demise of the monumental scale ragstone quarrying industry here in the mid-3rd century, it would similarly have been turned over to agriculture to help feed not only the provinces here but also the continental Empire. The use of the military to facilitate agriculture here is very likely. (see Chapter 7) Simon Elliott.

> the Provincial administration, it seems likely that the quarry area was part of an 'imperial estate' owned by the Emperor, for this would guarantee output of the quarries over a long period on this scale.

Prior to the advent of my research into this region, however, through my 'Medway Formula' MA Dissertation at UCL's Institute of Archaeology (2011, 33 and 42, also see 2016b, 267) which argued for the use of Roman locks and weirs on the upper Medway to allow access to the quarries, and more recently my PhD research, which has located them, the body of evidence used to support the interpretations of Jones and Mattingly, Milne, Pearson and Marsden has been far less defined than that for the Weald. I address that here.

Background

The *metalla* ragstone quarries of the Upper Medway Valley provided much of the building material for the urbanisation and early fortification of the south and east of occupied Britain (Pearson, 2002a, 82). In my opinion, they represent one of the best examples of industrial supply and demand in pre-modern Europe, with a vast industry rising quite literally out of the ground from nothing to cater for those building the new urban environments of the south-east of Roman Britain, particularly London.

As detailed above in Chapter 4 and below in Appendix A, Kentish ragstone sits within the Hythe Beds of the Lower Greensand formation. It was the preferred building material as London grew to be the Provincial capital, given that it was hard-wearing but also workable, its ubiquity in this regard evident in the distance from which it was transported to its place of use, not only in the capital but across the south-east (see below). The draw for the worked stone from London in particular cannot be underestimated; its early demand was caused by the fact that vast quantities of brick and tile were already being manufactured from locally accessible materials, which stretched their availability to the limit, hence the need for another material of choice.

The sheer scale of the ragstone *metalla* in the Upper Medway Valley is particularly striking, with enormous quantities of stone being quarried. Key examples of its use are detailed below in the analysis of the evidential data, with the specific quarries as detailed above located at Allington, Boughton Monchelsea, Dean Street, Quarry Wood in West Farleigh and Teston.

In terms of chronology, Jones and Mattingly (1990, 217) believe that industrial scale quarrying in the Upper Medway Valley began early in the occupation, within 20 years of the conquest at the very latest, while Pearson (2002a, 82) goes further in arguing that stone was being quarried here from around AD 50. Evidence supporting such an early start includes the first forum in London (dated to AD 50, detailed above), and the Claudian temple in Colchester (Houliston, 1999, 163). Greene (1986, 155) argued that at this early date the geology of southern Britain was well enough understood for limestone and sandstone quarrying from a variety of sources to begin, hence such fine quality building stone appearing in Colchester and London shortly after Claudian invasion. Analogously, examples are abundant of early quarrying elsewhere in occupied Britain, with Hayward (2009, 112) pointing out the early quarrying for freestone while earlier Legg (1986, 55) highlighted similar extractive industrial activity in Dorset. Here, high quality Purbeck marble was being extracted to dress regional public buildings and to line public baths (for example in Exeter) early in the occupation (Bidwell, 1980, 11, and Pearson, 2006, 113). All of these examples support Goldsworthy's (2014, 239) hypothesis of a mercantile presence in the south-east of Britain well before the Claudian invasion.

Back to the Medway Valley, the ragstone quarrying quickly developed into industrial scale activity to fulfil the booming demand for building stone as the new stone-built urban environments blossomed, and also to facilitate the construction of the region's new villa estates and roads. This demand peaked in the late 2nd and early 3rd centuries when construction of the region's first fortified wall circuits began, the best example here again being the Severan land walls of Roman London (see below for review of the enormous scale involved here).

It is also the walls of London however which provide the first indication of a dramatic change taking place with regard to the Medway Valley ragstone quarrying industry, in the form of the later river wall built towards the end of the 3rd century to close the circuit, together with new bastions around the perimeter. Far from the new walls and towers being built with the carefully worked, uniform ragstone blocks evident in the land wall, they were constructed from roughly reworked local materials, re-used from demolished public buildings and mausoleums. The reuse in the river wall of finely detailed sculptured stones depicting classical scenes is well documented by Blagg (1980, 5), who believed that some originated in a monumental arch featuring ornamental screens. Sheldon (2011, 230) also highlights the reuse in one bastion of material from the mausoleum of the province's third procurator, Julius Classicianus. Pearson (2006, 30) argues that the reuse of materials rather than building with newly-quarried ragstone is a manifestation of the ending of the era of major public building in towns in Britain, excepting some limited activity in York (where at least one large public building was built in the later 3rd century) and in Carausian/Allectan London where another large public building has been interpreted as a possible palace (Williams, 1993, 31). Even with this latter building, however, change from the earlier construction regime is evident, as it once again re-used building material in a similar manner to the river wall and bastions (Rogers, 2011, 96). Similarly, where ragstone was used for the construction of some of the later Saxon Shore forts, it is evident that they are actually built from re-used material from earlier nearby structures (with Richborough a prime example, Fields, 2006, 33, and see Chapter 5 above).

As is evident in the above analysis, with re-used material taking the place of newly quarried ragstone, a major change seems to have taken place in the Medway Valley quarrying industry from the mid-3rd century, with the latest use of freshly worked stone being for the wall circuit of Canterbury dating to around AD 270. Even here the quantity of ragstone used is limited when compared to earlier regional requirements given it is only visible in the context of footings and lower wall facings (flint being the preferred main facing), with the stone also being potentially re-used. After that time, enormous quantities of building stone would no more be extracted in the Upper Medway Valley and sent downriver to the Thames Estuary. Pearson (2006, 30) says that this is part of a broader picture of quarrying and building in the later provinces and *diocese*, where such activity by that time was small in scale, and one of repair and refurbishment when compared to the intense urbanisation of the earlier period. Everitt (1986, 51) says that in this later, local phase of regional quarrying, one can see the origins of a new local phenomenon in the Upper Medway Valley, with the 'great quarries' of the earlier phase being replaced by much smaller 'stone pits' known locally in more recent times as 'petts', which catered for local demand.

Evidence for Military Presence/Imperial Estate Interpretation

In the first instance, the most prominent evidence cited to link the ragstone quarries of the Upper Medway Valley with state-run *metalla* is the sheer scale of their output. The best example remains the original late 2nd-/early 3rd-century 3.2km Severan land wall circuit in London, detailed above in Chapter 5, which Hall and Merrifield (1986, 28) said comprised more than one million squared and dressed ragstone blocks. Merrifield (1965, 48) earlier estimated the ragstone volume for this original circuit to be around 35,000m^3, while based on the 100,000 man days estimated to have been needed to build the much shorter 760m wall circuit at the Saxon Shore fort at Pevensey (Pearson, 1999, 102), I estimated in Chapter 5 that some 420,000 man days would have been required for the land walls of London. To this high-profile use, Marsden (1994, 84) also adds Upper Medway Valley ragstone being used in the construction of the *basilica*, forum, at least three public baths, the governor's palace and a wide variety of public buildings in London, with Bateman (2011, 31) adding the second phase of the amphitheatre and Hall and Merrifield (1986, 10) a pre-Boudiccan revolt temple for emperor worship. It should also be remembered at this point that the ragstone was not just being used for such grand projects, but also to facilitate the more day-to-day aspects of the built environment. Examples include the 2nd-century town house located at Billingsgate in the south-eastern corner of the city, where ragstone was used as the principal foundation and building material, and also for the foundations of the slightly later associated bath house at the same location (Rowsome, 1996, 421). Meanwhile, ragstone cobbles were also used as the foundation of the walled mausoleum associated with the discovery of a large oolitic limestone-carved eagle found in 2013 in the Minories outside the Roman wall to the east (Pitts,

Beautifully worked ragstone wall-facing blocks on the inner face of the Severan land wall of Roman London (near Tower Hill underground station), quarried in the upper Medway Valley and transported down the Medway and up the Thames. This industry was very likely run by the Classis Britannica. Simon Elliott.

2014, 9). Most recently, two post-Hadrianic fire ragstone-built town houses have been found on the eastern banks of the Walbrook by MOLA (Watson, 2015) as part of the Bloomberg excavation.

Upper Medway Valley ragstone can also be found across the south-east of the province, its use as a building material not just restricted to London. Examples include the occupation-period walls of Canterbury (see above and below), the stone-built walls of Rochester dating to AD 225, early Saxon Shore forts, such as that at Reculver where the facing of the defences comprised ragstone blocks (Pearson, 2002a, 79), and in many of the villas in the region. This was especially the case in the Medway Valley, examples here including those at Snodland, Eccles, the Mount, East Farleigh and Teston to name but a few. Further afield, upper Medway Valley ragstone was also used in the pre-Boudiccan Claudian temple (see above) and 2nd century circus in Colchester, and the early Saxon Shore fort at Bradwell, both in Essex.

To the scale of the output of the quarries – thanks to my PhD research – we can now add the scale of the quarries themselves to illustrate the grandiosity of this industry. These have respective areas as follows, suggesting activity far beyond the capability of occupation period entrepreneurs acting alone:

- 61,600m^2 for Allington.
- 54,600m^2 for Boughton Monchelsea.
- 356,400m^2 for Dean Street.
- 215,000m^2 for Quarry Wood.
- 35,830m^2 for Teston.

These were clearly industrial (in the modern sense of the word) in scale, with that at Dean Street being comparable in size to the largest *metalla* across the entirety of the Roman Empire, for example at Rio Tinto (Jones, 1980, 148). It is here where analogy is useful, given mining and quarrying operations on this scale were heavily supported by the state elsewhere in the empire (Hirt, 2010, 106, Cleere and Crossley, 1995, 66, de la Bédoyère, 1992, 100 and Jones and Mattingly, 1990, 192).

From the consideration of scale hinting at state involvement, the existing commentators next turn to the importance of maritime transport to the success of the ragstone quarrying industry for further evidence (this bringing the *Classis Britannica* into view). Roman London expert Merrifield (1965, 49) was concise on the subject, saying:

> The best means of transport for bulk of this kind was by boat, and the Medway and the Thames provided a water-way from quarry to City.

We have hard data to support this view, in the form of Marsden's enigmatic Blackfriars 1 vessel found on the bed of the River Thames in 1962, with a load of 26 tonnes of upper Medway Valley ragstone still in its hold (which was capable of carrying up to 50 tonnes, Marsden, 1994, 80). The ship was 14m in length and 6.5m wide, with a shallow draught of 1.5m and a maximum speed of around 7 knots in favourable conditions (Pearson, 2002a, 85). Built of oak, it had no keel but featured two broad keel-planks, a stempost with corresponding sternpost and hazel twig caulking for the carvel planking. The mast was supported by a rectangular socket mast-step in the base of which a bronze coin of Domitian was found. Dendro-analysis has dated the vessel to around AD 140 and identified that it was built in the south-east of Britain. Milne (2000, 131) argues that this vessel, together with others of similar design found in the area of operations of the *Classis Britannica*, were specific to the regional fleet and therefore indicators of its involvement with the ragstone quarrying industry here. The distribution map in Appendix B shows the wide range of the uses of the stone from the Upper Medway Valley in the south-east of occupied Britain (noting the exponential demand from London) and also speaks to the organisational presence of the *Classis Britannica*.

Sticking with this maritime transport theme, most recently a major breakthrough in demonstrating a specific link between the occupation-period upper Medway Valley ragstone quarries and the State has come through the location of the 'Medway Stones' site in the River Medway between Tovil and East Farleigh (S. Elliott, 2014c, 11). Found in 2014, this features four blank millstones or columnal bases on the bed of the River Medway, with an initial underwater investigation suggesting a spread of such stones over a distance of 200m in the river, with the piles for a wharf having also been located set 5m out into the river and tracking the stone spread. This suggests a wreck with load and its associated wharf at the point where the Dean Street Roman quarry meets the river (Elliott, 2016b, 199). Further significant investigation is planned to confirm its Roman provenance.

The final piece of newly generated data from my PhD research regarding this extensive maritime transport network is the recreation of the typical 254km four day return journey (a two day, 127km journey each way) for a load of such stone from its place of extraction (not including Allington given this was on, or more likely just upriver, of the tidal reach during the Roman period, see Snodland reference by Kaye, 2015b, 232, above) to London and back in a Blackfriars 1-type vessel (Elliott, 2016b, 262). I argue that a military presence was likely to ensure its smooth running, in order to provide the huge quantities of stone required (a core theory advanced by Marsden, 1994, 83). This hypothesis is based on two key predications:

- The vessel would have to be capable of getting under sail with a 50-tonne load of ragstone, but with a shallow enough draft to operate upriver of Allington (more likely Snodland, see above) on the Medway.
- Such a vessel would have had to be able to navigate the 'Medway Formula' river infrastructure, which I argue made the Medway upriver of Snodland/Allington navigable in the first place.

Taking these into account, seen in print here for the first time is the journey as I believe it would have been undertaken thousands of times over the two centuries of operations of the quarries:

- Load (of finished stone, rough cuts or rubble) taken aboard a Blackfriars 1 type vessel at or near the quarries at Boughton Monchelsea (the nearest wharfing likely associated with one of the four villas known to have existed in Maidstone), Dean Street (the likely wharfing at the westernmost Maidstone villa at Florence Road/ Bower Lane or that at East Farleigh), Quarry Wood in West Farleigh (the likely wharfing either associated with the East Farleigh villa or that at Teston) and Teston (with the wharfing at the villa located there, Elliott, 2013, 40). Marsden (1994, 80) and Merrifield (1965, 49) are clear that the wharfing used to load the ragstone would have been as close to the quarries as possible.
- The ship uses sails, towers or rowers, and the flow of the river, to get to the tidal reach at Allington. The predominantly southwesterly winds would have allowed the use of a square sail (Marsden, 1995, 70), though the use of such sails above the tidal reach would have necessitated cutting back the vegetation on both sides of the river. Ausonius (Mosella, 7) is insightful here, speaking of the banks of the Moselle being cleared of vegetation and covered in hard, compacted sand. (I do note that the Moselle is clearly a broader river than the Medway, but believe the analogy still stands.) This would also have facilitated towing. Wilkinson (2006, 14) described the Medieval practice of towing vessels with loads of up to 80 tonnes the three miles from Hollow Shore on the Swale to the dockside at Faversham, with rowers being used if saving money was a necessity. Ellis Jones (2012, 91) similarly points out the use from the early Medieval period of 'bow-hauliers' on the Severn when conditions prevented the use of sails. In a Medway context, such towers would also have assisted navigating the occupation period 'Medway Formula' hydraulic river infrastructure. Wilkinson (2006, 14) adds with regard to using the flow of the river that if this were too swift, perhaps after heavy rain, then a capsize anchor would have been used to control the speed. To cover the 8km from Teston, the speed would have been around 2 knots and the journey would have taken up to 3 hours, including the use of any riverine hydraulic infrastructure.
- Having reached the tidal reach of the Medway at Allington (or more likely Snodland during the occupation, after which the width of the river and the tides would have precluded the use of towers) the vessel would then have waited for a falling tide to navigate the tidal section of the river up to Sheerness, a total journey of 45km taking in the twists and turns of the river, taking upwards of 6 hours assuming a reasonable wind and a speed of some 4 knots. Given that the distance between the tidal reach and the Thames Estuary is greater than it was possible to navigate with one tide, even a high spring tide, sails would have been essential. From personal experience, I can attest that to navigate the lower reaches of the river successfully, the boat crews would have needed an exceptional knowledge of the local tides and winds, especially given that their sail technology would have been deficient when compared to modern examples. The vessel would then have entered Morris' southern North Sea and Eastern Channel connectivity system (2010, 10), or Evans' east coast trade route (2013, 433), see Chapter 5.

- By this point, even in summer, the vessel would have been struggling with the light and it is inconceivable that any journey would have been attempted from this point without reasonable visibility. Therefore, it seems likely that the vessel would have used an overnight anchorage before continuing the journey the next day. Sheerness seems the most likely candidate, though an interesting option here is presented on pre-modern maps that show a creek called The Dray (interestingly, Old English for 'to pull') isolating the Isle of Grain from the Hoo Peninsula. This is now silted up and, given the balance between rising sea levels and silting, it is difficult to know if this creek existed in Roman times or not. If it did, it would have provided ideal shelter for this overnight section of the journey and would also have provided a short cut to avoid travelling to Sheerness before entering the Thames Estuary. Kaye (2015a, 29) goes further here, showing that the Isle of Grain could have been even further detached from the mainland during the occupation as a full (and diminished in size) island, presenting even more possibilities for an overnight stay.
- The following morning the vessel would again wait for the early tide before sailing up the River Thames to London, a journey of some 74km which at 5 knots would take around 8 hours.
- Travelling back, perhaps with exotic goods and pottery (for example south Essex and north-west Kent sandy grey wares, Houliston, 1999, 163) for the elites and artisans living along the north Kent coast and in the Medway Valley, the vessel would have used its sails, the current and the tide to reach the River Medway. Specific insight for the types of exotic goods carried comes from the work of Andrews *et al* at Northfleet (2011, 223). Here, archaeological evidence has been found of amphora carrying fish products from Portugal and olive oil from Spain and North Africa at a villa estate with a quayside on the Ebbsfleet. One should note here also the remains of Spanish amphora found at the large villa site at Teston.
- Following a further overnight stop on the Isle of Grain or Sheerness, sails and the tide would then have then been used to travel upriver to Allington, with a number of vessels perhaps being tied together.
- Finally, above the tidal reach again, towers or rowers would again have been employed to facilitate travel along the short distance to the ragstone quarries while navigating the 'Medway Formula' hydraulic river infrastructure.

The adherents to the military running this *metalla* in the Upper Medway Valley next turn to non-maritime transport infrastructure as evidence, particularly the Rochester–Wealden road linking the north Kent coast with the major iron working sites in the eastern/coastal Weald (Marsden, 1994, 83). Margary (1967, 44) showed how closely this road tracked the upper Medway Valley with its quarries before heading south, it being utilised more for administration than for the transport of regionally extracted natural resources which would, as suggested above, have principally used maritime routes. Further, in my PhD research I also determined that a Roman road running from the

Dean Street quarry to the Roman ford at Barming on the River Medway might actually be a spur of the Rochester–Wealden road. It was then a very specific and direct link between the Wealden iron working sites with their likely *Classis Britannica*/imperial estate provenance, as argued above, and the Upper Medway Valley ragstone quarries.

My MA and PhD research has also specifically linked for the first time the elite settlements in the Upper Medway Valley (in the form of up to eight villa estates ranging from Allington through to Teston) with an associated quarry, arguing that they may have been the country residences of those actually managing the quarrying activity through to the mid-3rd century. As such they would have formed an elite enclave where the owners competed with neighbouring friends to display wealth and culture via architectural form, at the same time exhibiting conspicuous consumption. It should be noted however that no structures to house the quarry workers themselves have yet been found, though one should note these would have been far more ephemeral given they would probably have been constructed from wooden and canvas.

Meanwhile other occupation-period industrial activity has been identified amid the Roman quarries and associated villas. This comes in the form of the Gallants Lane iron-working site between the Dean Street and Quarry Wood quarries found by the author, featuring a collection of ash heaps including tap slag and occupation-period pottery. This is also set out in my PhD research (Elliott, 2016b, 204).

Going back to analogy, this is also used by those arguing for a military presence exploiting the ragstone resources of the Upper Medway Valley. Examples include the

Ash heap from the Roman iron working site on Gallants Lane in the Upper Medway Valley. Simon Elliott.

Mons Claudianus granodiorite mine in the eastern Egyptian desert and the activities of the *Classis Germanica* with its quarrying activities along the Rhine and its tributaries, both detailed above. Evidence of the *Classis Britannica* carrying out quarrying activities comes from even closer to hand, for example, from the inscription at Benwell fort on Hadrian's Wall that shows the regional fleet constructing the granary. Further, on the doorstep of the Upper Medway Valley ragstone industry is, of course, the Wealden iron industry referenced above, which Marsden (1994, 83) argues was a direct analogy in terms of state-presence with the *metalla* of the Upper Medway Valley.

Finally, anecdote has also been used by existing commentators to support the state presence in this region, specifically in the context of chronology. Milne (2000, 131) for example has pointed to the synergy between the ending in the mid-3rd century of industrial scale ragstone quarrying in the Upper Medway Valley and the disappearance of the *Classis Britannica* (which he argues was the state representative facilitating the quarrying).

Determination

In the above case study discussion, I have considered existing and new data to determine whether a case can be made that the state – through the *Classis Britannica* as its military representative – controlled the ragstone quarrying industry in the Upper Medway Valley until the demise of both in the mid-3rd century. When one considers the sheer scale involved, both in terms of the of the quantity of ragstone quarried and the parallel scale of the maritime commitment to facilitate this industry, together with the facilitating administrative land links to the eastern/coastal Weald with its known military association, the wider emerging industrial landscape with at least one potential iron working site, the emerging link between elite and other settlement with the ragstone quarries, and the wealth of supporting analogy (not least the proximity to the *Classis Britannica* controlled *metalla* in the Weald as mentioned) and anecdote, then a case begins to emerge. Certainly, this industry was part of the imperial economy rather than the provincial economy, with again the sheer evident scale pushing towards the imperial estate interpretation as believed by Marsden (1995, 84).

As with the Weald, however, where the evidence for a link between the military and iron manufacturing in the eastern/coastal region is stronger, there is as yet no definitive evidence, for example in the form of undisputable epigraphy. It so happens that Kentish ragstone was not favoured for inscriptions, and the main floruit of its employment occurs at a time when inscriptions in stone were becoming less common. Furthermore, quarries and villas are not normally locales with stone inscriptions, which is another reason why epigraphic indications have not to date been forthcoming. The question, therefore, is how strong the case is today for a military presence running an imperial estate in the occupation-period Medway Valley *metalla*, based on the available data. Here I again turn to the model set out in Chapter 1 to help interpret a geographic economic entity as an imperial estate, with its five paradigms. What emerges is a largely positive though confusing picture. The region does feature unusual transport networks, for example the riverine hydraulic infrastructure necessary to allow the River Medway to be used above the tidal reach on this industrial scale. It also features unusual land use patterns, for example the concentration of enormous quarries, most uncommon during the occupation. Furthermore, an association with other industry such as the newly-found iron working site is present, and also the likely (based on the scale of the required maritime commitment and proximity to the Weald) presence of the Roman military in the form of the regional fleet. These are positive points. What counts against the imperial estate interpretation in terms of the five paradigms is the lack of unusual settlement patterns, since there is a dynamic range of villa estates along the banks of the Upper Medway Valley, together with other settlement. To counter this, I make the case above that these may have been associated with the quarries themselves. Mattingly (2006, 371, see discussion on the Roman economy in Chapter 1) also argues that there is no good reason that villas would not feature in an imperial estate landscape (though common senses here indicates this would have been more likely in agricultural imperial estates).

The honest answer here is that the evidence for the ragstone quarrying industry in the Upper Medway Valley being a military-run imperial estate is less clear-cut than that for the iron-manufacturing industry in the Weald, excepting perhaps its scale and the enormous maritime commitment to ensure its success. I think one can certainly say that it was part of the imperial economy under state control (the exploitation of natural resources as part of the imperial economy in a province was a matter of state control, Mattingly, 2006, 494), and further that it was under direct control of the procurator through his *procurator metallorum* using tightly controlled contractors at the very least (based in London in this interpretation rather than under some form of looser indirect control). Over and above that, though, based on existing data and interpretations, I am reduced to expressing an informed opinion. In that regard, I think a strong case can be made that the *Classis Britannica* was involved in some way in this enormous industry, if only to facilitate the required transport network, though with the imperial estate interpretation being at present unprovable.

Chapter 7

The Roman Military and Agriculture

Agriculture was a vital component of the Roman economy, and the military engaged directly with it both as beneficiaries (given their immense size within wider Roman society) and as facilitators. Here the relationship between agriculture and the Roman military is reviewed in detail, beginning with an examination of Roman agricultural practices, using Britain as an example once more, then considering agricultural imperial estates where there is much scope to see interaction with the military, before looking specifically at the military and its relationship with agriculture in the context of its own subsistence, and finally the negative effect it could also sometimes have on agricultural activity.

Roman Agriculture

Despite the focus in Chapter 6 on Roman industry, agriculture was actually the most significant component of the Roman economy (Greene, 1986, 142) and involved most of the empire's populace (Millett, 1990a, 186), whether in terms of trying to generate a surplus or purely for subsistence. Brown (2012, 11) gives specific figures, saying that:

> every year, 60% of the wealth of the Roman Empire was gathered at harvest time by a labour force that amounted to over 80% of the overall population.

However, agriculture during the occupation is also one of the most complicated areas to study due to imbalances in both primary and modern literary sources, particularly their focus on villa estates (Jones, 1982, 97). Greene (1986, 67) argues that to establish an accurate picture of agricultural practices, one has to cross-reference information from these literary sources with art and archaeology (including scientific analysis of materials), and I try to reflect that here.

In the Mediterranean core of the Roman Empire, the three principal agricultural products were grain, olive oil and wine (the 'Mediterranean triad'). Looking at Britain once more to provide a provincial example (a distant and late addition to the family of imperial provinces and thus a useful cipher to view the spread of Roman agricultural practices and the use of the military therein), given its north-west European geographical position grain was the most important in the economy here. In this regard, two factors would have facilitated the major increase in arable production which occurred during the LIA and the occupation period.

The first is climate. Conditions for agriculture would have been benevolent throughout much of this time; Greene (1986, 83) explains that the climate during the occupation was comparatively warm and analogous with warm periods in medieval times and today, while Tacitus (Agricola, 1970, 62) emphasised the climate as being wet, though not cold. This corresponds with Grainge's (2005, 37) view that the weather during the occupation would have been broadly similar to today's, though wetter earlier in the occupation. Greene adds (1986, 127) that the climate was one of the factors that led – alongside good communications, a cash payment/taxation economy and a proliferation of military/civilian consumers – to the rapid and substantial post-conquest growth in British settlement.

The second is the expansion during this period of agriculture into previously marginal land, driven by population growth, new technology and new agricultural techniques. When the Romans arrived in Britain they were faced with a patchwork of differing agricultural landscapes, some already mature but others much less so (Dumayne-Peaty, 1998, 319), with Jones (1982, 98) arguing that it is in these less-developed areas that the impact of the occupation is most visible, principally in the new crop types cultivated there. He says the prevalence of crops such as bread wheat and spelt wheat, tolerant of damp soils and frost, in addition to rye and oats, which can grow on acidic and infertile soils, are indicators of this trend.

Luxury foodstuffs also become evident in the occupation period. Such horticultural cash crops included fennel, flax, lentils, millet, grapes (see discussion below), dates, coriander, mulberry, cabbage, dill and anise, as well as orchard crops, which were also used to provide dried fruits and to make cider. These would have catered for the needs of new consumers who emerged during the occupation, for example townspeople, the military and occupation-period craft specialists, who used foodstuffs as a medium of demonstrating their status and sophistication (van der Veen, Livarda and Hill, 2008, 12), an expression of their *Romanitas.*

One area of great debate regarding horticulture in occupied Britain is whether viticulture was successfully practiced. There is some archaeological data to support such a hypothesis, together with supporting anecdote. Specific examples of potential viticulture include North Thoreseby in Lincolnshire, Wollaston in Northamptonshire and north-west Cambridge. In North Thoreseby, evidence of intensive attempts to drain heavy clay soils with ditches lined with old pottery and stones (and containing high phosphate levels indicative of manuring) have been interpreted as an attempt to grow a high-value crop, specifically vines (Webster, Webster and Perch, 1967, 10). Meanwhile, at Wollaston, an arguably stronger case has been made (Brown *et al*, 2001, 756) after the identification of a series of parallel trenches of occupation period provenance that are remarkably similar to viticultural examples on the continent. Pollen analysis at the time also indicated that very few other plants were allowed to prosper in the proximity of these trenches, again similar to both Roman and modern viticultural practices. Most recently, Evans and Newman (2014, 142) detail that excavations in north-west Cambridge have uncovered planting beds linked by ditches to pit wells, which they have identified as evidence of vineyards, though they also concede the beds may have been for growing asparagus. Meanwhile, Creighton (2013) adds that five further sites are currently under investigation (in Northamptonshire, Buckinghamshire and Nottinghamshire) for potential occupation period viticulture, though to date the evidence here is inconclusive and is still being reviewed. Finally, amphora forms associated in Gaul with wine are known to have been produced in Britain, as at Brockley Hill near St Albans (Castle, 1978, 383). However, study of these vessels requires synthesis before their association with local wine manufacturing can be allowed to contribute to the debate.

Anecdotally, the Medway Valley also provides modern evidence of Kent's suitability for viticulture. Chapel Down's vineyard at Kits Coty is a current example, while West Farleigh was the site of vine growing experiments during the 1980s by Courage Eastern (Ltd).

The data from the above potential sites for occupation-period viticulture, together with the anecdotal evidence in the Medway Valley, to my mind build only a limited case to support the view that wine manufacturing thrived in Roman Britain. Particularly telling is the total lack of any *falx vinitoria* (a tool associated with Roman vineyards across the empire) amongst material culture finds in Britain (Skelton, 2010, 4). Tacitus (Agricola, 1970, 62) adds a primary source voice here, saying that the climate in Britain was not warm enough for such Mediterranean crops, while van der Veen, Livarda and Hill (2008, 12) argue that grapes (along with figs and olives) were a largely imported exotic food type, adding that although attempts at viticulture in Britain may have been carried out, evidence is lacking to prove its success.

Perhaps the real answer as to whether viticulture was successfully practiced during the occupation lies with the British experience of wine manufacturing today. Vines do grow and there are successful vineyards producing very palatable wines, but on nowhere near the scale of activities on the continent. We can therefore perhaps discount any analogy with Ausonius' Mosella and its bucolic scenes of riverbanks and hillsides dripping with vineyards (1933, 15) in occupied Britain.

Moving from viticulture to sylviculture, the systematic management of woodland resources is also an identifiable feature of the Roman landscape during the occupation and a vital part of both the imperial and provincial economy. Matthews (1989, 3) details that evidence of three concepts are indicators that a woodland management system is in operation. These are:

- A method to regenerate the crops that constitute the forest.
- The specific types of crops that constitute the forest.
- The arrangement of the crops that constitute the forest (such that there is an orderly procedure to facilitate protection and harvesting).

All of these can be found to varying degrees in four different silvicultural systems used in the Roman period in Britain and elsewhere. These systems are:

- Clear cutting, the most basic silvicultural system, whereby every tree of all types within a large area of woodland is felled and left to regrow. Visser (2009, 10) says that a good occupation-period example of this can be found at Valkenburg in the Netherlands in the form of material used for a roadway, and also an early fort at nearby Velsen.
- Selection, whereby certain tree types within a wood are selected for felling, but not all. Visser (2009, 11) says that the presence of selection silviculture is indicated by the presence in funerary inscriptions of *salturarii* estate workers. These are freedmen or slaves who are associated with the protection of estate boundaries and, significantly, tree selection. Though none are known from occupied Britain, a regional analogy has been found at Heidelsburg in Westfischbach, Germany, relating to one Titus Publicus Tertius.
- Coppicing, whereby young tree stems are cut down near the ground to promote the growth of new shoots from the resulting 'stool', these then being harvested at a certain age before the whole process starts again. Visser (2009, 12) says that this type of silviculture is particularly appropriate for providing a steady supply of smaller constructional timber or firewood.

In the case of clear cutting, Goodburn (1991, 190) says that in London:

> a regular, large scale...supply of (wood) raw material must have been available. Such timber cannot be found in quantity in natural or little disturbed wildwood so we can suggest that the (in this case) oak selected must have been cut from coppiced...woodland managed on a long rotation.

Coppicing was ideal for producing charcoal to support iron production, as charcoal was a vital component of the occupation-period iron industry in the Weald, detailed in Chapter 6. In this context, Hodgkinson (2009, 17) says:

> some form of woodland management was essential to satisfy the demand for charcoal for some of the larger ironworks of the Roman period.

Again, as detailed above in Chapter 6, Cleere and Crossley (1995, 78) say that to maintain the level of iron output at Bardown in the Weald, one of the larger sites, 15ha of coppiced woodland would have been needed annually. Rackham (1997, 30) has estimated that, for the whole occupation-period iron manufacturing industry in the Weald, 9,300ha of permanently managed, coppiced woodland would have been needed to satisfy the overall demand for charcoal. This level of coppicing activity is evident elsewhere across the empire, with Visser (2009, 12) detailing the 50km^2 of coppiced woodland that has been identified around the major Roman settlements in Picardie. He says that research there has identified a deliberate 40-year cycle used for the coppicing during the Roman period.

- Agro-forestry, whereby the growing of timber trees, shrubs and fruit trees is combined in the same area with the animal husbandry and the growing of agricultural crops. Visser (2009, 12) explains the attraction of this arrangement:

> When combined with crops the trees protect the plants from strong winds, and the branches or stems can be used to build fences or (be) used as poles to grow for example beans...Woodlands can also be used as pasture. In this case the animals remove the undergrowth and their dung fertilizes the soil.

This agro-forestry is well attested in the historical record, and indeed specific types of mixed woodland had their own bespoke names in the Roman world. For example, combining oak (and possibly Beech) woodland with agriculture was called *silva glandaria*. As detailed above in Chapter 4, Tomlin (1996, 209) has provided Kentish occupation-period insight here, with the case of the sale of the 2ha of woodland in the land of the *Cantiaci* from Titus Valerius Silvinus to Lucius Julius Bellicus.

Turning to fauna, pigs, cattle and sheep are the most common farm animals across Roman-occupied Britain, for example as evidenced at the Barton Court villa estate (Jones, 1986, 41) and in the Norfolk fenlands (Malim, 2005, 169). Citing data from the Rural Settlement in Roman Britain Project, Smith (2013, 53) says that there is evidence that cattle became increasingly dominant in the mix later into the occupation. He does speculate, however, that, based on archaeological evidence illustrating animals living to a later age, this was perhaps because they were being increasingly used for traction rather than purely as a food source. With regard to fish, Locker (2007, 27) details that the most common types evidenced by data from fish bones during the occupation were eel, herring, plaice/flounder, cyprinids (such as carp) and salmonids. This is supported by the recent excavations at Church Street, Maidstone where Locker (2014, 141) says bones of eel, herring and plaice/flounder were the most common types found in occupation-period rubbish pits, comprising 40 of the 49 bones found.

Intriguingly, as detailed in Chapter 6, Biddulph (2013, 20) also reports on evidence for the industrial use of juvenile herrings, sprats and juvenile smelt for manufacturing fish sauce at the occupation-period salt manufacturing site at Stanford Wharf in Essex. He believes the types of sauce made would have been *liquamen* or *allec* to service demand in nearby London, also the market for the salt produced at this site. Meanwhile, the huge quantities of shells from oysters and other molluscs discarded around many occupation-period sites is testament to the Roman appetite for shellfish (they being very prominent at sites throughout the Medway Valley for example and doubtless being supplied to order).

Agricultural Imperial Estates

In terms of imperial estates (to recap, land specifically owned by the emperor and a key feature of the imperial economy), there is more evidence for those of an agricultural nature than those focusing on industrial activity, though less for the involvement military involvement therein. Nevertheless, suggestions have been made, for example by Malim (2005, 126) in the case of Stonea in the Fens, regarding the use of the military on such agricultural imperial estates, and so they are detailed here.

Agricultural imperial estates were particularly extensive in the eastern empire where they seem to have tracked crown land previously owned by earlier Hellenistic rulers (for example in the inland river valleys in Asia Minor, and also land reclaimed and cultivated by the Ptolemies in Egypt, Crawford, 1976, 37). They were also a particularly important feature of the economy in North Africa where estates such as the *saltus Burunitanus, saltus Philomusianusm, saltus Nerionianus, saltus Massipianus* and villa *Magna Variana* made up a sixth of the entire territory there under cultivation.

One of the best understood imperial estates was that at Vagnari in the valley of the River Basentello east of the Appenine Mountains in ancient Apulia, south-eastern Italy, and this provides a useful template to understand other such estates. Linked directly to Rome by the via Appia, the extensive agricultural land here was transformed into an imperial estate during the 1st century AD (it also previously having been a Hellenistic estate) and featured an extensive central *vicus* (a settlement type usually associated in the British Romanist tradition with a military site, though elsewhere and in this context with a central village) where the estate workers lived. This was at the heart of the estate, effectively being its administrative and economic core and featuring all of the various economic activities which supported the estate, including extensive metal working in the form of iron manufacturing and lead processing, and also tile and brick manufacture (Carroll, 2016, 31). This latter gives the clearest indication of the estate being imperially owned, given they feature the stamp of the imperially owned slaves who made them. The estate at Vagnari appears to have had a particular focus on wine production, with a stone-built complex excavated in 2015 featuring a *cella vinaria* wine fermentation room with large plastered circular basins set into a mortared floor. Each of the basins featured *dolium defossum* pitch-lined containers with a rim diameter of over half a metre and a capacity of over 1,000 litres. Meanwhile, on a hill overlooking the *vicus* and other settlement on the imperial estate, was the villa where resided the *vilicus* who ran the estate (see above reference in Chapter 6 to a similar individual at the iron working site at Beauport Park).

Moving to the province of Britannia, here we have already considered in Chapter 1 the possible agricultural imperial estate at Stonea in the Fens in East Anglia. Based on the five tests set out in that chapter to determine a geographic economic entity as an imperial estate, this featured unusual settlement patterns in the form of the central multiple-story stone tower, unusual transport networks with new and often raised roadways and new canals, unusual land use patterns featuring extensive land reclamation, an association with industry in the form of localised iron working, and finally the (speculated) presence of the Roman military. In that regard, Malim (2005, 126) says:

> Supervision of imperial estates and tax collection were jobs often undertaken by military personnel. Its administrative importance is further demonstrated during the 4th century (after the Principate) when this official presence is reflected not only in new stone buildings with hypocaust and similar luxury elements, but also in the discovery of eight crossbow-type brooches, some in silver and gilt, which represent a significant concentration of a relatively rare type generally associated with officials or soldiers. Military belt fittings of this period also exist at Stonea...

As discussed in Chapter 2, however, even if a strong case can be made here for Stonea, common sense indicates that it would be more likely for the military to play a role running agricultural imperial estates in the east where military formations tended to be more closely embedded within the civilian population (often in the larger urban conurbations).

The Military and Agriculture

The Roman military engaged with direct and indirect agricultural activity in a variety of ways and these are now considered below.

Subsistence

In the first instance the legionaries, auxiliaries and naval *milites* needed to be fed, both when in camp and when on campaign. Even in the case of the former, Goldsworthy (2003, 97) says considerable effort was needed to supply the garrisoned troops. In that regard the land around each permanent fortification would have been turned over to providing the supplies required to feed the troops, a substantial task when one considers the large size of many Roman military formations (see background in the Introduction above regarding the differing types of permanent Roman fortification). The troops ate two set meals per day, the *prandium* breakfast and the *cena* evening meal. In terms of the staples of the soldier's diet, as set out in Chapter 2, Vegetius (1995, 3.3) says the troops should never be without corn, wine, vinegar and salt, with other basics including bread (most commonly referenced as a wholemeal type called *panis militaris*), various *pulmentum* porridges, beans, vegetables and eggs. Fresh local foods and dried fruit would then have been added, with Goldsworthy (2003, 98) going to great lengths to overturn notions that the troops had a predominantly vegetarian diet, he saying they ate large quantities of pork and beef (the balance dependent on the origins of the military unit and its location). Mutton and fish were also popular, again depending on the locale. All would have been liberally covered in the ubiquitous Roman *garum* fish sauce when available!

Elsewhere (Elliott, 2016a, 60), I have set out the diet of the sailors and marines of the Principate regional navies which would have been slightly different from that of the legionaries and auxilia given the different daily working environment when not on campaign (involving much patrolling over short and long periods in the littoral and open ocean maritime zones). Staple foods here would again have included bread when available and porridges but with the ubiquitous *bucellatum* hard tack biscuits added. Specifically for the *remiges* oarsmen in the galleys of the regional navies, one reference to the diet of Greek galley crews speaks of their subsisting on a mix of barley meal with wine and oil while rowing. Once again, locally available fresh and dried fruit and vegetables would have been added to the diet when available, as well as meat and fish.

It should be noted here of course that when one considers the permanent garrisons of the Roman military, we are not just talking about the troops themselves. The soldiery of Rome didn't live in isolation, but were always part of their own wider community, with many civilians living alongside them through both choice and obligation (Mattingly, 2006, 171). When the military were stationed in their permanent bases, such civilians (up to 200,000 in number by some calculations in Britain, by way of example) most often resided in the surrounding *vicus* settlements featuring all of the trades and supporting activities to maintain the regional military presence, including those engaged in agriculture. In that regard it is therefore likely that even if the military were directly engaged in agriculture to provide their own subsistence (at the very least through its management), it would have been as part of this wider community.

It was when on campaign however that the Roman military machine really swung into action in terms of subsistence, it being crucial to ensure the troops were sustained well enough to be at their martial best. As Goldsworthy says (2003, 97):

> During a campaign, the need to keep his army adequately supplied was one of the greatest concerns of the Roman commander.

Provisioning was carried out through three types of base: supply bases provisioned by the provincial governor, operational bases which were often located at substantial ports, and tactical bases. The latter were often the marching camps described in Chapter 4, and it was not uncommon for these to be converted into supply depots, often becoming permanent fortifications in this capacity. Meals were taken in the marching camps once again in the morning and evening, though with the latter taking priority given the usual necessity for an early start. The legionaries were required to carry three days' worth of rations when on campaign, their nature dependent on the location of the campaign. The supplies were requisitioned from the surrounding populace/countryside (and thus not specifically the produce of the military engaging in agriculture themselves) when the supply chain was stretched. The principal difference between provisions when on campaign and when in garrison seems to have been a switch in the use of the grain ration, from making bread to making the *bucellatum* as used by the naval *milites.*

Active Agricultural Activity

Moving on from subsistence we can now look at how the Roman military contributed to agricultural practices in the wider community. We have already touched on the most prominent example of this in Chapter 4, namely the military *agrimensores*, *libratores* and *mensores* in using their *decempeda*, *groma*, and *chorobates* to lay out *centuriae*, divided and assigned parcels of 'official land' around 706m by 706m in size (20 by 20 Roman *actus* units of measurement, giving an overall area of some 50.4ha). Given the official nature of this activity it was always the military who carried out this surveying task, and the output of their work can still be seen across the empire, particularly in Italy, southern Gaul, Africa and Spain where huge land surveys created a dense networks of centuriated land, these agricultural units often being assigned to retired veteran troops as part of their *praemia* retirement gratuity (though noting that over time, changing ownership enabled individual landowners to accumulate patterns of land under cultivation, they becoming an essential part of the provincial economy).

In Britain, Wilkinson (2009, 40) has carried out an extensive analysis of centuriation along Watling Street as it tracks through northern Kent, showing how this activity (carried out by the military surveying teams) was an essential part of bringing a given territory into the Provincial Roman family. He says:

> The Roman administration in a newly conquered territory such as Britannia had extensive responsibilities and wide-ranging powers and the (military) surveyors were closely involved with everything they did. Roman surveyors would have had to decide boundaries, distribute individual allocations, lead settlers to their plots and were at the centre of activities crucial to Roman political, economic, and social life.

Centuriation was a key feature of the Roman agricultural experience and a very specific manifestation of *Romanitas*, with the intention being to deliberately and visibly divide the landscape into these equal plots. Wilkinson (2009, 40), through his Kent Archaeological Field School (KAFS), found that in the landscape around his Hog Brook and Deerton Street research there are 17 centuriation squares running in sequence along Watling Street in the vicinity of Hog Brook, with another 12 clustered around them. He adds that in his most recent research, yet to be published, he has identified a direct correlation between land surveying for villa estates, Roman milestones and centuriation, all using Watling Street as a base line. Thus, one can see that the use of the military surveyors (here using Britain as an example) engaging directly in agricultural activity by planning out field systems, and then facilitating their purchase under cultivation, was not just a component of agrarian activity within the provincial economy but also a key part of putting the stamp of the empire on a province.

The military again come into view in the context of agriculture in another example from occupied Britain, once more as facilitators using their specialist skills, in this case though not only surveying but through their construction expertise. This involves the large size of the granaries at four key sites in the Darent Valley in Kent, these structures being classified as 'military' by Morris (1979, 32) with, as evidence, their floors being raised on small stone walls or pillars. I also interpret these granaries as most likely having been laid out and constructed by the military, in this case to facilitate regional agriculture, perhaps reflecting their closeness to the governor and procurator in London. In this regard, elsewhere (Elliott, 2016a, 87) I argue that Kent was more militarised through much of the occupation than the rest of the south and the east of the province. The four villas were at Darenth, Horton Kirby, Lullingstone and Farningham respectively, and each of these featured a granary with a floor area of up to 280m^2, much larger than the usual occupation-period granary size of 70m^2 (Perring, 1991, 119, Blanning 2014, 298, and Philp, 1972). A number of theories have been put forward for these unusual features, for example Black (1987, 57) arguing that they represent hard evidence that the Darent Valley villas were able to take full economic advantage of their proximity to London (especially given the riverine proximity of some, for example at Horton Kirby, Scott, 1993, 105). Blanning (2014, 298) suggests that their large size and military architecture may also reflect an official association, with the villas perhaps supplying grain to the military in the south-east, or being run by *decuriones* facilitating the collection of the *annona* (see discussion regarding this in Chapter 8). There is also a chronological aspect to the narrative of these exponentially large granaries, with that at Horton Kirby having been expanded in the mid-3rd century to the size of the structure excavated by Brian Philp in 1972, while that at Lullingstone was constructed unusually late in the story of this villa site, towards the end of the 3rd century. Blanning (2014, 298) suggests that in the case of the former, this may be associated with the 'crisis of the 3rd century'. For the latter, a strong case can be argued for a link to the tax reforms of the Diocletianic reformation and the later increase in regional agricultural activity as the Rhine armies, and more broadly the troubled continental north-west of the empire, began to look to the *diocese* (as it became at this time, with its four and later possibly five smaller provinces) across the Channel for a reliable source of grain and other produce. One could argue that the nucleation of settlement around Folkestone (Parfitt, 2013, 54) is also evidence of this transition from industry to agriculture, as the regional elites exploited the opportunity created by the new continental demand. In that sense, the armies on the Rhine certainly had a major impact on agriculture in Britain, the south and east of the *diocese* responding by turning over more and more land to agriculture to meet demand (to the detriment of military-run industry, see Chapter 6 above). This becomes clear in AD 359 when Julian (then caesar of the western empire, later emperor AD 361–363) built 700 ships to transport grain from Britain to feed the Rhine army.

Negative Impact

Building on this impact of demand by the Roman military on regional agriculture, the last consideration in this chapter is actually how this could negatively impact a territory. For example, in Britain, there was clearly a divide between a south and east of the province (later *diocese*), which were fully functioning parts of the empire, and a north and west, which were to a large extent frontier zones. This economic border effectively ran along a line stretching from the Severn in the west to the Humber in the east (Mattingly, 2006, 149). Millett (1990a, 100) says that, in this regard, within the north and west border zone the military was the dominant economic presence, and I argue (2016a, 19) that the entire economy there (including agriculture) would have been given over to supporting this martial presence, to the detriment of all else.

There is also evidence of this phenomenon elsewhere in the Empire, with, for example a recent review of the data for the multiperiod site of Gordion in Anatolia identifying a very noticeable pattern of intensive and unsustainable land use in the Roman period (Bennett, 2013, 315). One interpretation of this is that they were attempting to meet a requirement for over-production by the agricultural estate-owners (within both the imperial and the provincial economies) in order to comply with onerous taxation levels to supply food for the legionaries and auxiliaries based in the provinces of Cappadocia and Galatia from the mid-1st century AD onwards.

Chapter 8

Conclusion

My aim in this work has been to show the military forces of the Roman Empire, whether the legionaries, auxiliaries or naval *milites* of the regional fleets, in a light different to that in which they are usually considered, that most often being as the elite fighting force of the ancient world. With that in mind, in this conclusion I aim to create a synthesis based on what has been considered in the preceding chapters, followed by a review of the changing nature of the Roman military and their use in a non-conflict capacity as the Principate became the Dominate, before finally considering how viewing the Roman military in roles not associated with fighting can help us see them as something more than 'other' within their own wider society.

To recap, in an age before a modern civil service able to carry out an administrative function, nationalised industries directly run by the state, or the use of the free market to facilitate commercial solutions to capital expenditure programmes, it was the Roman military to which the state turned on every occasion to facilitate all aspects of building (physically and otherwise) and maintaining the empire. In that regard, I have considered them in a variety of roles, set initially against detailed background sections, starting with their role as administrators who managed the empire on behalf of the emperor, enabling the smooth running of the imperial machine. To reflect, for the majority of the Principate (the main chronological focus of this book) a given province would only have had 80 or fewer senior officials to run the territory legally and financially, and this only when combining the staffs of both the governor and procurator. It was therefore the military who supplied all of the additional manpower needed, whether the *beneficiarii* running the *stationes* waystations on the major trunk routes, or carrying out official censuses, as with the cavalry commander Priscus in Arabia, the cavalry prefect Titus Haterius Nepos in Dumfries and Galloway (both in the 2nd century AD), or the centurion T. Floridius Natalis of the *legio* VI *Victrix* who was the regional administrator at Ribchester. The narrative of the book then moved to cover the military in other roles that would have been their daily lot, for example policing the empire, providing firefighting resources and helping to organise the games in the arena (particularly in the case of the regional navies), the latter a central part of Roman life.

Central to this book, however, is the consideration of the military literally building the Empire, in their roles as surveyors and engineers, whether in the case of the individual trooper who was skilled in this regard as a matter of course, or the specialists embedded within each military unit (for example the *agrimensores*, *libratores* and *mensores* whose work initiated each such project). Today, the world of Rome is best known through the results of this activity, whether in the case of modern roads that track the routes of their imperial forebears, or the great building projects that still excite attention today, for example Hadrian's Wall in the north of Britain or the Aurelian wall circuit of Rome itself.

A key focus in this work has also been on the role of the Roman military running major industrial enterprises, particularly large scale *metalla* mining and quarrying operations. In the context of the imperial economy, the role of the military here cannot be understated, ensuring the success on these industries on a scale not seen again for at least 1,400 years. In Chapters 1 and 6 I have endeavored to set out formulas that those wishing to continue this research can use to determine not only whether the military did indeed run a given enterprise, but also the scale of their role up to and including managing imperial estates. Finally, I have also considered the role of the military in agriculture, the central feature of the Roman economy – and one in which the armed forces of Rome participated fully.

A common theme running through all of the above is that of scale, for example the 3.2km Severan land wall circuit of Roman London, which was built from more than one million squared and dressed ragstone blocks as outlined in Chapter 5, extracted from five quarries with a total area of 723,430m^2 and then transported 127km in boat loads of up to 50 tonnes down the River Medway and up the River Thames, as set out in Chapter 6. One thing is clear: when the Roman military was involved in any type of operation, whether conflict related or not, the scale was epic.

Chronology is also an important part of this book, given its focus on the Roman military engaging in non-conflict activities throughout the Principate period of the empire. After this time, as we head into the Dominate period of Roman history, the military's activities in this regard began to change. This was partly due to the changing nature of the military themselves. The initial reforms of the Roman war machine were initiated by Septimius Severus in the early 3rd century AD (still within the Principate), but were substantially accelerated as the empire traversed the 'Crisis of the 3rd Century' (see Chapter 1), and then formalised from the time of Diocletian, finally coming to fruition under Constantine in the early 4th century AD. The army that emerged by this time was very different to that of the Principate, with the formal, large legions and auxiliary formations replaced by *comitatenses* field army troops and *limitanei* border troops (called *ripenses* when guarding river frontiers), all increasingly bolstered by *foederate* 'barbarian' mercenaries. MacDowall (1994, 4) says that this new system was designed to provide a defence in depth against the external threats that, by this time, were putting pressure on all of the borders of the empire, particularly along the Rhine and Danube, and in the east from Sassanid Persia. In this system, the border troops were deployed to act as a trigger system, tasked with delaying any incursions into imperial territory until the crack field armies could be deployed from deep with the empire to provide an effective counter. This imbalance in the capabilities of the border troops and field army troops became more marked as the Dominate progressed. MacDowall (1994, 4) says the former eventually became little more than part-time militia, while Gardner (2007, 257) adds that this change was evolutionary and occurred over time, rather than being the result of a dramatic event.

Concentrating on the elite troops, while still including legionaries and auxilia (including new auxilia palatina troops), the field armies were very different from their Principate forebears. For a start, the component formations were smaller than the previous legions, no more than 1,200 troops in number. Next, mounted troops made up a significantly larger percentage of the armies, reflecting the greater need for flexibility and speed. These included fully armoured (man and horse) cataphracts, the result of the eastern arms race against the Sassanids, in whose armies they played a key role (as they previously did with the Parthians).

The result of all of this change over a 100-year period was that the military was less used by the state for non-conflict activity in the later Empire than under the Principate. One reason was simply that there was more fighting to be done, in endless civil wars and to deal with deep incursions into imperial territory on a regular basis. However, change was also taking place elsewhere in the Roman state and economy, and these impacted on the military also. In that regard, the nature of the empire had changed by this time from one of expansion to one of consolidation and, to put it bluntly, survival. A manifestation of this was the slowing – and in the case of peripheral provinces such as Britain, ending – of the era of major public buildings being constructed as an expression of *Romanitas*. Further, a new layer of administration was added within the empire as part of the Diocletianic reforms of the late 3rd and early 4th centuries, removing some of the roles previously carried out specifically by the military.

Kulikowski (2016, 5) has recently argued that the roots of these later reforms of the Roman state and economy are to be found actually much earlier, in the Principate. He says the causational event was the gradual displacement of power away from the leading, hierarchical senatorial classes in Rome in favour of:

- Leading noble families from elsewhere in the growing empire.
- The equestrian classes broadly, who were taking on a greater role in the running of the empire.
- A new *nouveau riche* class of meritocrats, who had benefited from the outward expansion of the Principate.

The first real manifestation of a significant economic change, however, was the appearance of what might be viewed in retrospect as the beginnings of a recognisable Roman civil service. This was in the context of the permanent *annona* tax instigated by Septimius Severus as the Principate entered the 3rd century AD. The term originated with the *Cura Annonae* detailed in Chapter 1, with *annona* coming to represent types of *ad hoc* taxation in kind (both direct and indirect, see Chapter 1 discussion on the nature of the Roman economy) in the 2nd century, when it was raised in times of crisis to support the army as a supplement to regular taxes. Levied on landowners, this tax was indemnified by the state (though not always at the full price).

Early in his reign, Severus realized that the financial institutions of the empire were still struggling to keep up with demand, particularly with regard to the cost of the military, as he began to institute serious increases in their pay and reward. To alleviate this financial pressure, Severus increased the number of *praesides* (government officials) and procuratorial staff, particularly increasing the number on the Danube frontier (his power base), in the East and in Africa. This reflected a similar pattern with regard to the Senate, where he also favoured the promotion on non-Italians, a deliberate move to water down any opposition from the traditional Italian senatorial classes to his reign. He further increased the importance of the equestrian class, incorporating more members into his *Consilium Principus*. He then regularised the *annona*, instituting it as a regular tax in kind (in effect a recurring requisition) across the empire, including Italy, which had previously had some privileges of exception. He opted for this new layer of taxation to be paid in kind as that protected it to some extent from the affects of the inflation which was beginning to gather pace with regard to the Roman economy in the early 3rd century AD (the *denarius* had already been devalued in AD 194). A key difference with this new Severan tax compared to earlier manifestations of the *annona* was that it was no longer indemnified by the state.

The Severan *annona* was managed by the wealthiest *decuriones* (municipal councillors) within the cities and towns of the empire, who were increasingly taking a leading role in administering the empire (a phenomenon originating in the Antonine period in the mid-2nd century). These *decuriones* were financially responsible for the levying and collection of the taxes, with *boulē* (municipal Senates) being set up in the cities and towns to facilitate their activities in this regard, and to help monetise the collected taxes in kind to ensure their ultimate payment into the *fiscus*. The actual day-to-day running of the *annona* was performed by a new '*annona* service' of civil servants, who took on some of the administrative tasks previously managed by the military.

An obvious flaw with the Severan *annona* was the ability of the *decuriones* to abuse their positions for their own betterment. To that end, the state appointed *curatores rei publicae* (central government officials) to oversee the whole system, though predation of the lower classes certainly took place (who faced restrictions on shipping and commercial activities). Another flaw was the fact that the institution of the '*annona* service' imposed another cost on the state.

However, as the century progressed, the weaknesses of this Severan *annona* system and existing taxation were exposed by the turbulence of the 'Crisis of the 3rd Century', and also the increasing costs of maintaining an ever-larger military establishment. Heather (2005, 64) says that the imperial response as the Principate moved towards its end was threefold. First, starting at some stage between AD 240 and AD 260, the state began to confiscate city revenues such as local tolls, taxes and endowments. The next step to manage the financial crisis was to debase the currency again, specifically by reducing the silver context in the *denarii* with which the troops were paid. Finally, at times of extreme pressure during the crisis (which were frequent), additional emergency taxes were raised.

Further economic stress was then caused by Aurelian's attempt to mark his reunification of the Empire by launching new gold and silver coinage, apparently with the aim of replacing much of the money then in circulation. The result however was to almost demonetise the Empire, given the poor quality of particularly the silver coins they replaced.

It was in these circumstances that Diocletian, as part of his wider reformation of the political, economic and social systems of the Roman Empire, instituted his fully systemised taxation system on all economic production, this called the *annona militaris* which replaced all that had gone before. To run this effectively, he doubled the number of civil servants (confusingly often given military titles, and sometimes serving with military units), further reducing the need to use the military in this context.

I finish this conclusion by looking at the identity of the Roman military to determine if we can consider them in a different way (other than as a fighting force) given we have now seen the output of their work in other areas in the preceding chapters in detail. The Roman military, as with all militaries, was definitely 'other' when compared to the rest of society, being separate and available to be deployed for military or other purposes as required. This 'otherness' was at its most pronounced when a territory was first taken within the empire, and in times of extreme crisis. In this regard, Hill (2016, 29) shows the building on the Plantation Place temporary fort in the heart of London in the immediate aftermath of the Boudiccan Revolt as an example of such extreme 'otherness', saying:

> the fort was raised over what had been, before AD 60/61, several blocks of clay and timber domestic buildings, separated by a side road. The military could clearly impose themselves on the landscape, requisitioning land and altering the road layout to suit their purpose.

Within this concept of 'otherness', in Chapter 2 I detailed the lively debate taking place currently among Roman academia about whether the troops were a single, homogenous whole or instead featured a variety of differing identities. I then set out three paradigms to allow the study of such identities, including capability and specialisation (very relevant here given the specialist troops detailed in Chapter 4), chronology (again relevant given the focus on the Principate, and noting the changes above with the onset of the Dominate) and geography (noting the foreign origins of the many of the troops serving in a province, and, in the case of Britain, the vast majority).

A useful example to enable us to view any of these potential differentiated military identities, and thus to take a view about how 'other' such troops were from the rest of society, are the various sized fortresses, forts and fortlets detailed in the Introduction. These sites are important because they allow the examination both of the interaction within the military unit itself, and of that unit with the surrounding local communities (for example in a bespoke *vicus*).

Gardner (2013, 11), in the case of the first, talks of the 'dialectic of control' in a military unit whereby power is exerted both over the trooper, but also being contested by him. Here he argues we get visibility of differing identities emerging. Using the example of the baths at the major legionary fortress at Caerleon, he says (2013, 12):

> evidence...speaks to both the imposition of discipline and the potential for discord that defined military practice in dynamic ways over time. The baths were a priority in the construction of the fortress...and although later modifications would expand the complex, the importance of bathing as a practice which promoted both solidarity and bodily transformation (in conjunction with equipment and training) was clearly paramount. Yet the baths were also an area for more unstructured interaction, with the finds providing evidence of gambling, casual food consumption and the potential for socializing with non-soldiers.

Such a dialectic became even more pronounced when the Principate transformed into the Dominate Empire, with, for example (as detailed above) the extra layers of public administration introduced through the Diocletianic Reformation increasing the coercive experience of being within the Roman military (they still retaining some roles in this area, even if more at the enforcement end of the relationship with wider

Barrack blocks, with ovens in the foreground, of the Roman legionary fortress at Caerleon, home of the legio II Augusta for much of the occupation. Simon Elliott.

society). On the other hand, different building styles emerging in military sites show more evidence of individuality. Using his research at Caerleon as an example again, Gardner (2013, 12) references the differing ways in which the barracks were rebuilt here as an example of the latter.

Meanwhile, and more importantly when considering the nature of military 'otherness', one of the best indicators is that of scale when comparing the military establishment of a given fortification with their garrison settlements (*vici* or otherwise). Millett (1990a, 185) and Mattingly (2011, 223) have both argued that such garrison settlements had a population at least twice that of the military establishment they were attached to.

The former believes that the army in Britain, as an example, numbered between 10,000 and 20,000 and attracted a garrison settlement population of up to 200,000 (though with a lower estimate of 50,000), while the latter argues that, when the military presence in Britain was at its peak in the 2nd century AD, it numbered between 45,000 and 55,000, with an associated garrison settlement population of 100,000. Of course, many of the inhabitants in these settlements were members of the military train, but many others would have been local. Mattingly (2011, 223) says of these communities:

> These were the families (official and unofficial) of the soldiery and veterans, the traders, the craftspeople, and servicers of the needs and desires of the army.

Common sense dictates that the presence of non-military communities on this scale so close to the soldiery would have impacted on the identity of the latter. As we have seen in the above chapters, this process would then have been a two-way street, given that such communities, and indeed wider contemporary society, would have seen first-hand the handiwork of the military formations in their non-conflict related capacities, whether as Principate administrators, carrying out major construction projects, running industry or helping with agriculture. As an example, Parfitt (2013, 45) described the *Classis Britannica* regional fleet in Britain as being more akin to an army service corps than being a purely combat organisation. To that end, I believe this work has enabled us more definitively than in the past to view the Roman military as being more visibly part of wider Roman society and as something more than simply the military 'other'.

Appendix A

Geological Formations of South-East Britain to Inform Roman Regional Use of Stone as a Building Material

As I have used the south-east of Britain as an example of the use of local building stone in a Roman province in Chapter 4, I provide here an overview of the regional geology and its impact on the economy and settlement in the region during the Roman period to provide context.

The geology of south-east Britain, then and now, is surprisingly simple, especially given the wide variety of landscapes evident across the region. It also provides the key to understanding the resource exploitation in each of the two case studies in Chapter 6. McRae and Burnham (1973, 9) described the underpinning macro-geology of the south-east of Britain as sedimentary rock laid down during the Cretaceous and Tertiary periods, which has since been forced into a dome (known as the Wealden anticlinorium) by earth-movements culminating in the Miocene period. This geological process created the two complimentary compound synclines now known as the London Basin and the Hampshire Basin. Subsequent erosion, the development of the Thames Estuary and associated drainage systems (including principal Kentish rivers the Stour, Medway and Darent, for millennia the principal means of accessing the county inland from the north coast), and the formation of the English Channel have then resulted in the pattern of rocks shown on the geological map of the south-east of Britain today.

These macro geological processes translate into nine geological formations (Croft, Munby and Ridley, 2001, 1–4), which from uppermost to lowermost (generally) are as follows:

- London clays in the north, which in terms of relief are generally flat and which include the foothills of the North Downs. Lawson and Killingray (2004, 2) explain that much of the surface geology of northern Kent from the Hoo Peninsula to the Isle of Sheppey is formed from these London clays.
- The Thanet Beds, also flat and comprising of calcareous sandstone, pale grey sandstone and clayey sands.

- Chalk, forming the west–east horseshoe of the North and South Downs, which defines the region. The North Downs comprises the chalk base overlain by extensive deposits of clay-with-flint.
- The Upper Greensand, comprising sandy lithoacies originally deposited in stronger currents than the subsequent Gault clay, hence the separation. This layer is not present beneath the entire London Basin, passing laterally into Gault clay east of a line between Tatsfield and Dunstable, with the Upper Greensand being completely absent on the eastern Kentish coast and thus not featuring as a building material there.
- Gault clay, on which sits the Holmesdale on the south slope of the North Downs, the most fertile land in the county of Kent (Everitt, 1986, 49).
- The Lower Greensand, otherwise known as the Greensand Ridge. This comprises, in descending order, the Folkestone Beds, Sandgate Beds and Hythe Beds which, together with the underlying Atherfield Clay described below, form the geographical region known as the Chart Hills in Kent. The Lower Greensand formation was particularly important in terms of regional extractive industry during the occupation, for example the coastal outcropping of the very hard Folkestone Beds being exploited for millstone and quern production, while within the Hythe Beds sits the Kentish ragstone which is so important to the Upper Medway Valley case study in Chapter 6.
- Atherfield and Wealden Clay (sometimes called the Wealden Beds), on which sits the Low Weald and which is the least fertile part of Kent and the south-east. The former clay (often described as a sub-division of the Lower Greensand) overlies the latter, difficult to differentiate except for the presence of marine fossils. These clays were much used for pottery, tile and brick manufacture during the occupation (see Chapters 4 and 6). It is worth noting here that siderite ironstone mined as iron ore for the occupation-period iron manufacturing industry sits within at least two horizons of the Wealden Clay and is therefore of direct relevance to the industrial case study in Chapter 6.
- The Hastings Beds, on which sit the High Weald. This geological unit includes inter-bedded clays, silts, siltstones, sands and sandstones. These specific strata make up the component geological formations known as the Ashdown Formation, the Wadhurst Clay Formation and the Tunbridge Wells Sand Formation. These deposits were particularly important during the occupation as within them sat further siderite deposits exploited by the Wealden iron industry, with the greatest concentration in the whole region being found within the lower levels of the Wadhurst Clay Formation. Additionally, the Fairlight Clay, which seems to have been the material of choice used to manufacture the *Classis Britannica* bricks and tiles in the Weald (Peacock, 1977, 237, see Chapters 4 and 6), sits within the Ashdown Formation.
- On the south-eastern periphery, the alluvial, wind-blown sand deposits and pebble banks of Romney Marsh. Only a few localities were economically utilised here

during the occupation, though since that time large tracts have been brought into productivity through reclamation and aggregate extraction.

This geological sequence had a formative impact on the geography and soils (and thus settlement and land-use) in the south-east of Britain during the occupation. In that regard, Everitt (1986, 43) explains that while the changes in geology are less visible when travelling along the modern east–west routes (for example the M2 and M20 in Kent), they become much more overt when traversing traditional north–south drove ways in that county when at least six different landscapes become visible in the space of no more than 65km.

The above geological formations were exploited to maximum effect in the south-east during the occupation, providing siderite for the iron industry as detailed and, principally, a wide variety of building materials, hence their consideration here in this Appendix. Construction using the latter was one of the key manifestations of *Romanitas* in the region, as it was elsewhere in Britain – and indeed the Empire – where such materials were available. Examples of the use of stone as a building material do appear in the region in the Late Iron Age, for example the Ightham Stone used as revetting material and strengthening ballast at the Oldbury *oppida* in western Kent (Thompson, 1986, 270), but it is with the advent of Rome that we see a dramatic proliferation of its use on a grand scale. As outlined by Blagg (1990, 33), demand would have initially been driven by the need for major urban centres to provide the administration required by the new province, and clearly grand stone built structures in this new built environment were intended to put the stamp of Rome on the local populace (especially the elites) as part of a package which included other manifestations of the Roman experience. Tacitus (The Agricola, 1970, 72) is explicit about the use of stone-built structures as part of this cultural suite, saying of Agricola after his two years of campaigning in Wales and the north of Britain from AD 77:

> Agricola had to deal with people living in isolation and ignorance, and therefore prone to fight: and his object was to accustom them to a life of peace and quiet by the provision of amenities. He therefore gave private encouragement and official assistance to the building of temples, public squares and good houses. He praised the energetic and scolded the slack. And competition for honour proved as effective as compulsion. Furthermore, he educated the sons of the chiefs in the liberal arts...the result was that instead of loathing the Latin language they became eager to speak it effectively.

A major early driver here behind this stone-built urbanisation was the societal obligation placed on elites by the State to invest in public buildings in their communities as an expression of their *Romanitas*. Halsall (2013, 90) explains:

> Spending private money on such projects brought important political rewards. It might bring success in the competition to control the curia (town council) of the civitas. The curia was responsible for tax collection...an important source of patronage. Success here

> [would] be a platform for the advancement on a broader political stage...and perhaps even promotion to the higher orders of Roman Society.

Such stone-built structures, later to be joined by fortifications as the imperial experience changed, were expressed in a variety of forms and locations across the south-east region, including:

- The provincial and later *diocesan* capital London.
- The *civitas* capital at Canterbury in modern Kent.
- The *colonia* at Colchester in modern Essex.
- The small towns of Rochester and Springhead in modern Kent.
- Conquest and post conquest period fortifications, including the various *Classis Britannica* and later Saxon Shore forts.
- The later fortification of key urban sites.
- The *phari* at Dover in modern Kent.
- Grand stone-built rural elite country houses in the form of villas and similar, from the later 1st century AD through to the end of the occupation.
- Industrial sites, for example the watermills at Ickham in modern Kent near Canterbury.
- The extensive road network across the region.

Building on this grand scale generated a huge demand for building stone and other materials, creating an explosion in the scale of quarrying together with associated industries such as construction and specialist heavy goods transport. These are all considered in detail in their various contexts in the above Chapters 4, 5 and 6.

Appendix B

Distribution Table for Upper Medway Valley Ragstone across the South-East of Britain during the Roman Occupation

Location	*Distance*	*Chronology*	*Context*
Bradwell-on-Sea, Essex	59km	3rd and 4th centuries AD	Building material in the Saxon Shore fort
Boughton Monchelsea, Kent	Within zone of extraction	1st through 4th centuries AD	Villa and remote bath house
Canterbury, Kent	42km	1st through 4th centuries AD	Town walls, public buildings, built environment
Colchester, Essex	75km	1st through 3rd centuries AD	Claudian temple, circus
Dover, Kent	60km	1st through 4th centuries AD	*Pharos*, built environment
East Farleigh, Kent	Within zone of extraction	1st through 4th centuries AD	Villa and temple
East Malling, Kent	Within zone of extraction	1st through 4th centuries AD	Villa
Eccles, Kent	7.5km	1st through 4th centuries AD	Villa
Faversham, Kent	30km	1st through 4th centuries AD	Hogs Brook aisled building, Stone-by-Faversham temple/ mausoleum
Keston, Kent	34km	1st through 3rd centuries AD	Cemetery
London	50km	1st through 4th centuries AD	Forum, basilica, governor's palace, amphitheatre, temples, wider built environment, 3.2km land wall circuit
Maidstone, Kent	Within zone of extraction	1st through 4th centuries AD	Villas

(Continued)

Location	*Distance*	*Chronology*	*Context*
Plaxtol, Kent	13km	1st through 4th centuries AD	Used as a building material in the three Roman villas here, as a platform in a funerary context and in a trackway
Reculver, Kent	52km	3rd and 4th centuries AD	Saxon Shore fort
Richborough, Kent	60km	1st through 5th centuries AD	Early built environment, monumental arch, later Saxon Shore fort
Rochester, Kent	15km	1st through 4th centuries AD	Public buildings, built environment, town walls
Snodland, Kent	10km	1st through 4th centuries AD	Villa
Southfleet, Kent	21km	1st through 3rd centuries AD	Walled cemetery
Springhead, Kent	22km	1st through 4th centuries AD	Temples, built environment
Swanscombe, Kent	24km	1st and 2nd centuries AD.	Non-villa settlement
Teston, Kent	Within zone of extraction	1st through 4th centuries AD	Villa
Teynham, Kent	24km	1st through 3rd centuries AD	Used as the principal construction material in the octagonal bath house at Bax Farm
Thurnham, Kent	8.5km	1st through 4th centuries AD	Villa

After Merrifield (1965), Marsden (1994), Pearson (2002a and 2002b) and Blanning (2015).

Appendix C

Distribution Table, Locations and Totals of *Classis Britannica* Stamps on Tile of Known Provenance

In alphabetical order, all Fabric 2 unless specified, together with site history. No distances given as exact place of origin ill defined.

Location	*Number of Stamps*	*Site History*
Bardown – eastern/ coastal Weald	28	The first *Classis Britannica* tile was found here by Brother Stephen Pepperell in 1951 and identified by Margary (Brodribb, 1969, 109). All subsequent tile was found during the excavations of Cleere in the late 1960s.
Beauport Park – eastern/ coastal Weald	1,600	The vast quantity of stamped tile found here was discovered during the investigations of Brodribb and Cleere in the 1970s and 1980s, most in association with the well-recorded bath house (Brodribb *et al*, 1988, 268).
Bodiam – eastern/ coastal Weald	31	Found between 1959 and 1969 in excavations by the Battle and District Historical Society (Brodribb, 1969, 111).
Boulogne	100 plus (approximately two thirds Fabric 1)	Mostly discovered in the 19th century, many of these tiles have since been lost though a number remain in Boulogne Museum (Crowley and Betts, 1992, 218).
Desvres	?	*Classis Britannica* tiles were reported at this site inland from Boulogne in the antiquarian record but the provenance of their finding is unclear (Crowley and Betts, 1992, 218).
Dover	1,000 plus (one Fabric 1)	First tile found in 1778, with many since, particularly in the context of the excavations of the *Classis Britannica* fort and the 'Painted House' (Philp, 1989, 57, and 2014, 38).

(Continued)

Location	*Number of Stamps*	*Site History*
Folkestone	21	Seven tiles featuring a *Classis Britannica* stamp were found during the initial excavations of S. E. Winbolt in 1923–1924 (Brodribb, 1969, 109). Since that time others have been recovered from successive excavations and from spoil (much from the first excavation) at the foot of East Cliff, East Wear Bay.
Kitchenham Farm – central Weald	31 (29 Fabric 1, most in pristine condition)	The Hastings Area Archaeological Research Group's recent investigations here have located 31 *Classis Britannica* tiles, 29 of which are of the Fabric 1 type originating in Boulogne. These tiles are the first and only ones located to date in the Central Weald.
Little Farningham – eastern/coastal Weald	53	Site located by the landowner in the 1950s and excavated by the Cranbrook and Sissinghurst Local History Society.
London	5	*Classis Britannica* stamped tiles have been found here at Nobel Street, Winchester Palace (Crowley and Betts, 1992, 218), Hunt's House (Taylor-Wilson, 2002, 10) and Garlick Hill.
Lyminge	2	Two re-used tiles have been found in the context of the Saxon palace under excavation by Reading University (unpublished at the time of writing, original provenance unknown).
Lympne	22	All *Classis Britannica* tiles located here were found during the Charles Roach-Smith excavations of the Saxon Shore fort in 1850. Others may have been found subsequently but have been lost (Brodribb, 1969, 108).
Pevensey	3	These tiles were found during the investigations at the site of Sussex antiquarian L. F. Salzman in 1906–1907. Others were apparently found between 1907 and 1939 but were lost at the outbreak of the Second World War (Brodribb, 1969, 109).
Richborough	1	One tile found in 1932 (Atkinson, 1933, 10).
St Catherine's Point, Isle of Wight	1 (Fabric 1)	Lyne (2000, 10) speculates that this single example found in a late period enclosure ditch may indicate the previous presence of a signal station on the southernmost point of the Isle of Wight.

Brodribb, 1969, 185, 1970, 25, and 1980, 191, Cleere and Crossley, 1995, 65, and Crowley and Betts, 1992, 218, updated by Elliott, 2015.

Appendix D

A Timeline of Roman Britain

Below I include a timeline of key events in the narrative of Roman Britain designed to act as a guide to many of the examples detailed above of the Roman military carrying out non-conflict related duties and activities. Chronologically, while the book has focused on the Principate period of imperial rule, I have also included events both before and after where I feel they have context to add. Meanwhile, in terms of geography, while the events detailed mainly focus on the province of Britain (later two provinces and, following the Diocletianic reformation, four and perhaps five provinces within the later *diocese*), key events elsewhere in the Roman Empire have also been included, again to provide context.

60 BC	The First Triumvirate is formed by Julius Caesar, Gnaeus Pompeius Magnus (Pompey) and Marcus Licinius Crassus.
58 BC	Julius Caesar begins his conquest of Gaul.
57 BC	The Veneti submit to Julius Caesar.
56 BC	The rebellion of the Veneti, with the Battle of Morbihan.
55 BC	The first Roman invasion of Britain, with Julius Caesar's first incursion.
54 BC	The second Roman invasion of Britain, with Julius Caesar's second incursion.
44 BC	Julius Caesar assassinated in Rome.
27 BC	Conquest of north-west Spain begins. Octavian becomes Augustus, effectively the first emperor.
AD 9	Varus' three legions and nine auxiliary units destroyed in Teutoberg Forest, Germany by the Cherusci tribe and others.
AD 40	Caligula's aborted invasion of Britain.
AD 43	The third, and successful, Roman invasion of Britain under the Emperor Claudius, with the troops commanded by Aulus Plautius. The landing took place on the eastern Kentish coast near Richborough. There followed a hard fought 'river crossing battle', widely believed to have been on the River Medway, which the Romans won. A further battle took place crossing the River Thames before the Roman legionary spearheads reached and captured Camulodunum (Colchester), capital

of the Catuvellauni tribe who had led the resistance. Claudius arrived in Britain around this time to proclaim victory, staying for 14 days. Aulus Plautius was then appointed first governor of new province.

AD 44 The future Emperor Vespasian successfully campaigns in south and south-west Britain, leading the *legio* II *Augusta*.

AD 47 Governor Aulus Plautius returns to Rome, being granted an *ovatio* lesser triumph, Vespasian returning also. The new governor is Publius Ostorius Scapula who campaigns in North Wales, then subduing the first revolt by Iceni tribe in the north of East Anglia.

AD 48 The first revolt of the Brigantes tribe in northern Britain.

AD 49 A *colonia* for veterans is founded at Colchester, with the *legio* XX *Valeria Victrix* moving to Gloucester. Governor Scapula's campaigns in the south and centre of Wales.

AD 50 Construction begins of first forum in the new-found city of London (Roman *Londinium*). The ragstone quarrying industry in the upper Medway Valley, detailed in Chapter 6 above, is established and is possibly run by the *Classis Britannica* regional fleet.

AD 51 The leader of the British resistance to Roman rule, Caratacus, is captured by the Romans after being handed over to them by the Brigantian Queen, Cartimandua.

AD 52 The Silures tribe in southern Wales is pacified by Governor Didius Gallus.

AD 54 Claudius is poisoned to death, Nero becomes emperor.

AD 57 Quintus Veranius Nepos becomes the governor of the province, dying in office. Meanwhile Rome intervenes in favour of Queen Cartimandua in a dispute over the leadership of the Brigantes.

AD 58 Gaius Seutonius Paulinus becomes the governor.

AD 59/60 The initial subjugation of the druids takes place in the far west, and the initial invasion of Anglesey by Governor Gauis Seutonius Paulinus. The campaign is cut short however by the Boudiccan revolt.

AD 60/61 The Boudiccan revolt takes place, featuring the destruction of Colchester, St Albans and London. The revolt is defeated by Gaius Seutonius Paulinus, followed by the suicide of Boudicca.

AD 61/63 Publius Petronius Turpilianus becomes governor, followed by Marcus Trebellius Maximus.

AD 68 Nero is overthrown, Galba becomes emperor.

AD 69 The Year of Four Emperors. In Britain, Cartimandua, Queen of the Brigantes and ally of Rome, is overthrown by her former husband Venutius. Marcus Vettius Bolanus is the governor.

AD 70 The *Classis Britannica* regional navy in Britain is named for the first time, by Tacitus and in the context of the Batavian Revolt of Civilis on the River Rhine.

AD 71 Emperor Vespasian orders the British Governor Quintus Petilius Cerialis to campaign in the north of Britain. The Brigantes are defeated, Venutius is captured and killed.

AD 74 The last in the series of northern garrison forts is built at Carlisle.

AD 74 Sextus Julius Frontinus is appointed as the new governor in Britain. Further campaigning in Wales follows, and Chester is founded.

AD 77 Gnaeus Julius Agricola becomes the new governor in Britain. Wales and western Britain are finally conquered by Agricola, this following a final, definitive attack on Anglesey.

AD 78 Agricola consolidates the Roman control of Brigantian territory in the north.

AD 79 Agricola attends the grand opening of the civic centre of St Albans, then mounting a 'hearts and minds' campaign designed to encourage the elites in British to embrace *Romanitas* by learning latin, wearing togas, and investing their surplus wealth in public buildings. He begins his campaign to subdue the whole of the north of Britain, including Scotland. Emperor Vespasian dies and is replaced by his son Titus.

AD 80 Agricola continues his campaigning in Scotland.

AD 81 Death of Titus who is succeeded by Domitian.

AD 82 Agricola continues his campaigning in Scotland.

AD 83 Agricola brings the combined Caledonian tribes to battle at *Mons Graupius* in the Grampians, south of the Moray Firth. The *Classis Britannica* circumnavigates northern Scotland, proving Britain is an island. The regional fleet reaches the Orkney Islands. The conquest of Britain is declared 'complete', construction begins on a monumental arch at Richborough in modern Kent to commemorate the event. The Chatti War takes place in Germany, building begins on the *limes* to link the Upper Rhine and Upper Danube.

AD 87 Roman troops are withdrawn from the far north of Britain because of pressures elsewhere in the Empire. As a result, the major legionary fortress of Inchtuthill in Tayside is abandoned and systematically dismantled.

AD 90 Both Gloucester and Lincoln become *coloniae*.

AD 96 Domitian is assassinated, bringing to an end the Flavian dynasty. He is succeeded by Nerva.

AD 98 Death of Nerva, who is succeeded by Trajan. In Britain, Publius Metilius Nepos is the Governor, followed by Titus Avidius Quietus.

AD 100 Emperor Trajan orders the full withdrawal of Roman troops from Scotland, and then establishes a new frontier along the Solway Firth–Tyne line. All defences north of this line are abandoned by AD 105.

AD 103 Lucius Neratius Marcellus is the governor.

AD 115 Marcus Atilius Bradua is the governor.
AD 117 Death of Trajan, who is succeeded by Hadrian as emperor. This coincides with major disturbances in the north of the province of Britain.
AD 122 Emperor Hadrian visits Britain, initiating the construction of Hadrian's Wall on the Solway Firth–Tyne line. Aulus Platorius Nepos is the governor.
AD 126 Lucius Trebius Germanus is the governor.
AD 131 Sextus Julius Severus is the governor.
AD 133 Publius Mummius Sisenna is the governor.
AD 138 Death of Hadrian, who is succeeded by Antoninus Pius. Quintus Lollius Urbicus is the governor in Britain. A major fire breaks out in London.
AD 142 Military engagement north of Hadrian's Wall recommences under Quintus Lollius Urbicus, on the orders of Antoninus Pius, in an attempt to subdue the tribes of northern Britain and southern Scotland, the latter region being conquered again. Construction begins of the Antonine Wall along Clyde–Forth line, the new northern frontier.
AD 145 Gnaeus Papirus Aelianus is the governor.
AD 155 Central St Albans is destroyed by fire.
AD 157 Gnaeus Julius Verus is the governor.
AD 160 The Marcomannic Wars break out on the Danube frontier, lasting for ten years.
AD 161 Antoninus Pius dies, and is succeeded by Marcus Aurelius.
AD 162 Marcus Statius Priscuss is the governor of Britain, followed by Sextus Calpurnius Agricola. The Antonine Wall is evacuated, with the northern border once again moving south to the line of Hadrian's Wall.
AD 169 There is more trouble in northern Britain.
AD 174 Caerellius is the governor.
AD 175 5,500 Sarmatian cavalry are sent to Britain.
AD 178 Ulpius Marcellus is the governor.
AD 180 Marcus Aurelius dies and is replaced by Commodus.
AD 182 The tribes on either side of Hadrian's Wall start raiding along and across the border, with Roman troops responding with counter-raids. Towns far to the south of the wall begin constructing the first earth-and-timber defence circuits at this time, indicating that the tribal raiding penetrated far into the province. This situation continues for some time.
AD 184 Emperor Commodus receives his seventh acclamation as imperator, taking the title Britannicus. The *Classis Britannica* regional fleet transports two of the three legions based in Britain to the Amorican Peninsula to help defeat a rebellion.
AD 185 Some 1,500 picked troops from Britain travel to Rome with a petition for the Emperor Commodus to dismiss the Praetorian Prefect Perennis. The new governor in Britain is the future Emperor Publius Helvius Pertinax.

AD 191/192 Decimus Clodius Albinus becomes the new governor in Britain.

AD 193 The 'Year of the Five Emperors', Severus emerges as victor.

AD 196 British Governor Albinus invades Gaul and is proclaimed emperor by the legions from Britain and Spain.

AD 197 Albinus is defeated by Septimius Severus at the closely fought Battle of Lugdunum (modern Lyons) and is killed. Planning begins to divide the province of Britain into two, *Britannia Superior* and *Britannia Inferior.* Virius Lupus is the new governor in Britain.

AD 197/198 Emperor Severus sends military commissioners to Britain aiming to quickly suppress the supporters of Albinus. Roman troops rebuild parts of Hadrian's Wall (some of which may have actually been destroyed) and other parts of the northern defences which had been damaged by an increase in tribal raiding after Albinus had travelled to Gaul with his troops. Construction of the land walls of London also starts around this time. Severus begins his reforms of the military, while he himself campaigns in Parthia for two years.

AD 202 Gaius Valerius Pudens is the governor in Britain.

AD 203 Severus campaigns for a year in North Africa.

AD 205 Lucius Alfensus Senecio is the governor in Britain.

AD 208 Ongoing raiding along the northern frontier in Britain prompts Severus to arrive with the imperial household and additional troops, he planning a major campaign against the Maeatae and Caledonian tribal confederations north of Hadrian's Wall. St Alban is martyred.

AD 209 The first Severan campaign in Scotland.

AD 210 The second Severan campaign in Scotland, led by Caracalla.

AD 211 Severus dies at York, with his sons Caracalla and Geta becoming joint emperors. The campaign in the north of Britain is suspended with the brothers returning to Rome. Britain is officially divided into two provinces, *Britannia Superior* and *Britannia Inferior.*

AD 212 Citizenship given to all freemen in the empire under the *Constitutio Antoniniana.*

AD 213 *Brittones dediticii* are recorded at the fort of Walldurn on the *limes Germanicus.*

AD 215 The last Severan outposts in Scotland are abandoned.

AD 216 Marcus Antonius Gordianus is the governor of *Britannia Inferior.*

AD 222 Tiberius Julius Pollienus Auspex is the governor of *Britannia Superior.*

AD 223 Claudius Xenephon is the governor of *Britannia Inferior.*

AD 224 Ardashir I of Persia defeats his Parthian overlords over a two-year period, bringing the Sassanid Persian Empire into being.

AD 225 Maximus is the governor of *Britannia Inferior.*

AD 226 Calvisius Rufus becomes the governor of *Britannia Inferior*, being followed by Valerius Crescens and then by Claudius Appelinus.

AD 233	Alamanni and other German confederations raid Roman provinces for a year.
AD 235	Assassination of Severus Alexander, beginning the 'Crisis of the 3rd Century'. Maximinus Thrax becomes emperor.
AD 237	Tuccianus becomes the governor of *Britannia Inferior*. York becomes a *colonia* town.
AD 238	Marcus Martiannius Pulcher becomes the governor of *Britannia Superior*. Maecilius Fuscus becomes the governor of *Britannia Inferior*, quickly followed by Egnatius Lucilianus.
AD 242	Nonius Phillipus becomes the governor of *Britannia Inferior*.
AD 244	Aemilianus becomes the governor of *Britannia Inferior*.
AD 249	The last potential mention of the *Classis Britannica* regional fleet, on epigraphy commemorating *Saturninus*, an ex-captain in the British fleet.
AD 250	Irish raiding takes place along the west coast, with Germanic raiding along the east coast. The first use of the term 'Pict' to describe the confederation of tribes in northern Scotland.
AD 253	Desticius Juba becomes the governor of *Britannia Superior*.
AD 255	London's wall circuit is completed around this time with the building of the river wall and bastions.
AD 260	The 'Gallic Empire' is declared by Postumus, splitting Britain, Gaul and Spain away from the empire for 14 years.
AD 262	Octavius Sabinus becomes the governor of *Britannia Inferior*.
AD 268	Postumus is murdered by his own troops.
AD 274	Emperor Aurelian defeats the 'Gallic Empire', with Britain, Gaul and Spain rejoining the empire.
AD 277	Vandals and Burgundian mercenaries are settled in Britain, with Victorinus defeating a British usurpation.
AD 284	Diocletian becomes emperor, beginning of Diocletianic reforms of the military. End of the 'Crisis of the 3rd Century'.
AD 287	The usurpation of Carausius, which splits Britain and northern Gaul away from the empire.
AD 293	The western *caesares* Constantius Chlorus recaptures northern Gaul from Carausius who is then assassinated by Allectus, the latter then taking over control from his former master in Britain.
AD 296	The fourth Roman invasion of Britain, with Constantius Chlorus invading to defeat Allectus, the western *caesares* then returning the two provinces to the empire. Britain is declared a *diocese* as part of the Diocletianic Reformation, with four provinces: *Maxima Caesariensis*, *Britannia Prima*, *Flavia Caesariensis* and *Britannia Secunda*.

AD 306 Constantius Chlorus campaigns in the north of Britain, then dies in York. His son Constantine is proclaimed emperor by the troops.

AD 312 Constantine becomes the sole emperor in the west, with his military reforms beginning around this time.

AD 314 Constantine's Edict of Milan ends the persecution of Christians, while three British bishops attend the Council of Bishops at Arles.

AD 324 Constantine becomes the sole emperor of the whole empire.

AD 337 Constantine prepares for war with Persia but falls ill in Nicodemia and dies.

AD 343 Emperor Constans makes a winter crossing of the English Channel to Britain following the defeat of his brother Constantine II three years earlier, possibly in the context of a military emergency in the north of the islands.

AD 350 The military leader Magnentius (born in Britain) usurps power in Gaul, with the provinces in Britain and Spain quickly supporting him, and ultimately the whole of the Western Empire.

AD 351 Magnentius is defeated by Eastern Emperor Constantius II at the Battle of Mursa Major, then retreats to Gaul. Magnentius is defeated again at the Battle of Mons Seleucus, after which he commits suicide. Constantius II sends Paul Catena ('The Chain') to Britain to purge the aristocracy after the revolt of Magnentius. The *vicarius* of the *diocese*, Martinus, commits suicide rather than face trial.

AD 358 Alypius becomes the *vicarius* of the *diocese*.

AD 359 British bishops attend the Council of Rimini. Emperor Julian builds 700 ships to transport grain from Britain to feed his Rhine army.

AD 367 Civilis becomes the *vicarius* of the *diocese*. The 'Great Conspiracy' of Picts from Scotland, Attecotti from the Western Isles, Irish and Germanic raiders attack Britain, overwhelming the frontier defences.

AD 369 Count Theodosius arrives in Britain to suppress the revolt and restore order, with Magnus Maximus serving under him. The northern frontier is rebuilt yet again.

AD 383 Magnus Maximus (now the British military commander, and possibly the *vicarius* of the *diocese*) campaigns against Pictish and Irish raiders. He is then proclaimed the emperor by his troops, invading Gaul which declares its support for him, as does Spain.

AD 387 Magnus Maximus invades Italy where he ousts the emperor, Valentinian II.

AD 388 Magnus Maximus is defeated and executed by Theodosius I, Emperor in the East.

AD 391 Theodosius I bans pagan worship, though the practice persists in Britain.

AD 395 Chrysanthus becomes the *vicarius* of the *diocese*.

AD 400	The Western Empire *Magister Militum* (overall commander) Stilicho campaigns in Britain and defeats Pictish, Irish and Germanic raiders. He then withdraws many troops from the *diocese* to help defend Italy against the Goths, with Britain left dangerously exposed to further attack. Victorinus becomes the new *vicarius*.
AD 402	Last import of base coins into Britain takes place.
AD 405	Heavy Irish raiding on the south-western coast of Britain occurs, this being a possible date for the capture of St Patrick.
AD 406	Vandals, Burgundians, Alans, Franks and Suevi overrun the *limes Germanicus* near Mainz and invade Gaul.
AD 407	In swift succession, the military in Britain declare Marcus, then Gratian and finally Constantine III to be the emperor. The latter crosses to Gaul with the remaining *comitatenses* field army troops from Britain, he setting up his capital at Arles.
AD 409	The British aristocracy throw out their Roman administrators, with the *diocese* cut adrift from the remaining parts of the Western Empire.
AD 410	Western Emperor Honorius tells the Britons to look to their own defences.
AD 411	Constantine III is captured and executed on the orders of Honorius.
AD 429	St Germanus visits Britain to debate with the Pelagian Christians resident there. There is further conflict with the Picts and Irish.
AD 430	The effective end of coin use in Britain.
AD 454	The Britons appeal to the *Magister Miletum* Flavius Aetius by letter in 'the groans of the Britons' request for military assistance, but no troops are available to help.
AD 476	The last western emperor, Romulus Augustulus, is deposed. End of the Roman Empire in the west.

Bibliography

Ancient Sources

Decimus Magnus Ausonius, *The Mosella*. 1933, trans. Blakeney, E. H., London.

Julius Caesar, *The Conquest of Gaul*. 1951, trans. Handford, S. A., London: Penguin.

Marcus Cato, *De Agri Cultura*. 1934, trans. Ash, H. B. and Hooper, W. D., Harvard: Loeb Classical Library.

Cassius Dio, *Roman History*. 1925, trans. Cary, E., Harvard: Loeb Classical Library.

Sextus Julius Frontinus, *De aquis Urbis Romae*, 1925, trans. Bennett, C. E., Harvard: Loeb Classical Library.

Herodian, *History of the Empire*. 1989, trans. Whitakker, C. R., Harvard: Loeb Classical Library.

Quintus Horatius Flaccus (Horace), *The Complete 'Odes' and 'Epodes'*. 2008, trans. West, D., Oxford: Oxford Paperbacks.

Tarrentenus Paternus, *Digest*, 1994, trans. Bowman. A. K., London: The British Museum.

Pliny the Elder, *Natural History*. 1940, trans. Rackham, H., Harvard: Harvard University Press.

Pliny the Younger, *Correspondence with Trajan from Bithynia: Epistles X*. 1990, trans. Williams, W., Oxford: Aris & Phillips.

Strabo, *The Geography*. 2014, trans. Roler, D. W., Cambridge: Cambridge University Press.

Cornelius Tacitus, *The Agricola*. 1970, trans. Mattingly, H., London: Penguin.

Cornelius Tacitus, *The Annals of Imperial Rome*. 2003, trans. Grant, M., London: Penguin.

Marcus Terentius Varro, *Rerum Rusticarum*. 1932, trans. Ash, H. B. and Hooper, W. D., Harvard: Loeb Classical Library, 1932.

Publius Flavius Vegetius Renatus, *Epitoma rei militaris*, 1995, trans. Milner, N. P., Liverpool: Liverpool University Press.

Marcus Vitruvius, *De Architectura*, 2016, trans. Hicky, M., Charleston: CreateSpace Independent Publishing Platform.

Marcus Vitruvius Pollio, *De Architectura*, 1931, trans. Granger, F., Heinemann.

Modern Sources

Allen, J. R. 2010. The Alkali–Metal Ratio in Romano-British Bloomery Slags, Severn Estuary Levels, South West Britain: Values and Implications. *Archaeology in the Severn Estuary 2009. Annual Report of the Severn Estuary Levels Research Committee* 20, 41–45.

Allen, J. R. and Fulford, M. G. 1999. Fort Building and Military Supply along Britain's Eastern Channel and North Sea Coasts: The Later Second and Third Centuries. *Britannia* 30, 163–184.

Allen, J. R. and Fulford, M. G. 2004. Early Roman Mosaic Materials in Southern Britain, with Particular Reference to Silchester: A Regional Geological Perspective. *Britannia* 35, 9–38.

Anderson, J. D. 1992. *Roman Military Supply in North East England*. Oxford: BAR, Tempus Reparatum

Andrews, C. 2001. Romanisation: A Kentish Perspective. *Archaeologia Cantiana* 121, 25–43.

Andrews, P. and Buss, B. 2011. Fairlawne Estate Roman Building Investigation: Phase 2. Wessex Archaeology (unpublished).

Andrews, P. Biddulph, E. Hardy, A. and Brown, R. 2011. *Settling the Ebbsfleet Valley, Sites 1*. Oxford: Oxford Wessex Archaeology.

Allen, J. R. and Fulford, M. G. 2004. Early Roman Mosaic Materials in Southern Britain, with Particular Reference to Silchester: A Regional Geological Perspective. *Britannia* 35, 9–38.

Atkinson, D. 1933. *Historical Essays in Honour of James Tait*. Manchester: Manchester University Press.

Bang, P. 2008. *The Roman Bazaar: A Comparative Study of Trade and Markets in Tributory Empire*. Cambridge: Cambridge University Press.

Bateman, N. 2011. *Roman London's Amphitheatre*. London: Museum of London Archaeology.

Beard, M. 2016. *SPQR*. London: Head Zeus.

de la Bédoyère, G. 1992. *Roman Towns in Britain*. London: Batsford.

de la Bédoyère, G. 1999. *The Golden Age of Britain*. Stroud: Tempus.

de la Bédoyère, G. 2000. *Pottery in Roman Britain*. Princes Risborough: Shire Publications.

de la Bédoyère, G. 2015. Face to Face with the Past: Uncovering the Real Lives of Roman Britain. *Current Archaeology* 25(304), 26–33.

Bennett, J. 2013. Agricultural strategies and the Roman military in central Anatolia during the early Imperial period. *Olba* 21, 315–344

Bennett, P., Ridler, I. and Sparey-Green, C. 2010. *The Roman Watermills and Settlement at Ickham, Kent*. Canterbury: Canterbury Archaeology Trust.

Betts, I. 1987. Ceramic Building Material: Recent Work in London. *Archaeology Today* 8, 26–28.

Biddulph, E. 2013. Salt of the Earth: Roman Industry at Stanford Wharf. *Current Archaeology*, 24(276), 16–22.

Bidwell, P. 1980. *Roman Exeter: Fortress and Town*. Exeter: Exeter City Council.

Bidwell, P. 1995. Review of Anderson 1992. *Britannia* 26, 395–396.

Birley, A. R. 2005. *The Roman Government of Britain*. Oxford: Oxford University Press.

Bishop, M. C. 2016. *The Gladius*. Oxford: Osprey Publishing.

Black, E. W. 1982. The Roman Villa at Darenth. *Archaeologia Cantiana* 97, 159–183.

Black, E. W. 1987. *The Roman Villas of South East England*. Oxford: BAR/Tempus Reparatum

Black, E. W. 2013. Roman Relief: Patterned Tiles at Dover and Elsewhere in Kent. *Kent Archaeological Review* 191, 40–42.

Blagg, T. 1976. Tools and Techniques of the Roman Stonemason in Britain. *Britannia* 7, 152–172.

Blagg, T. 1980. The Sculptured Stones. In: Dyson, T. ed. *The Roman Riverside Wall and Monumental Arch in London - Special Paper No 3*. London: London and Middlesex Archaeological Society, 125–193.

Blagg, T. 1990. Building Stone in Roman Britain. In: Parsons. D. ed. *Stone: Quarring and Building in England. AD 43-1525*. Chichester: Phillimore, 33–50.

Blagg, T. 2002. *Roman Architectural Ornament in Britain*. Oxford: BAR

Blanning, E. 2008. Towards an Interpretation of the Detached and 'Isolated' Bath Houses of Roman Kent. Unpublished MA dissertation, University of Kent.

Blanning, E. 2014. Landscape, Settlement and Materiality: Aspects of Rural Life in Kent during the Roman Period. Unpublished PhD thesis, University of Kent.

Bonifay, M. 2014. Africa: Patterns of Consumption in Coastal Regions Versus Inland Regions. The Ceramic Evidence. *Late Antique Archaeology* 10(1), 529–566.

Booth, P. 2001. The Roman Shrine at Westhawk Farm. *Archaeologia Cantiana* 121, 1–41.

Booth, P., Bingham, A. M. and Lawrence, S. 2008. *The Roman Roadside Settlement at Westhawk Farm, Ashford, Kent*. Oxford: Oxford Archaeology.

Borsos, E., Makra, L., Beczi, R., Vitanyi, B. and Szentpeter, M. 2003. Anthropogenic Air Pollution in the Ancient Times. *ACTA Climatologica Et Chorologica, Universitatis Szegediensis* 36–37, 5.15.

Breeze, D. J. and Dobson, B. 2000. *Hadrian's Wall*. London: Penguin.

Brigham, T., Goodburn, D., Tyers, I. and Dillon, J. 1995. A Roman Timbered Building on the Southwark Waterfront. *The Archaeological Journal* 152, 1–72.

Brodribb, G. 1969. Stamped Tiles of the Classis Britannica. *Sussex Archaeological Collections* 107, 102–125.

Brodribb, G. 1970. Stamped Tiles of the Classis Britannica. *Kent Archaeological Review* 21, 25. Available from: http://cka.moon-demon.co.uk/KAR021/KAR021_CB.htm [accessed 2nd December 2015].

Brodribb, G. 1979. A Survey of Tile at the Roman Bath House at Beauport Park, Battle, East Sussex. *Britannia* 10, 139–156.

Brodribb, G. 1980. A Further Survey of Stamped Tiles of the Classis Britannica. *Sussex Archaeological Collections* 118, 183–196.

Brodribb, G., Cleere, H., Henig, M., MacKreth, D. F. and Greep, S. J. 1988. The 'Classis Britannica' Bath-House at Beauport Park, East Sussex. *Britannia* 19, 217–274.

Brooks, N. P. 1994. Rochester Bridge AD43 to 1381. In: Yates, N. and Gibson, J. H. ed. *Traffic and Politics - The Construction and Management of Rochester Bridge AD42-1993*. Woodbridge: The Boydell Press, 1–35.

Brown, A. G., Meadows, I., Turner, S. D. and Mattingly, D. 2001. Roman Vineyards in Britain: stratigraphic and palynological data from Wollaston in the Nene Valley, England. *Antiquity* 75, 745–757.

Brown, P. 2012. *Through the Eye of a Needle*. Princeton: Princeton University Press.

Burnham, B. C., Wacher, J. 1990. *The Small Towns of Roman Britain*. London: Batsford.

Campbell, B. 2011. *Rivers and the Power of Ancient Rome*. Chapel Hill: University of North Carolina Press.

Carroll, M. 2009. Cologne. In: Gagarin, M. ed. *The Oxford Encyclopaedia of Greece and Rome*. Oxford: Oxford University Press, 251–260.

Carroll, M. 2016. Vagnari. *Current World Archaeology* 7(76), 30–33.

Carruthers, W. J. 2014. The Charred and Mineralised Plant Remains. In: O'Shea, L. and Weeks, J. ed. Evidence of a Distinct Focus of Romano-British Settlement at Maidstone? Excavations at Church Street 2011–2012. *Archaeologia Cantiana* 135, 143–147.

Castle, S. A. 1978. Amphorae from Brockley Hill, 1975. *Britannia* 9, 383–392.

Catling, C. 2013. Chedworth Roman Villa: Life in the Cotswolds Then and Now. *Current Archaeology* 24(284), 43.

Catling, C. 2014. Excavating Earth: Was the Roman Fenland an imperial estate. *Current Archaeology* 25(295), 20–25.

Chaplin, R. E. 1962. Excavations in Rochester, Winter 1961–1962. *Archaeologia Cantiana* 77, i–li.

Cleere, H. 1970. *The Romano-British Industrial Site at Bardown*. Lewes: Sussex Archaeological Society.

Cleere, H. 1974. The Roman Iron Industry in the Weald and its Connections with the Classis Britannica. *Archaeological Journal* 131, 17–31.

Cleere, H. 1977. The Classis Britannica. In: Johnston, D. E. ed. *The Saxon Shore*, London: CBA Research Report No 18, 16–19.

Cleere, H. and Crossley, D. 1995. *The Iron Industry of The Weald*. Cardiff: Merton Priory Press.

Coles, Mr Coles Observation of Nuisances on the Medway. 15th June 1630. *An Account of the Proceedings of the Commissioners of Sewers towards making the River Medway navigable between Maidstone and Penshurst 1627-1630*. Medway Archives and Local Studies Centre. AZ1 (a late 18th-century reproduction of the original, within the Medway Navigation Company's papers for the year 1800). Strood.

Connolly, P. 1988. *Greece and Rome at War*. London: Macdonald Phoebus.

Cool, H. E. M. and Mason, D. J. P. 2008. *Roman Piercebridge, Excavations by D. W. Harding and Peter Scott 1969-1981*. Durham: The Architectural and Archaeological Society of Durham and Northumberland.

Cooper, C. 2008. *Maidstone: A History*. Chichester: Phillimore.
Cornell, T. J. 1993. The End of Roman Imperial Expansion. In: Rich, J. and Shipley, G. eds. *War and Society in the Roman World*. London: Routledge, 139–170.
Cornwell, K., Cornwell. L. and Pagham, D. 2007. Castle Croft, Ninfield. *Hastings Area Archaeological Research Group* 23, 3.
Cornwell, K. and Cornwell. L. 2008. A Roman Site on Kitchenham Farm, Ashburnham. *Hastings Area Archaeological Research Group* 24, 10.
Cornwell, K. and Cornwell. L. 2008. A Roman Site on Kitchenham Farm, Ashburnham – 2nd Interim Report – Ceramic Building Material. *Hastings Area Archaeological Research Group* 25, 1–10.
Cornwell, K. and Cornwell. L. 2010. The Stamps of the *Classis Britannica from Kitchenham Farm, Ashburnham. Hastings Area Archaeological Research Group* 29, 16–18.
Cornwell, K. and Cornwell. L. 2013. Footlands Farm, Seddlescombe: A geophysical survey of the iron-production complex and its transport links. *Hastings Area Archaeological Research Group* 33, 1–22.
Cowan, C., Seeley, F., Wardle, A., Westman, A. and Wheeler, L. 2009. *Roman Southwark, Settlement and Economy: Excavations in Southwark 1973-1991*. London: Museum of London Archaeology.
Cowan, R. 2003a. *Roman Legionary, 58 BC–AD 69*. Oxford, Osprey Publishing.
Cowan, R. 2003b. *Imperial Roman Legionary, AD 161–284*. Oxford, Osprey Publishing.
Cowan, R. 2015. *Roman Legionary, AD 284–337*. Oxford, Osprey Publishing.
Crawford, D. J. 1976. Imperial Estates. In: Finley, M. I. ed. *Studies in Roman Property*. Cambridge: Cambridge University Press, 35–70.
Croft, A., Munby, J. and Ridley, M. 2001. *Kent Historic Landscape Characterisation*. Maidstone: Oxford Archaeology.
Crowley, N. and Betts, I. 1992. Three Classis Britannica Stamps from London. *Britannia* 23, 218–222.
Cunliffe, B. 1969. Roman Kent. In: Newman, J. ed. *The Buildings of England, West Sussex and the Weald*. London: Penguin, 22–24.
Cunliffe, B. 1980. The Evolution of Romney Marsh: A Preliminary Romney Statesmen. In: Thompson, F. H. ed. *Archaeology and Coastal Change*. London: The Society of Antiquities, 37–55.
Cunliffe, B., Reece, R., Henig, M., Chadwick Hawkes, S., Care, V. and Young, C. J. 1980. Excavations at the Roman fort at Lympne, Kent 1976–1978. *Britannia* 11, 227–288.
Cunliffe, B. 1988. *Greeks, Romans and Barbarians. Spheres of Interaction*. London: Batsford
Cunliffe, B. (1988). Romney Marsh in the Roman Period. In: Edisson, J. and Green, C. ed. *Romney Marsh: Evolution, Occupation, Reclamation*. Oxford: Oxford University Committee for Archaeology, 83–87.
Cunliffe, B. 2009. *Iron Age Communities in Britain – An Account of England, Scotland and Wales from the 7th century BC Until the Roman Conquest*. London: Routledge.
Cunliffe, B. 2013. *Britain Begins*. Oxford: Oxford University Press.
D'Amato, R. 2009. *Imperial Roman Naval Forces 31BC–AD500*. Oxford: Osprey Publishing.
D'Amato, R. 2016. *Roman Army Units in the Western provinces (1)*. Oxford: Osprey Publishing.
Dark, K. and Dark, P. 1997. *The Landscape of Roman Britain*. Stroud: Sutton Publishing.
Dannell, G. and Mees, A. 2015. Getting Samian Ware to Britain: Routes and Transport Possibilities. *Journal of Roman Pottery Studies* 16, 77–92.
Davies, M. 2009. The Evidence of Settlement at Plaxtol in the Late Iron Age and Romano-British Periods. *Archaeologia Cantiana* 129, 257–278.
Dise, R. L. 1997. Trajan, The Antonines, and the Governor's Staff. *Zeitschrift fur Papyrologie und Epigraphik* 116, 273–283.
Driessen, M. and Besselsen, E. 2014. *Voorburg-Arentsburg. Een Romeinse Havenstad tussen Rijn en Mass*. Amsterdam, University of Amsterdam.
Dumayne-Peaty, L. 1998. Forest Clearance in Northern Britain during Romano-British Times: Re-addressing the Palynological Evidence. *Britannia* 29, 315–322.

Durham, A. and Goormachtigh, M. 2015. Greenwich and the Early Emporia of Kent. *Archaeologia Cantiana* 136, 163–176.
Dworakowska, A. 1983. *Quarries in Roman provinces.* Wroclaw: Zaklad Narodowy im. Ossolinskich.
Elliott, P. 2014. *Legions in Crisis.* Stroud: Fonthill Media
Elliott, S. 2011. The Medway Formula. Unpublished MA dissertation, University College London.
Elliott, S. 2013. A Roman Villa at Teston. *British Archaeology* 133, 40–46.
Elliott, S. 2014a. The Medway Formula – A Search for Evidence That the Roman Authorities Improved the River's Navigability to Facilitate Their Extensive Ragstone Quarrying Industry. *Archaeologia Cantiana* 135, 251–260.
Elliott, S. 2014b. Britain's First Industrial Revolution. *History Today* 64(5), 49–55.
Elliott, S. 2014c. The Mystery of the Medway Stones. *Current Archaeology* 25(298), 11.
Elliott, S. 2016a. *Sea Eagles of Empire: The Classis Britannica and the Battles for Britain.* Stroud: The History Press.
Elliott, S. 2016b. Change and Continuity in the Exploitation of Natural Resources (such as stone, iron, clay and wood) in Kent During the Roman Occupation. Unpublished PhD thesis, University of Kent.
Ellis Jones, J. 2012. *The Maritime Landscape of Roman Britain.* Oxford: BAR/Archaeological and Historical Associates Ltd.
Erdkamp, P. 2005. *The Grain Market in the Roman Empire: A Social, Political, and Economic Study.* Cambridge: Cambridge University Press.
Erdkamp, P. 2013. *The Cambridge Companion to Ancient Rome.* Cambridge: Cambridge University Press.
Esmonde Cleary, A. S. 1989. *The Ending of Roman Britain.* London: Batsford.
Esmonde Cleary, A. S. 2013. *Chedworth: Life in a Roman Villa.* Stroud: The History Press.
Esmonde Cleary, A. S. 2013. *The Roman West AD200–500.* Cambridge: Cambridge University Press.
Evans, C. and Newman, R. 2014. *North West Cambridge: University of Cambridge. Archaeological Evaluation Fieldwork.* Cambridge: Cambridge Archaeological Unit.
Evans, J. 1953. Archaeological Horizons in the North Kent Marshes. *Archaeologia Cantiana* 66, 103–146.
Evans, J. 2013. Balancing the Scales: Romano-British Pottery in Early Late Antiquity. *Late Antique Archaeology* 10(1), 1–11.
Everitt, A. 1986. *Continuity and Colonisation.* Leicester: Leicester University Press.
Farebrother, G. 1978. Bloomery at Rushlake Green. *Wealden Iron – Bulletin of the Wealden Iron Research Group* 1, 5.
Faulkner, N. 2001. *The Decline and Fall of Roman Britain.* Stroud: Tempus.
Fernando-Lozano, J., Gutierrez-Alonso, G. and Fernandez-Moran, M. A. 2015. Using Airborne LIDAR Sensing Technology and Aerial Orthoimages to Unravel Roman Water Supply Systems and Gold Works in NW Spain. *Journal of Archaeological Science* 53, 356–373.
Fields, N. 2003. *Hadrian's Wall AD 122–410.* Oxford: Osprey Publishing.
Fields, N. 2006. *Rome's Saxon Shore.* Oxford: Osprey Publishing.
Finley, M. 1999. *The Ancient Economy.* Berkeley: University of California Press.
Freeman, P. 2010. Ancient References to Tartessos. In: Cunliffe, B. and Koch, T. eds. *Celtic from the West.* Oxford: Oxbow Books, 303–334.
Frere, S. 1987. *Britannia: A History of Roman Britain* (3rd edn). London: Routledge.
Fuhrmann, C. J. 2011. *Policing the Roman Empire: Soldiers, Administration and Public Order.* Oxford: Oxford University Press.
Gardiner, M. 1996. An Archaeological Evaluation of Land adjacent to Pested Bars Road, Boughton Monchelsea, Maidstone, Kent. South Eastern Archaeological Service (unpublished).
Gardner, A. 2007. *An Archaeology of Identity.* California: Left Coast Press.

Gardner, A. 2013. Thinking about Roman Imperialism: Postcolonialism, Globalisation and Beyond? *Britannia* 44, 1–25.
Garrison, E. G. 1998. *History of Engineering and Technology: Artful Methods*. Boca Raton: CRC Press.
Goldsworthy, A. 2000. *Roman Warfare*. London: Cassell.
Goldsworthy, A. 2003. *The Complete Roman Army*. London: Thames and Hudson.
Goldsworthy, A. 2014. *Augustus: From Revolutionary to Emperor*. London: Weidenfeld and Nicolson.
Goodburn, D. 1991. A Roman Timber Framed Building Tradition. *The Archaeological Journal* 148, 182–204.
Grainge, G. 2005. *The Roman Invasions of Britain*. Stroud, Tempus.
Green, C. 2013. Quernstone Production Around Copt Point: Folkestone's First Industry. In: Coulson, I. ed. *Folkestone to 1500, A Town Unearthed*. Canterbury: Canterbury Archaeological Trust, 50–51.
Greene, K. 1986. *The Archaeology of the Roman Economy*. Berkeley and Los Angeles: University of Chicago Press.
Guest, P. and Young, T. 2009. Mapping Isca: Geophysical Investigation of School Field and Priory Field, Caerleon. *Archaeologia Cambrensis* 158, 97–111.
Gurney, D. 2002. *Outposts of the Empire. A Guide to Norfolk's Roman Forts at Burgh Castle, Caister-on-Sea and Brancaster*. Norwich: Norfolk Archaeological Trust.
Halkon, P. 2011. Iron Landscape and Power in Iron Age East Yorkshire. *The Archaeological Journal* 168, 134–165.
Hall, J. and Merrifield, R. 1986. *Roman London*. London: HMSO Publications for the Museum of London.
Halsall, G. 2013. *Worlds of Arthur*. Oxford: Oxford University Press.
Hamey, L. A. and Hamey, J. A. 1994. *The Roman Engineers*. Cambridge: Cambridge University Press.
Hanson, W. S. 1996. Forest Clearance and the Roman Army. *Britannia* 27, 354–358.
Harrington, S. and Welch, M. 2014. *The Early Anglo-Saxon Kingdoms of Southern Britain*. Oxford: Oxbow Books.
Hartley, B. R. and Hartley, K. F. Pottery in the Romano British Fenland. In: Phillips, C. W. ed. *The Fenland in Roman Times*. London: Royal Geographical Society, 165–169.
Hayward, K. M. J. 2009. *Roman Quarrying and Stone Supply on the Periphery - Southern England*. Oxford: BAR/Archaeological and Historical Associates Ltd.
Hill, J. 2016. After the Fire: A Roman Fort at Plantation Place. *British Archaeology* 152, 24–29.
Hingley, R. 1982. Roman Britain: The structure of Roman imperialism and the consequences of imperialism on the development of a peripheral province. In: Miles, D. ed. *The Romano-British Countryside: Studies in Rural Settlement and Economy*. Oxford: BAR/Archaeological and Historical Associates Ltd, 17–52.
Hirt, A. M. 2010. *Imperial mines and Quarries in the Roman World*. Oxford: Oxford University Press.
Hodges, R. 2014. Roman Goldmines in Transylvania. *Current World Archaeology* 68, 54–57.
Hodgkinson, J. 1987. Footlands Iron Working Site, Seddlescombe. *Wealden Iron - Bulletin of the Wealden Iron Research Group* 2, 22–32.
Hodgkinson, J. 1988. Two Roman Shoe Fragments from Seddlescombe. *Sussex Notes and Queries* 126, 231–233.
Hodgkinson, J. 1988. Field Notes. *Wealden Iron - Bulletin of the Wealden Iron Research Group* 2(1988), 2–11.
Hodgkinson, J. 1991. Field Notes. *Wealden Iron - Bulletin of the Wealden Iron Research Group* 2(1991), 2–7.
Hodgkinson, J. 1992. Field Notes. *Wealden Iron - Bulletin of the Wealden Iron Research Group* 2(1992), 8–9.
Hodgkinson, J. 1993. Field Notes. *Wealden Iron - Bulletin of the Wealden Iron Research Group* 2(1993), 2–3.
Hodgkinson, J. 1994. Field Notes. *Wealden Iron - Bulletin of the Wealden Iron Research Group* 2(1944), 2–3.
Hodgkinson, J. 1997. Field Notes. *Wealden Iron - Bulletin of the Wealden Iron Research Group* 2(1997), 2–9.
Hodgkinson, J. 1999. Romano-British Iron Production in the Sussex and Kent Weald: a review of current data. *The Journal of the Historical Metallurgy Society* 33, 68–72.
Hodgkinson, J. 2001. Field Notes. *Wealden Iron Research Group Bulletin* 2(2001), 3–5.

Hodgkinson, J. 2004. Field Notes. *Wealden Iron Research Group Bulletin* 2(2004), 2–6.

Hodgkinson, J. 2008. Waste as a Potential Indicator of Regional Iron Production and Organisation: An example from Southeast Roman Britain. Wealden Iron Research Group (unpublished).

Hodgkinson, J. 2009. *The Wealden Iron Industry*. Stroud: The History Press.

Hodgkinson, J. 2012. *Winter Meeting 2012. WIRG Newsletter 55*. Available from: http://www.wealdeniron.org.uk/Newsletters/Mar%202012%20col.pdf [accessed 1st December 2015].

Hopkins, K. 1985. *Death and Renewal*. Cambridge: Cambridge University Press.

Houliston, M. 1999. Excavations at the Mount Villa, Maidstone. *Archaeologia Cantiana* 119, 71–172.

Howell, I. 2014. Continuity and Change in the late Iron Age-Roman Transition Within the Environs of Quarry Wood Oppidum: Excavations at Furfield Quarry, Boughton Monchelsea. *Archaeologia Cantiana* 134, 37–66.

Howell, I., Blackmore, L., Phillpotts, C. and Thorp, A. 2013. *Roman and Medieval Development South of Cheapside. Excavations at Bow Bells House, City of London, 2005-2006*, London: Museum of London Archaeology.

Hughes, J. 1851. On the pneumatic method adopted in constructing the foundations of the new bridge across the Medway - Minutes of the Proceedings of the Institution of Civil Engineers. In: Yates, N. and Gibson, J. M. ed. *Traffic and Politics - The Construction and Management of Rochester Bridge AD43-1993*. Woodbridge: The Boydell Press, 9.

James, S. 2011. *Rome and the Sword*. London: Thames and Hudson.

Jessup, R. F. 1932. Romano-British Remains - Industries. In: Page, W. ed. *The Victoria History of the Counties of England - Kent*. London: St. Catherine Press, 127–133.

Jessup, R. F. 1956. The 'Temple of Mithras' at Burham. *Archaeologia Cantiana* 70, 168–172.

Jobson, J. J. 1921. The Roman Bridge at Rochester. *Archaeologia Cantiana* 35, 138–144.

Jones, A. H. M. 1953. Inflation Under the Roman Empire. *Economic History Review* 5, 293–318.

Jones, H. A. 1992. A Survey of Roman Fragments in Churches in S. E. Kent. *Kent Archaeological Review* 110, 230.

Jones, B. and Mattingly, D. 1990. *An Atlas of Roman Britain*. Oxford: Oxbow Books.

Jones, G. D. B. 1980. The Roman Mines at Rio Tinto. *The Journal of Roman Studies* 70, 146–164.

Jones, G. 1981. Field Reports 1980–1981. *Recologea Papers* 7, 68–72.

Jones, M. 1982. Crop Production in Roman Britain. In: Miles, D. ed. *Romano-British Countryside*. Oxford: BAR, 97–107.

Jones, M. 1986. Towards a Model of the Villa Estate. In: Miles, D. ed. *Archaeology at Barton Court Farm, Abingdon, Oxon. Council for British Archaeology Research Report* 50, 38–42.

Jones, B. and Mattingly, D. 1990. *An Atlas of Roman Britain*. Oxford: Oxbow Books.

Kaye, S. 2015a. The Roman Invasion of Britain AD, 43. Riverine, Wading and Tidal Studies Place Limits on the Location of the Two Day River Battle and Beachead. Available from: https://www.academia.edu/13579532/The_Roman_Invasion_of_Britain_AD_43_riverine_wading_and_tidal_studies_place_limits_on_the_possible_locations_of_the_two-day_river_battle_and_beachhead [accessed 1st February 2016].

Kaye, S. 2015b. The Roman Invasion of Britain AD, 43. Riverine, Wading and Tidal Studies Place Limits on the Location of the Two Day River Battle and Beachead. *Archaeologia Cantiana* 136, 227–240.

Kean, M. K. 2005. *The Complete Chronicles of the Emperors of Rome*. Ludlow: Thalamus.

Kolb, A. 2001. The Cursus Publicus. In: Adams, C. and Laurence, R. eds. *Travel and Geography in the Roman Empire*. London: Routledge, 95–106.

Kulikowski, M. 2016. *Imperial Triumph: The Roman World From Hadrian to Constantine*. London: Profile Books.

Lavan, L. 2014. Local Economies in Late Antiquity? Some Thoughts. *Late Antique Archaeology* 10(1), 1–11.

Laurence, R. 2012. *Roman Archaeology for Historians*. Abingdon: Routledge.

Laurence, R. 2013. Road To Success – How Money, Mules and Milestones Led to Roman Globalisation. *Current World Archaeology* 59, 42–46.

Lawson, T. and Killingray, D. 2004. *An Historical Atlas of Kent*. Chichester: Phillimore for the Kent Archaeological Society.

Le Bohec, Y. 2000. *The Imperial Roman Army*. London: Routledge.

Legg, R. 1986. *Exploring the Heartland of Purbeck*. Sherborne: Dorset Publishing Company.

Lemak, J. 2006. Review of 'The Grain market in the Roman Empire: A Social, Political, and Economic Study'. Available from: http://bmcr.brynmawr.edu/2006/2006-12-09.html [accessed 10th November 2016].

Ling, R. 1985. The Mechanics of the Building Trade. In: Grew, F. and Hobley, B. ed. *Roman Urban Topography in Britain and the Western Empire*. London: CBA Research Report No 59, 14–27.

Locker, A. 2007. In piscibus diversis: the Bone Evidence for Fish Consumption in Roman Britain. *Britannia* 38, 141–180.

Locker, A. 2014. The Fish Remains. In: O'Shea, L. and Weeks, J. ed. Evidence of a Distinct Focus of Romano-British Settlement at Maidstone? Excavations at Church Street 2011–2012. *Archaeologia Cantiana* 135, 141–142.

Lott, G. and Cameron, D. 2005. *The Building Stones of South East England; Minerology and Provenance*. Nottingham: British Geological Survey.

Lyne, M. 1994. Late Roman Handmade Wares in South East Britain. Unpublished PhD thesis, University of Reading.

Lyne, M. September 1996. *Roman Ship Fittings From Richborough: Speech at ROMEC X, Montpelier*. Available from: http://www.classis-britannica.co.uk/menu/shipping/shipping.htm [accessed 10th October 2011].

Lyne, M. 2000. *Roman Wight. Isle of Wight History Centre*. Available from: http://www.iwhistory.org.uk/resourceassessment/iow%20Roman.pdf [accessed 12th December 2012].

MacDowall, S. 1994. *Late Roman Infantryman: 236-565 AD*. London: Osprey Publishing.

McGrail, S. 2014. *Early Ships and Seafaring: European Water Transport*. Barnsley: Pen and Sword Archaeology.

McRae, S. G. and Burnham, C. P. 1973. *The Rural Landscape of Kent*. London: Wye College.

McWhirr, A. and Viner, D. 1978. The Production and Distribution of Tiles in Roman Britain with Particular Reference to the Cirencester Region. *Britannia* 9, 359–377.

Malim, T. 2005. *Stonea and the Roman Fenlands*. Stroud: Tempus.

Manco, J. 2015. *Blood of the Celts*. London: Thames and Hudson.

Margary, I. D. 1933. Objects Found at the Ironworks, Ridge Hill, East Grinstead. *Sussex Notes and Queries* 6, 177–178.

Margary, I. D. 1955. An Old Map of Cansiron in East Grinstead and Hartfield 1724. *Sussex Notes and Queries* 13, 100–102.

Margary, I. D. 1967. *Roman Roads in Britain*. London. John Baker Publishers

Marsden, P. 1994. *Ships of the Port of London, 1st to 11th Centuries*. Swindon: English Heritage.

Mason, D. J. P. 2001. *Roman Chester: City of the Eagles*. Stroud: Tempus Publishing

Mason, D. J. P. 2003. *Roman Britain and the Roman Navy*. Stroud: The History Press.

Mason, S. 1998. Land Adjacent to Pested Bars Road, Boughton Monchelsea, Maidstone, Kent – An Archaeological Evaluation. Museum of London Archaeology Service (unpublished).

Matthews, J. D. 1989. *Silvicultural Systems*. Wotton-under-Edge: Clarendon Press.

Mattingly, D. 2006. *An Imperial Possession, Britain in the Roman Empire*. London: Penguin.

Mattingly, D. 2009. The Imperial Economy. In: Potter, D. S. ed. *Companion to the Roman Empire*. Hoboken: Wiley-Blackwell.

Mattingly, D. 2011. *Imperialism, Power and Identity – Experiencing the Roman Empire*. Princeton: Princeton University Press.

Merrifield, R. 1965. *The Roman City of London*. London: Ernest Benn
Millett, M. 1990a. *The Romanization of Britain*. Cambridge: Cambridge University Press.
Millett, M. 1990b. Introduction: London as a Capital. In: Watson, B. ed. *Roman London: Recent Archaeological Work*. Portsmouth: Journal of Roman Archaeology, 7–12.
Millett, M. 1995. *Roman Britain*. London: Batsford.
Millett, M. 2007. Roman Kent. In: Williams, H. ed. *The Archaeology of Kent to 800AD*. Woodbridge: The Boyden Press and Kent County Council, 135–186.
Mills, P. J. E. 2013. The Supply and Distribution of Ceramic Building Material in Roman Britain. In: Levan, L. and Mulryan, M. eds. *Field Methods and Techniques in Late Antique Archaeology 10*. Leiden: Brill, 451–470.
Milne, G. 2000. A Roman Provincial Fleet; The Classis Britannica reconsidered. In: Oliver G., Brock, R., Cornell, T. and Hodgkinson, S. eds. *The Sea in Antiquity*. Oxford: Archaeopress 131.
Moorhead, S. and Stuttard, D. 2012. *The Romans Who Shaped Britain*. London: Thames and Hudson.
Moorhead, S. 2014. *A History of Roman Coinage in Britain*. Witham: Greenlight Publishing.
Moorhead, S., Anderson, I. and Walton, P. 2012. The Roman Coins from the Excavation at Whitefriars, Canterbury. The British Museum (unpublished).
Morris, F. M. 2010. *North Sea and Channel Connectivity during the Late Iron Age and Roman Period (175/150BC–AD 409)*. Oxford: Archaeopress.
Morris, P. 1979. *Agricultural Buildings in Roman Britain*. Oxford: BAR
Oleson, J. P. 2009. *The Oxford Handbook of Engineering and Technology in the Classical World*. Oxford: Oxford University Press.
Parfitt, K. and Philp, B. 1981. Building Materials. In: Philp, B. ed. *The Excavations of the Roman Forts of the Classis Britannica at Dover, 1970-1977*, Dover: Kent Archaeological Rescue Unit, 175–176.
Parfitt, K. 2004. The Roman Building at Harp Wood, Saltwood, Near Hythe. *Kent Archaeological Review* 158, 169–171.
Parfitt, K. 2011. The Rocky Road to the Iron Age: Excavations at Folkestone Roman Villa, 2011. *Kent Archaeological Society Newsletter* 92, 2–4.
Parfitt, K. 2013. Folkestone During the Roman Period. In: Coulson, I. ed. *Folkestone to 1500, A Town Unearthed*. Canterbury: Canterbury Archaeological Trust, 31–54.
Parry, D. 2005. *Engineering the Ancient World*. Stroud: Sutton Publishing
Peacock, D. P. S. 1977. Bricks and Tiles of the Classis Britannica: Petrology and Origin. *Britannia* 8, 235–248.
Peacock, D. P. S. 1982. *Pottery in the Roman World: An Ethnoarchaeological Approach*. Harlow: Longman.
Peacock, D. P. S. 1987. Iron Age and Roman Quern Production at Lodsworth, West Sussex. *The Antiquaries Journal* 67, 61–85.
Peacock, D. P. S. 2013. *The Stone of Life*. Southampton: The Highfield Press.
Pearson, A. F. 1999. Building Anderita: Late Roman Coastal Defences and the Construction of the Saxon Shore Fort at Pevensey. *Oxford Journal of Archaeology* 18(1), 95–117.
Pearson, A. F. 2002a. *The Roman Shore Forts*. Stroud: Tempus Publishing.
Pearson, A. F. 2002b. Stone Supply to the Saxon Shore Forts at Reculver, Richborough, Dover and Lympne. *Archaeologia Cantiana* 122, 197–222.
Pearson, A. F. 2003. *The Construction of the Saxon Shore Forts*. Oxford: BAR/Archaeopress
Pearson, A. F. 2006. *The work of giants. Stone quarrying in Roman Britain*. Stroud: Tempus Publishing.
Perring, D. and Roskams, S. 1991. *Early Development of Roman London West of the Walbrook*. London: CBA Research Report No 70.
Perring, D. 1991. *Roman London*. London: Routledge.
Perring, D. 2009. *The Roman House in Britain*. London: Routledge.
Petrikovits, H von. 1975. *Die Innenbauten römischen Legionslager während der Prinzipatszeit*. Warsaw: Westdeutscher Verlag.

Philp, B. 1968. The Roman Cemetery at Keston. *Kent Archaeological Review* 11, 10.

Philp, B. 1972. The Discovery and Preservation of the Roman Villa at Horton Kirby. (Online). Available from: http://cka.moon-demon.co.uk/KAR030/KAR030_Horton.htm [accessed 5th June 2015].

Philp, B. 1981. *The Excavations of the Roman Forts of the Classis Britannica in Dover 1970–1977*. Dover: Kent Archaeological Rescue Unit.

Philp, B. 1982. Romney Marsh and the Roman Fort at Lympne. *Kent Archaeological Review* 68, 175–191.

Philp, B. 1984. *Excavations in the Darent Valley, Kent*. Dover: Kent Archaeological Rescue Unit.

Philp, B. 1989. *The Roman House with Bacchic Murals at Dover*. Dover: Kent Archaeological Rescue Unit.

Philp, B. 1990. Excavations on the Roman Villa at Folkestone 1989. Available from: http://www.cka.moon-demon.co.uk/KAR099/KAR099_Folkestone.htm [accessed 14th June 2014].

Philp, B. 1994. *The Iron Age and Romano-British Site at Lenham, Kent*. Dover: Kent Archaeological Rescue Unit.

Philp, B. 2012. *The Discovery and Excavation of the Roman Shore-Fort at Dover, Kent*. Dover: Kent Archaeological Rescue Unit.

Philp, B. 2014. *Discoveries and Excavations Across Kent, 1970–2014*. Dover: Kent Archaeological Rescue Unit.

Philp, B. and Chenery, M. 1997. *A Roman Site at Springhead (Vagniacae) Near Gravesend*. Dover: Kent Archaeological Rescue Unit.

Pitts, M. 2014. London Eagle Watched Over Roman Tomb. *British Archaeology* 134(January/February 2014), 8.

Pollard, N. 2000. *Soldiers, Cities and Civilians in Roman Syria*. Ann Arbor: University of Michigan Press.

Potter, T. W, and Jackson, R. P. J. 1982. The Roman Site of Stonea, Cambs. *Antiquity* 217, 110–120.

Poulter, J. and Entwhistle, R. 2016. Charting the Roads. *Current Archaeology* 27(314), 12–18.

Rackham, O. 1997. *The Illustrated History of the Countryside*. London: Orion Publishing.

Reece, R. 1980. Town and country: the end of Roman Britain. *World Archaeology* 12(1), 77–92.

Reece, R. 1981. The Third Century, crisis or change? In: King, A. and Henig, M. eds. *The Roman West in the Third century*. Oxford: BAR

Richmond, I. A. 1955. *Roman Britain*. London: Penguin.

Rickman, G. 1980. *The Corn Supply of Ancient Rome*. Oxford: Oxford University Press.

Riddler, I. 2010. Querns. In: Bennett, P., Ridler, I. and Sparey-Green, C. eds. *The Roman Watermills and Settlement at Ickham, Kent*. Canterbury: Canterbury Archaeology Trust, 251–254.

Rogers, A. 2011. *Late Roman Towns in Britain. Rethinking Change and Decline*. Cambridge: Cambridge University Press.

Rodgers, N. and Dodge, H. 2009. *The History and Conquests of Ancient Rome*. London: Hermes House.

Rowsome, P. 1996. The Billingsgate Roman House and Bath – Conservation and Assessment. *London Archaeologist* 7(16), 421–422.

Rudling, D., Cartwright, C., Swift, G., Foster, S., Shepherd, J., Hinton, P. and Tebbutt, F. 1986. The Excavation of a Roman Tilery on Great Cansiron Farm, East Sussex. *Britannia*, V.17, 191–230.

Russel, A. and Elliott, G. L. 2013. Survey of Roman Structures in the River Itchen between Clausentum and St Denys, Southampton. Southampton Archaeology Unit (unpublished).

Russell, B. 2013a. *The Economics of the Roman Stone Trade*. Oxford: Oxford University Press.

Russell, B. 2013b. Gazetteer of Stone Quarries in the Roman World. Available from: www.romaneconomy.ox.ac.uk [accessed 12th January 2015].

Russell, C. and Staveley, D. 2012. A Geophysical Survey at Great Cansiron Farm, Butcherfield Lane, Hartfield, East Sussex. Chris Butler Archaeological Services Ltd (unpublished).

Salway, P. 1970. The Roman Fenland. In: Phillips, C. W. ed. *The Fenland in Roman Times*. London: Royal Geographical Society, 1–21.

Salway, P. 1981. *Roman Britain.* Oxford: Oxford University Press.

Selkirk, A. 2011. Folkestone: Roman Villa or Iron Age Oppidum? *Current Archaeology* 22(262), 23–30.

Selkirk, R. 1983. *The Piercebridge Formula.* Cambridge: Patrick Stephens

Selkirk, R. 1995. *On the Trail of the Legions.* Ipswich: Anglia Publishing.

Selkirk, R. 2001. *Chester-le-Street and Its Place in History.* Durham: CASDEC

Shaffrey, R. 2015. Intensive Milling Practices in the Romano-British Landscape of Southern England: Using Newly Established criteria for Distinguishing Millstones from Rotary Querns. *Britannia* 46, 55–92.

Shaffrey, R. and Allen, J. R. L. 2014. A Complete Whetstone of Wealden Lithology from the Roman Site at Tackley, Oxfordshire. *Britannia* 45, 288–293.

Shaffrey, R. 2006. *Grinding and Milling. A study of Romano-British rotary querns and millstones made from Old Red Sandstone.* Oxford: Archaeopress.

Sheldon, H. 2010. Enclosing Londinium. *London and Middlesex Archaeological Society Transactions* 61, 227–235.

Skelton, S. 2010. *UK Vineyards Guide.* London: Stephen Skelton.

Smallwood, E. M. 1981. *The Jews Under Roman Rule: From Pompey to Diocletian: A Study in Political Relations.* Leiden: Brill.

Smith, A. 2013. Roman Britain...As You've Never Seen It Before. *British Archaeology* 132, 20–23.

Smith, D. J. 1984. Roman Mosaics in Britain: a synthesis. In: Favioli Campanati, R. ed. *III Colloqoquio Internazionale su Mosaico Antico.* Ravenna: Edizioni del Girasole, 357–380.

Smith, J. 1839. *The Topography of Maidstone and its Environs.* Maidstone: J. Smith Publisher.

Smythe, C. T. 1883. A Walled Roman Cemetery in Joy Wood, Lockham, Near Maidstone. *Archaeologia Cantiana* 15, 81–88.

Smythe, J. A. 1937. Ancient Sussex Iron Blooms. *Transactions of the Newcomen Society* 17, 197–203.

Southern, P. 2007. *The Roman Army: A Social and Institutional History.* Oxford: Oxford University Press.

Southern, P. 2013. *Roman Britain.* Stroud: Amberley Publishing.

Sowan, P. W. 1977. Reigate Stone in Kent. *Kent Archaeological Review.* Available from: http://cka.moon-demon.co.uk/KAR048/KAR048_Reigate.htm [accessed 10th February 2014].

Spain, R. J. and Riddler, I. 2010. Millstones. In: Bennett, P., Ridler, I. and Sparey-Green, C. eds. *The Roman Watermills and Settlement at Ickham, Kent.* Canterbury: Canterbury Archaeologogical Trust, 277–283.

Taylor, J. 2000. Review of 'Stonea in its Fenland context: moving beyond an imperial estate.' *Journal of Roman Archaeology* 13, 647–658.

Taylor, J. 2007. *An Atlas of Roman Rural Settlement in England.* York: CBA Research Report No 151.

Taylor, M. V. 1932. Country Houses and Other Buildings. In: Page, W. ed. *The Victoria History of the Counties of England - Kent,* London: St. Catherine Press, 102–127.

Taylor, M. V., Jessup, R. F., and Hawkes, C. F. C. 1932. Topographical Index. In: Page, W. ed. *The Victoria History of the Counties of England - Kent.* London: St. Catherine Press, 144–177.

Taylor-Wilson, R. 2002. *Excavations at Hunts House, Guy's Hospital. London Borough of Southwark.* London: Pre-Construct Archaeology Monograph 1.

Tebbutt, C. F. 1971. Blacklands, Cansiron Bloomery. *Wealden Iron - Bulletin of the Wealden Iron Research Group* 1, 11.

Tebbutt, C. F. 1972. A Roman Bloomery at Great Cansiron, Near Holtye, Sussex. *Sussex Archaeological Collections* 110, 10–13.

Tebbutt, C. F. 1973. A Roman Site at Howbourne Farm, Hadlow Down. *Sussex Archaeological Collections* 111, 115.

Tebbutt, C. F. 1976. Kitchenham Farm, Ashburnham, Hadlow Down. *Sussex Archaeological Collections* 114, 324.

Tebbutt, C. F. 1978. Mid Sussex Water Company Pipelines. *Sussex Archaeological Collections* 116, 402–406.
Tebbutt, C. F. 1978. Reports on Fieldwork. *Wealden Iron - Bulletin of the Wealden Iron Research Group* 1, 6–15.
Tebbutt, C. F. 1979. A Roman Coin from Great Cansiron Bloomery. *Wealden Iron - Bulletin of the Wealden Iron Research Group* 1, 14–15.
Tebbutt, C. F. 1981a. Wealden Bloomery Smelting Furnaces. *Sussex Archaeological Collections* 119, 57–64.
Tebbutt, C. F. 1981b. Field Reports. *Wealden Iron - Bulletin of the Wealden Iron Research Group* 2, 20–23.
Tebbutt, M. and Tebbutt, C. F. (1982). Oldlands Roman Bloomery. *Wealden Iron - Bulletin of the Wealden Iron Research Group* 2, 12–15.
Temin, P. 2012. *The Roman Market Economy*. Princeton: Princeton University Press.
Thompson, F. 1986. The Iron Age Hillfort of Oldbury, Kent. Excavations 1983–1984. *The Antiquaries Journal* 66, 267–286.
Todd, M. 1970. The Small Towns of Roman Britain. London. *Britannia* 1, 114–130.
Todd, M. 1996. Ancient Mining on Mendip, Somerset: A Preliminary Report on Recent Work. *The Bulletin of the Peak District Mines Society*, 13(2), 47–51.
Tomlin, R. S. O. 1996. A Five Acre Wood in Kent. In: Bird, J., Hassall, M. W. C. and Sheldon, H. eds. *Interpreting Roman London: Papers in Memory of Hugh Chapman*. Oxford: Oxbow Books, 209.
Tomlin, S. O. 2016. *Roman London's First Voices*. London: Museum of London Archaeology.
Turnbull, S. 2004. *The Walls of Constantinople AD 324-1453*. Oxford: Osprey Publishing.
Tyers, P. 1996. *Roman Pottery in Britain*. London: Batsford
van der Veen, M., Livarda, A., and Hill, A. 2008. New Foods in Roman Britain – Dispersal and Social Access. *Environmental Archaeology* 13, 11–36.
Visser, R. M. 2009. Growing and Felling Romans: Theory and Evidence Related to Silvicultural Systems. In: Moore, A., Taylor, G., Girdwood, P., Harris, E. and Shipley, L. eds. *TRAC 09: Proceedings of the 19th Annual Theoretical Roman Archaeology Conference, Ann Arbor and Southampton*. Oxford: Oxbow Books, 11–22.
Warry, J. 1980. *Warfare in the Classical World*. London: Salamander Books.
Webster, D., Webster, H. and Perch, D. F. 1967. A Possible Vineyard of the Romano-British Period at North Thoresby, Lincolnshire. *Lincolnshire History and Archaeology* 2, 55–61.
Wheeler, R. E. M. 1932. Romano-British Remains – Towns. In: Page, W. ed. *The Victoria History of the Counties of England - Kent*. London: St. Catherine Press, 60–101.
Wild, J. P. 2002. The Textile Industry of Roman Britain. *Britannia* 33, 1–42.
Wilkinson, P. 2006. *The Historical Development of the Port of Faversham, Kent 1580-1780*. Oxford: BAR/ Archaeopress
Wilkinson, P. 2008. The Interim Results of an Archaeological Investigation at Stone Chapel Field, Faversham, Kent. Kent Archaeological Field School (unpublished).
Wilkinson, P. 2009. An Archaeological Investigation of the Roman Aisled Stone Building at Hog brook, Deerton Street, Faversham, Kent, 2004–2005. Kent Archaeological Field School (unpublished).
Wilkinson, P. 2012. *Excavation of Octagonal Roman Bath-House at Bax Farm, Teynham*. Kent Archaeological Field School (unpublished).
Williams, J. H. 1971. Roman Building Materials in South East England. *Britannia* 2, 166–195.
Williams, T. 1993. *The Archaeology of Roman London, Volume 3: Public Buildings in the South West Quarter of Roman London*. York: CBA Research Report 88.
Willis, S. 2005. *Samian Pottery, a Resource for the Study of Roman Britain and Beyond: The Results of the English Heritage Funded Samian Project. An e-monograph*. Internet Archaeology No. 17.
Willis, S. 2007. Roman Towns, Roman Landscapes: The Cultural Terrain of Town and Country in the Roman Period. In: Fleming, A. and Hingley, R. eds. *Prehistoric and Roman Landscapes*. Oxford: Windgather Press, 143–164.

Willis, S. 2010. Brief Interim Report on ongoing Archaeological works and Observation at Harp Wood, Pedlinge. University of Kent (unpublished).

Willis, S. 2011. Samian Ware and Society in Roman Britain and Beyond. *Britannia* 42, 167–242.

Willis, S. 2012. Review of 'The Roman Roadside Settlement at Westhawk Farm, Ashford, Kent'. *Britannia* 43, 433–434.

Windrow, M. and McBride, A. 1996. *Imperial Rome at War*. Hong Kong: Concord Publications.

Woodiwiss, S. 1992. General Discussion. In: Woodiwiss, S. ed. *Iron Age and Late Roman Salt Production and the Medieval Town of Droitwich*. York: CBA Research Report No 81, 183–193.

Worssam, B. C. 1963. *Geology of the Country Around Maidstone*. Nottingham: British Geological Survey.

Worssam, B. and Tatton-Brown, T. 1993. Kentish Rag and Other Kent Building Stone. *Archaeologia Cantiana* 112, 93–126.

Worssam, B. 1995. The Geology of Wealden Iron. In: Cleere, H. and Crossley, H. eds. *The Iron Industry of The Weald*. Cardiff: Merton Priory Press, 1–30.